THE WORKS OF JOHN HELD JR

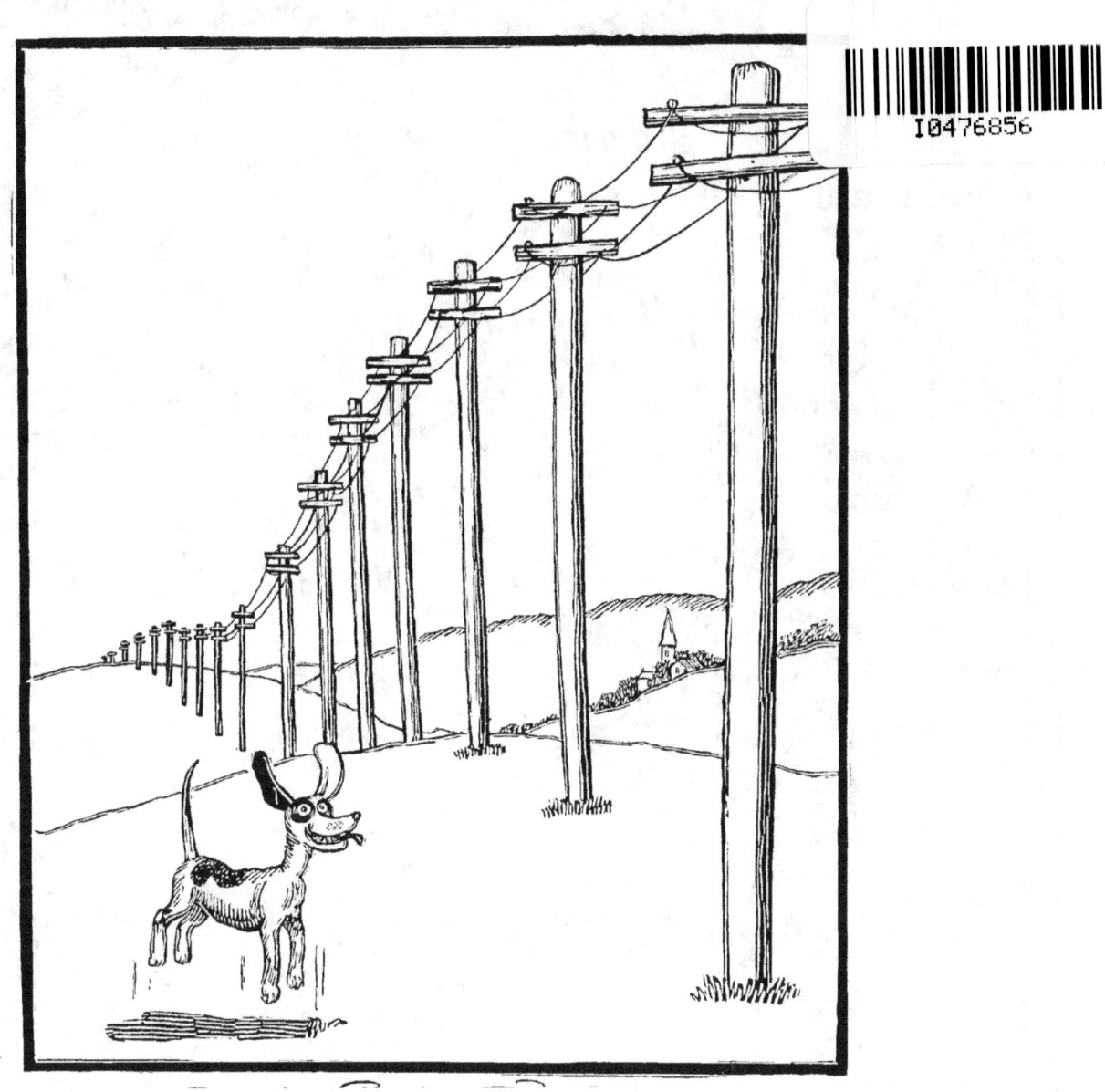

Prepared for publication by Jane Peppler

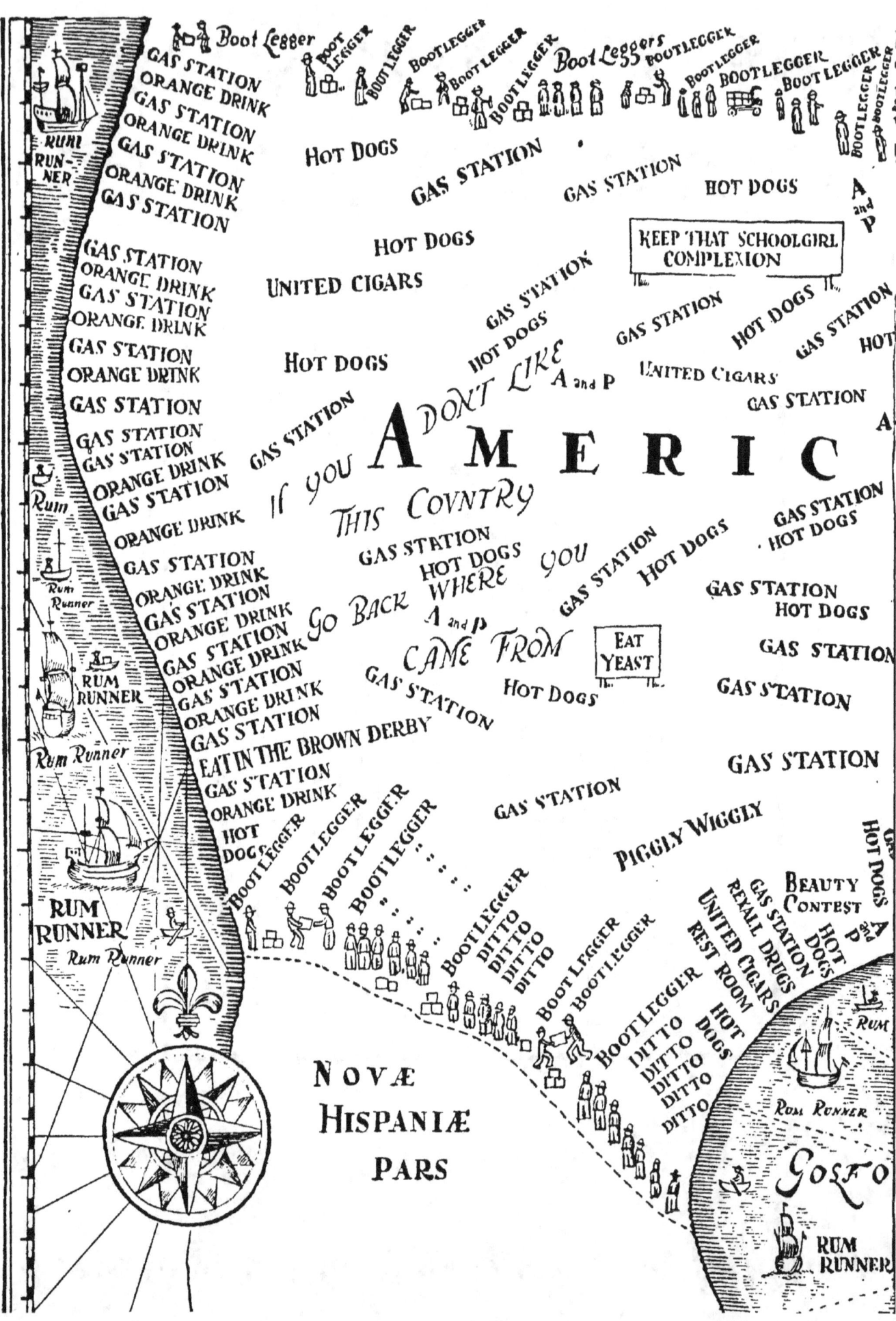

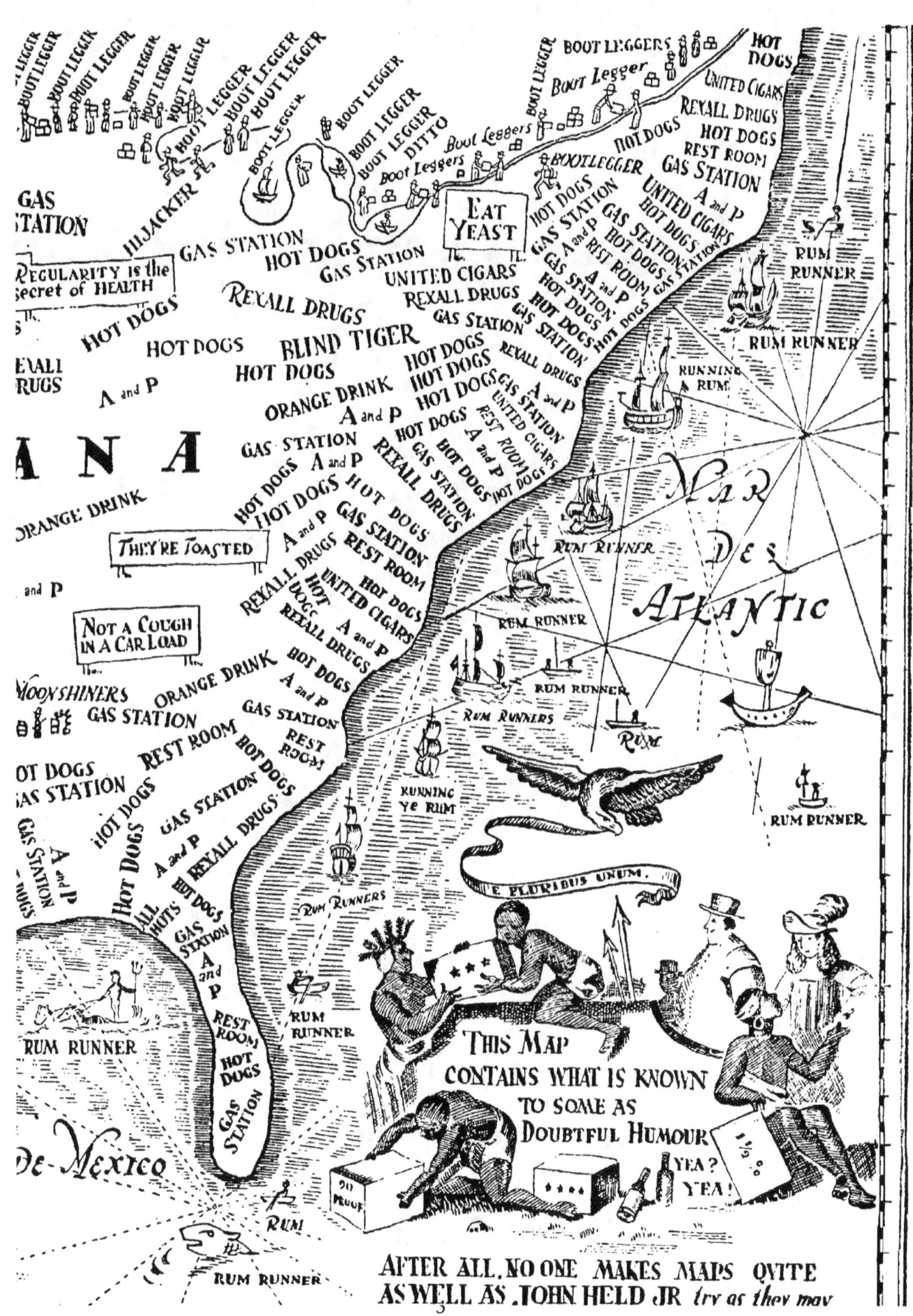

For more copies visit
Uncle Shlomo's Pushcart
http://uncleshlomo.com

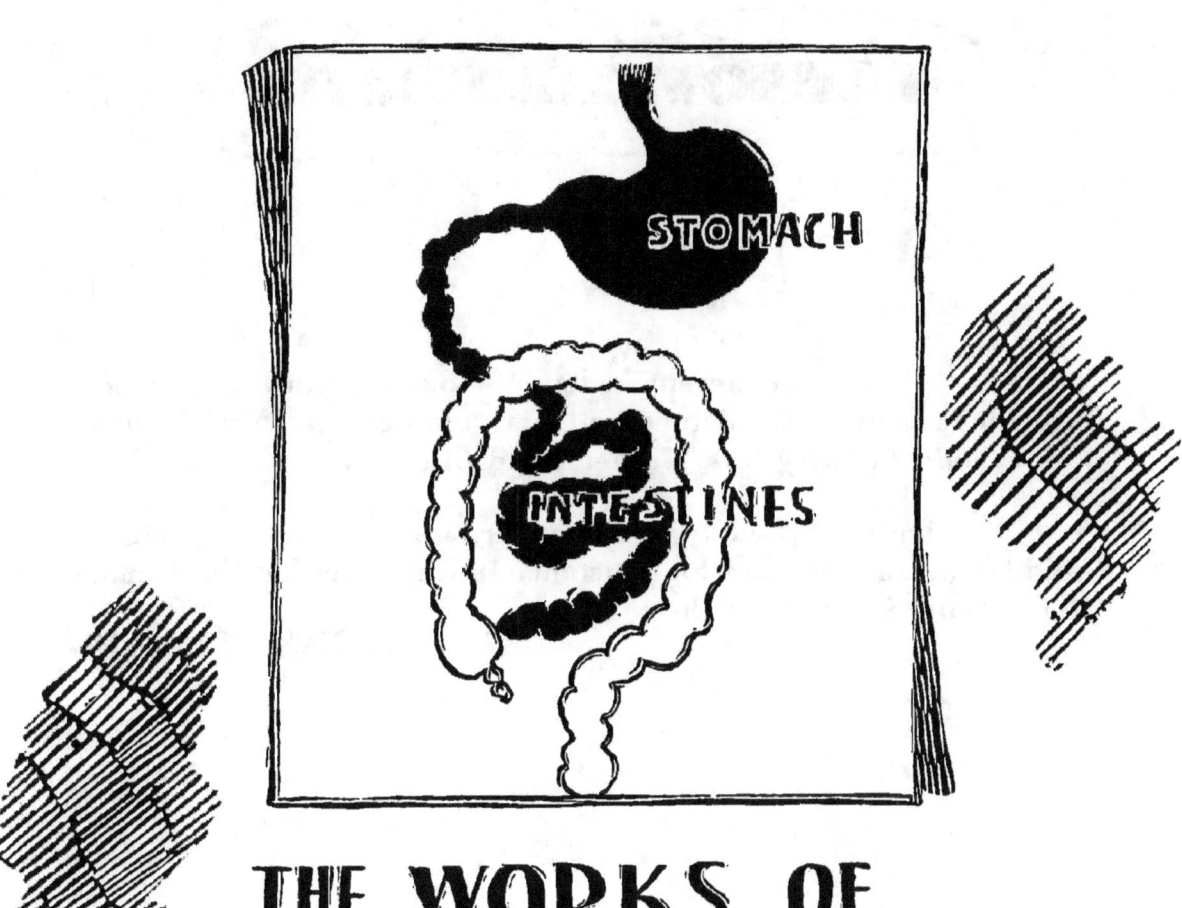

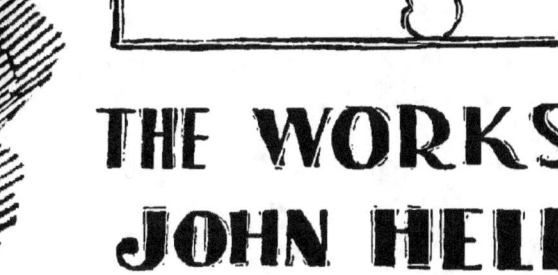

THE WORKS OF
JOHN HELD JR

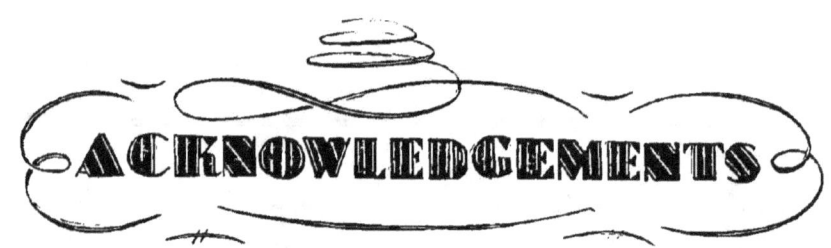

Thanks are hereby extended to the following for permission to reproduce pictures in this volume: *The New Yorker, Vanity Fair, Country Life, Colliers,* and *Life.*

I wish especially to thank Mr. Hal Burrows, he being a kind friend and true, for his assistance in the somewhat illegitimate conception of several of the pictures.

JOHN HELD JR

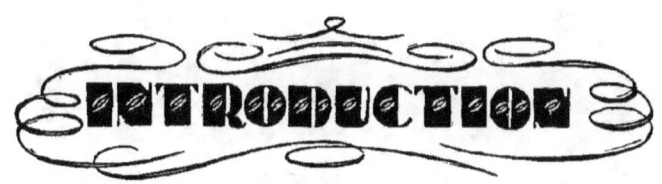

INTRODUCTION

I have known John Held Junior ever since he was born. His first official job, which was witnessed by the city editor of the Salt Lake Tribune on which he was working at the time, was— what? Oh, all right, perhaps we had better not be too explicit about that first job. His second official job was—please don't interrupt,— there is nothing wrong with a cartoonist's being hungry. That's perfectly natural, isn't it? His third official act was to shout, "Where the hell is my pencil?" and placing it in the left side of his tiny mouth, (Held was always left handed and still is, for that matter) he thereupon drew his first picture on what later turned out to be a brand new diaper which his mother had placed there in anticipation of his first official job. So there you are, I got it in after all. I've always said, if I'm allowed to coin a phrase, where there's a will there's a way.

As I was about to say I have known John Held, Jr. ever since he was born and I get pretty sick of him sometimes.

JOHN HELD JR

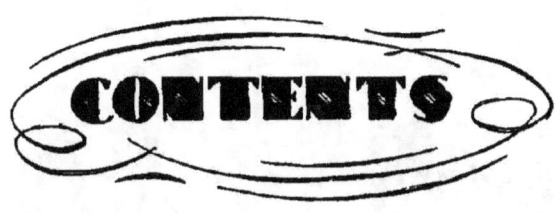

CONTENTS

THE WORKS OF
JOHN HELD JR

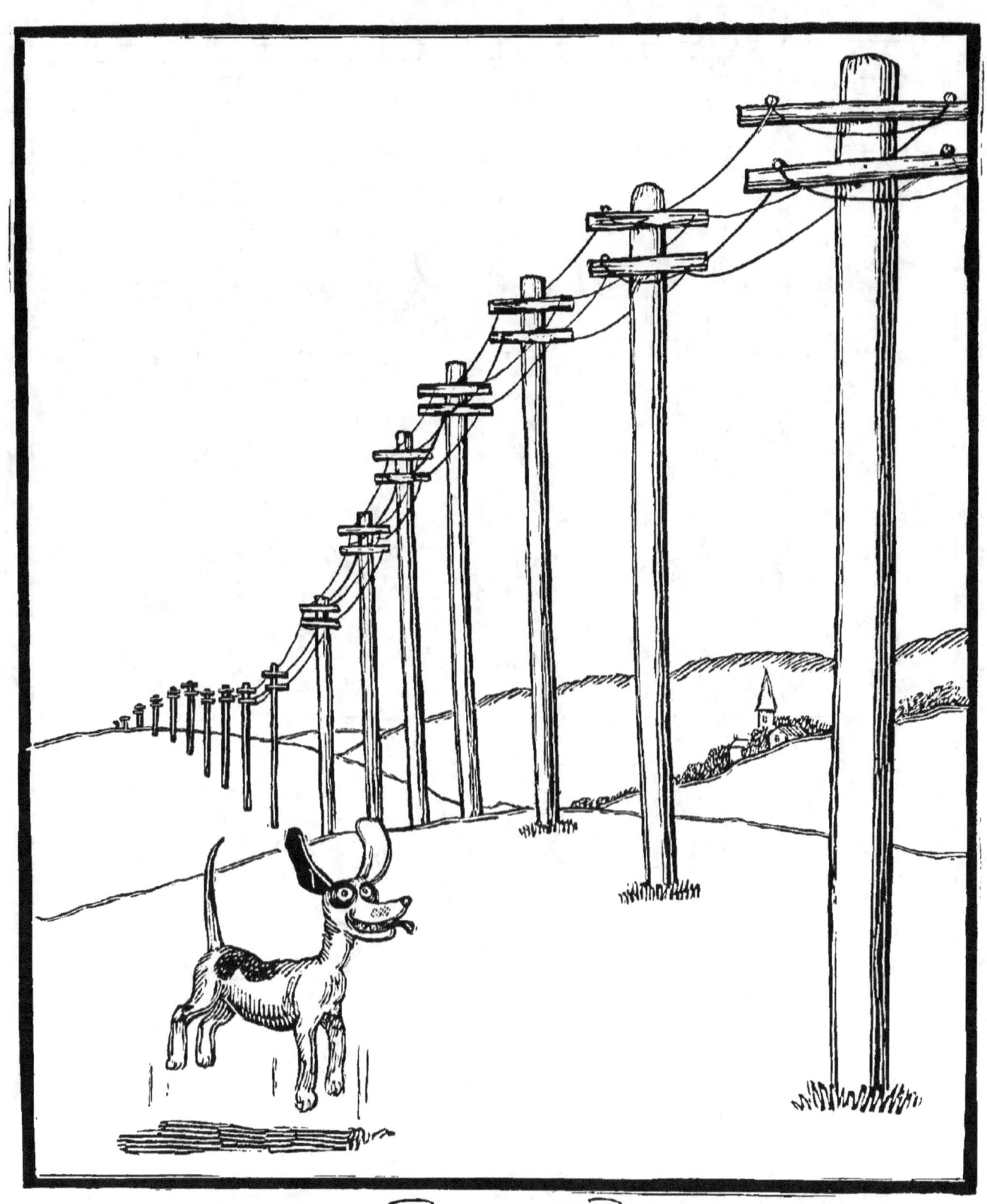

PARADISE

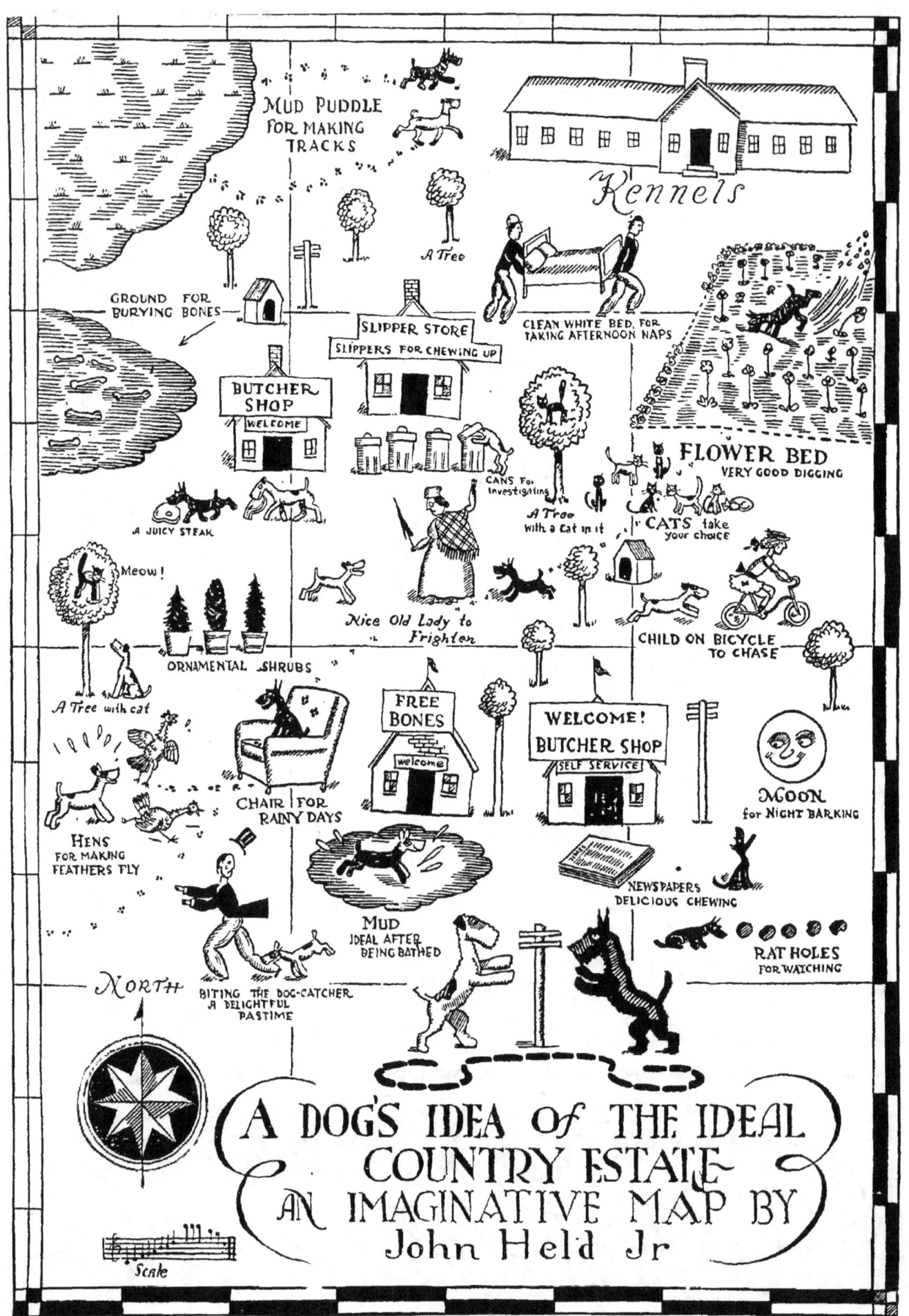

A DOG'S IDEA of THE IDEAL COUNTRY ESTATE—AN IMAGINATIVE MAP BY John Held Jr

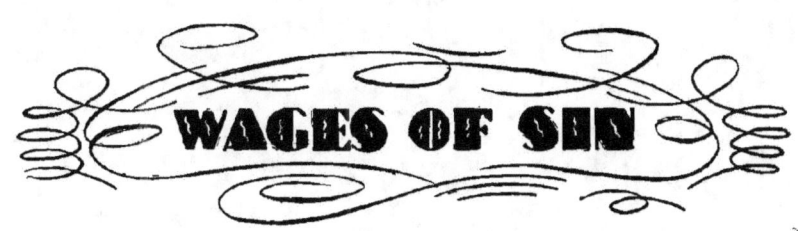

WAGES OF SIN

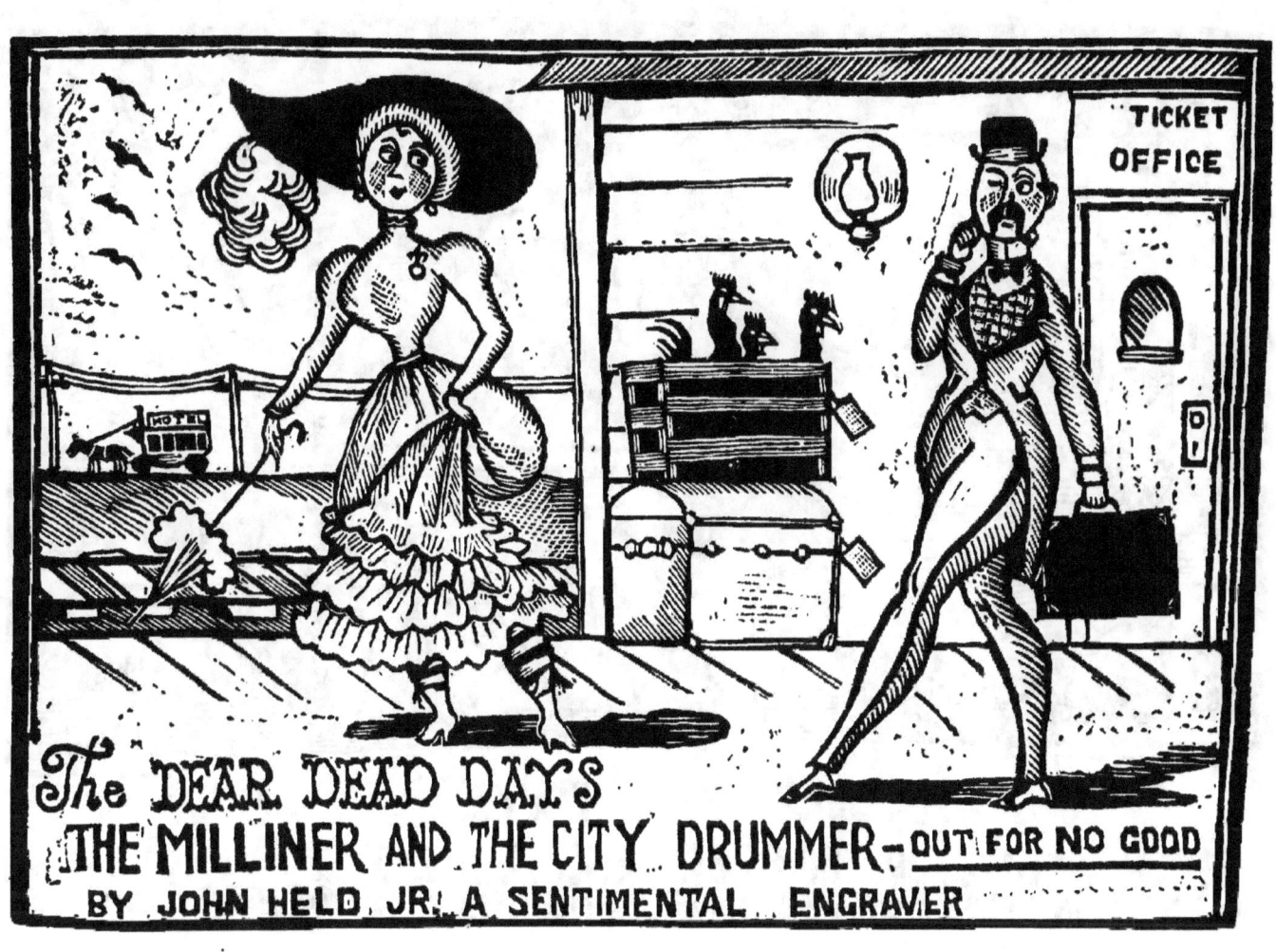

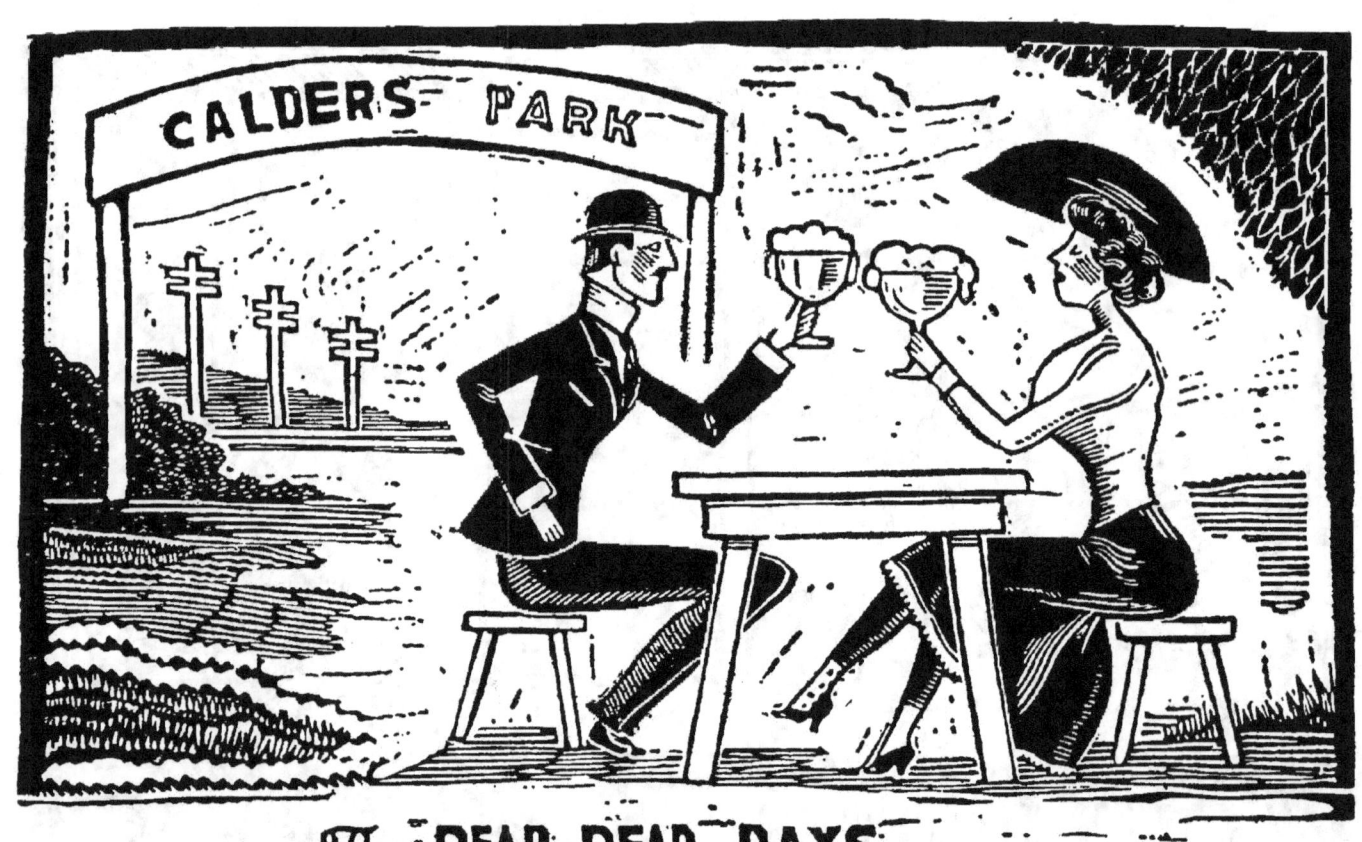

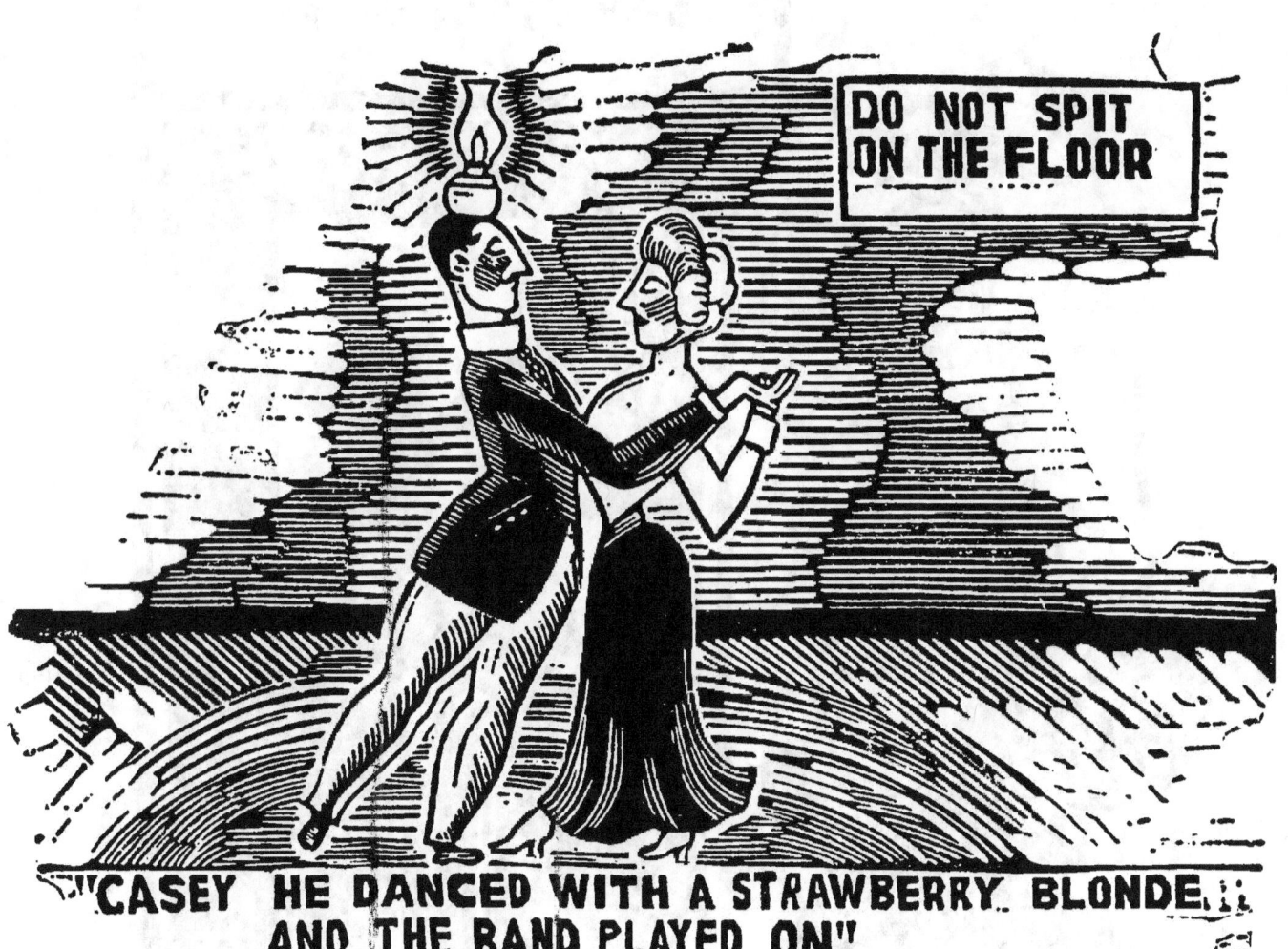

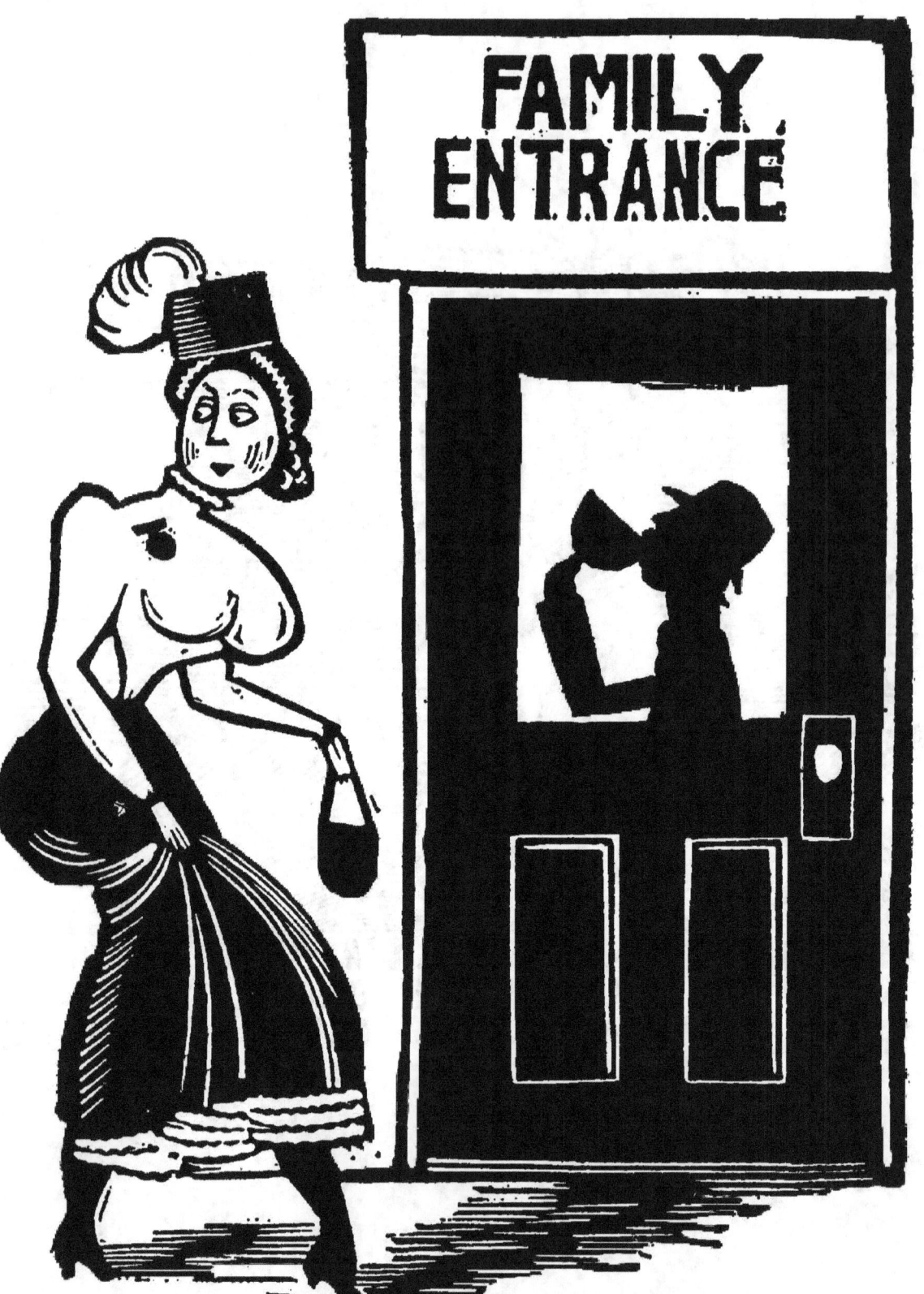

THE ROAD TO RUIN

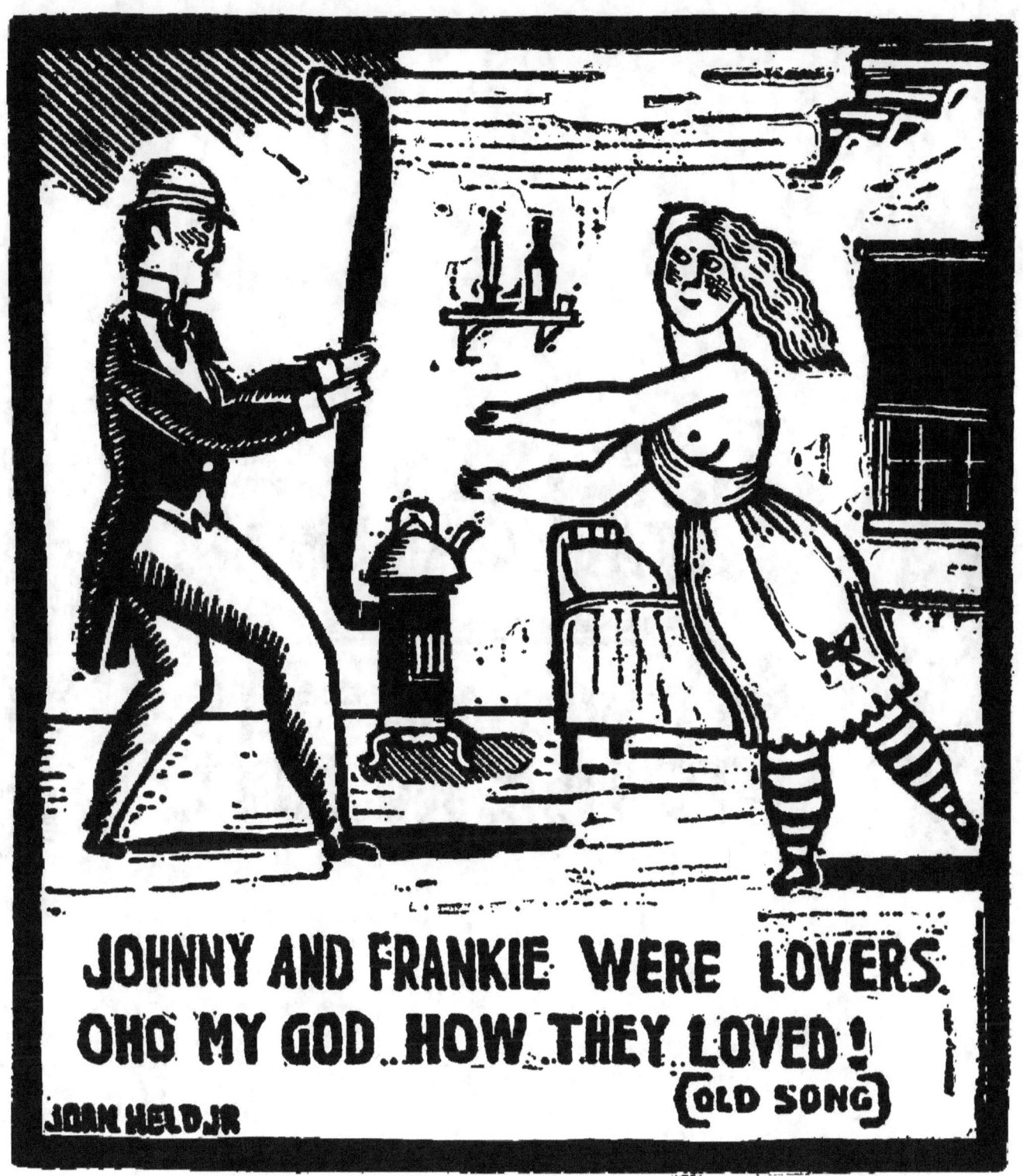

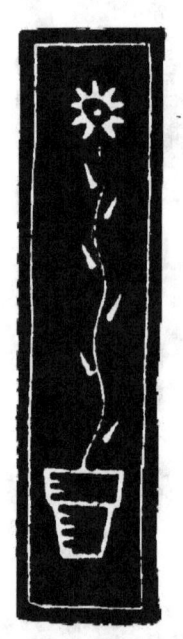

THE FALLEN MAN AGAIN CAN SOAR

BUT WOMAN FALLS TO RISE NO MORE

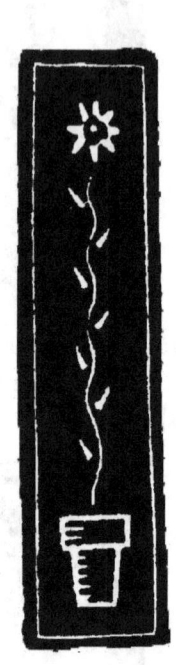

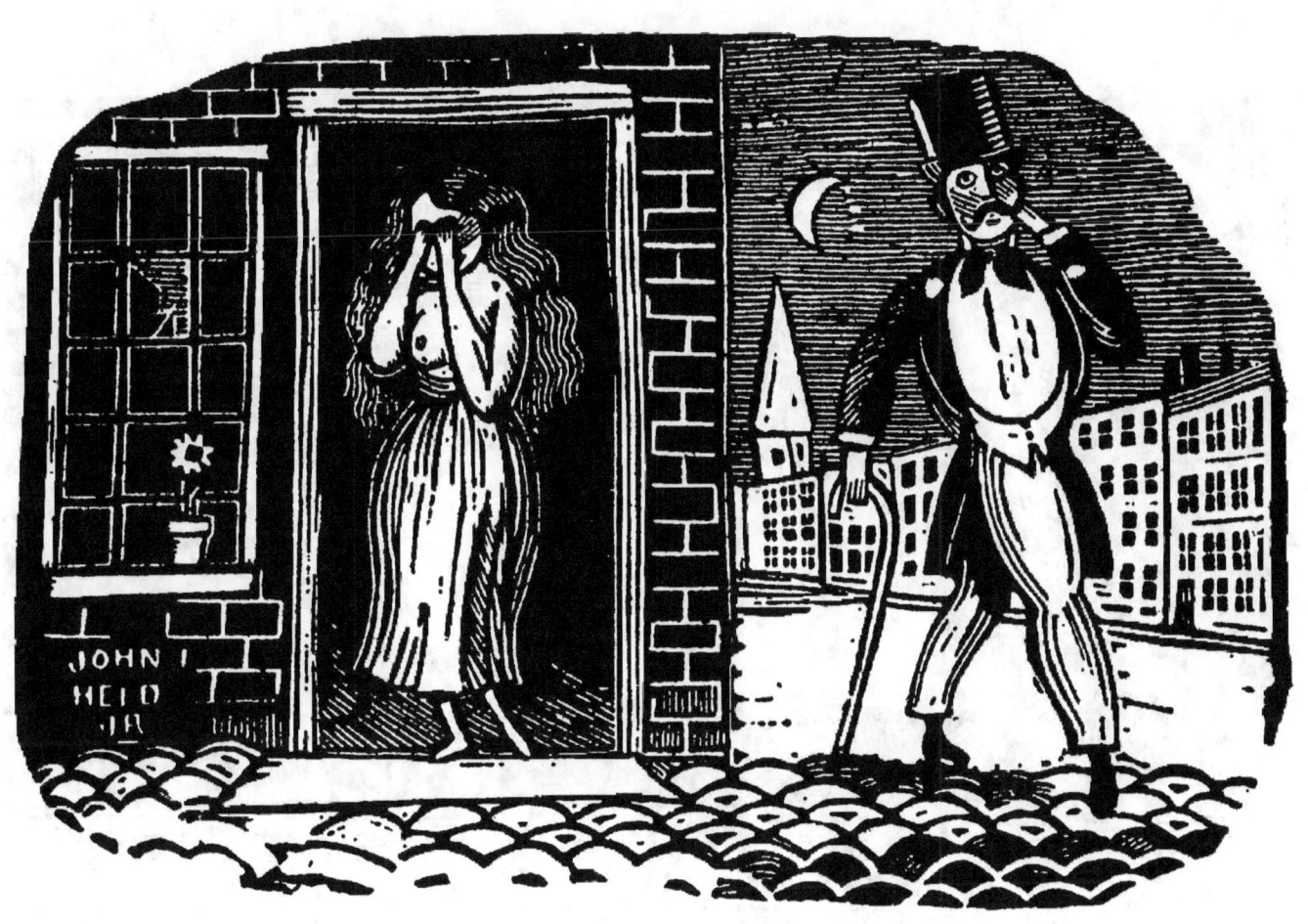

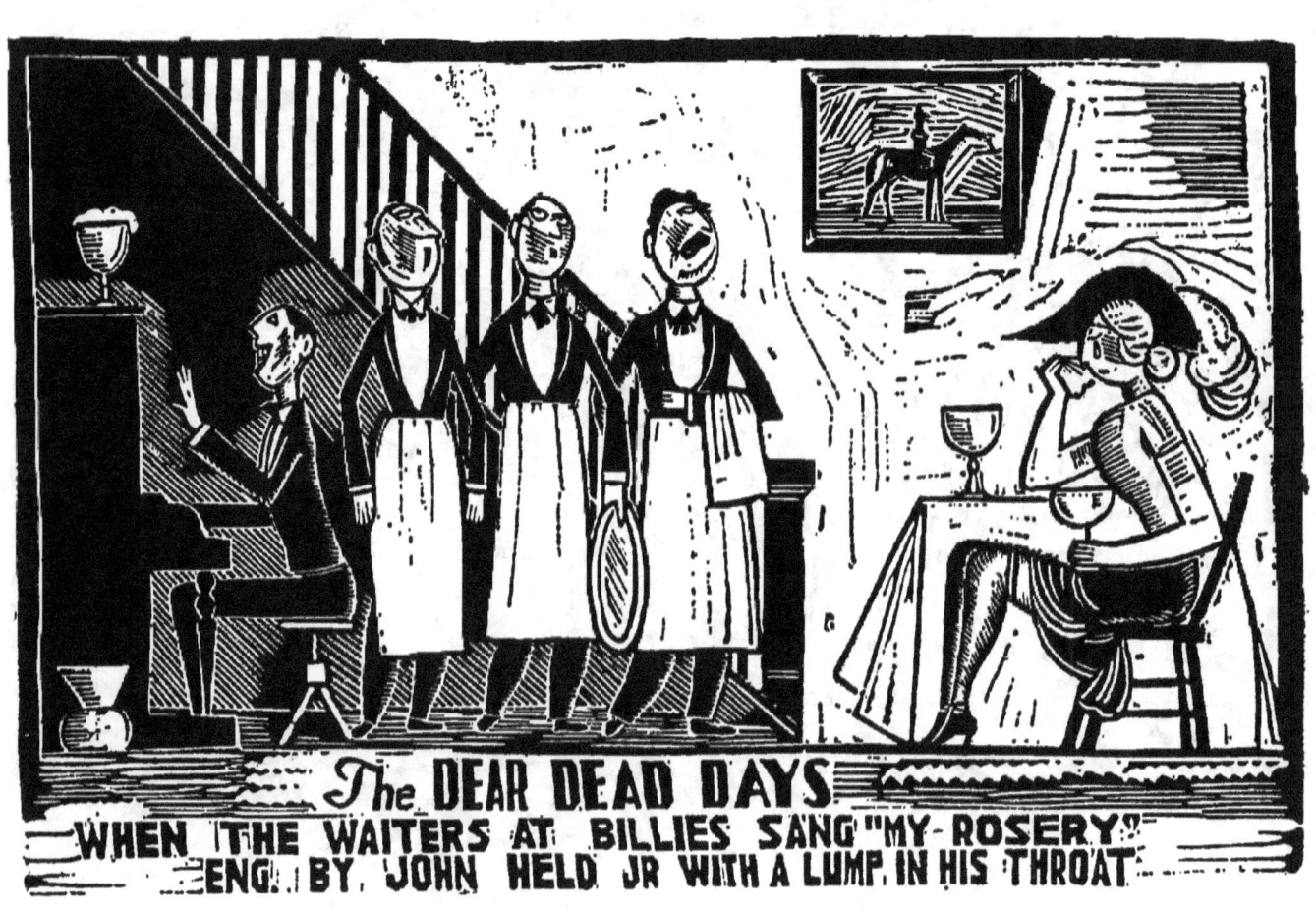

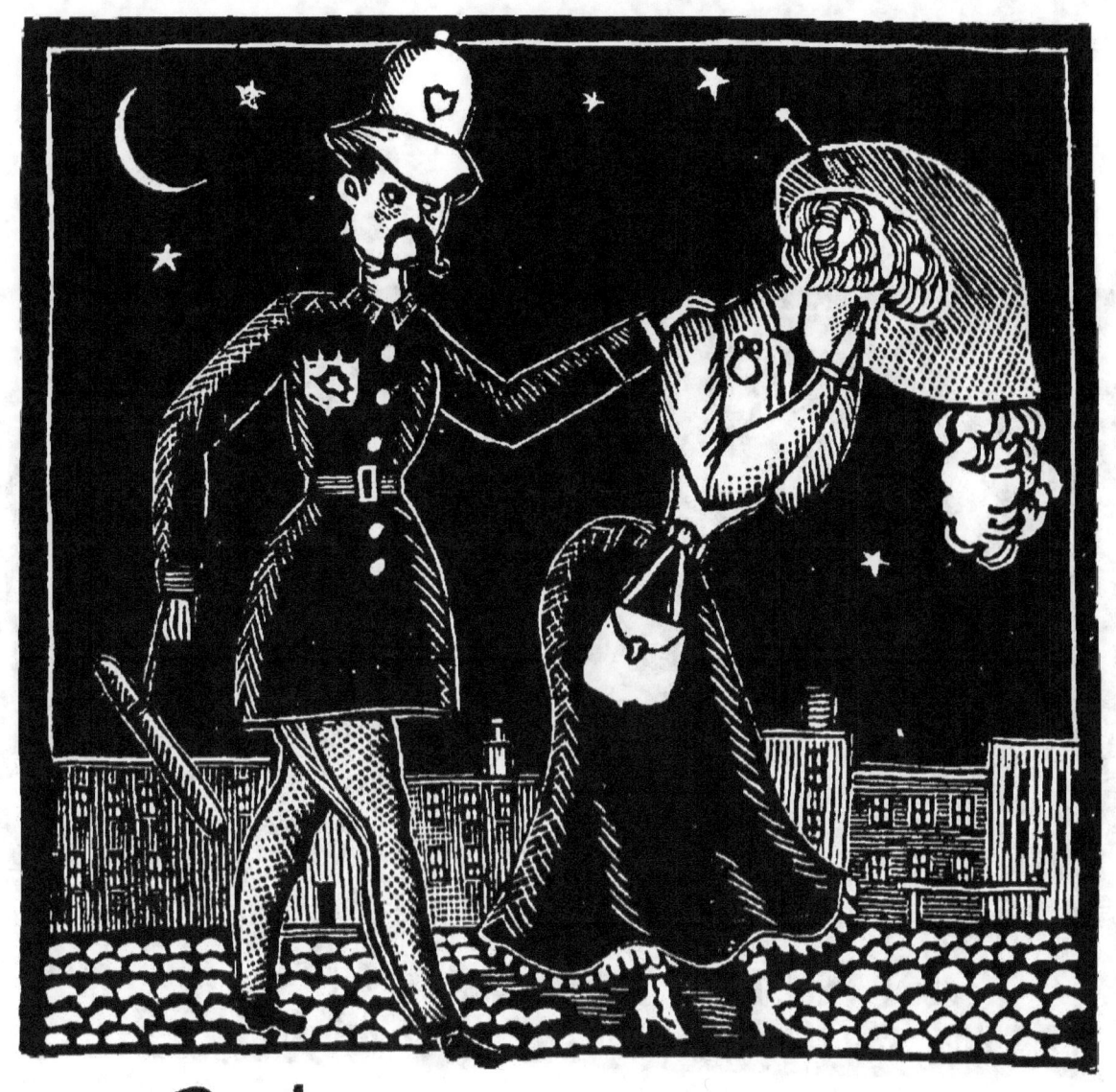

SHE'S ONLY A LASSIE WHO VENTURED ON LIFE'S STORMY PATH ILL-ADVISED

ENG. BY JOHN HELD JR WITH A HEART FULL OF PITY

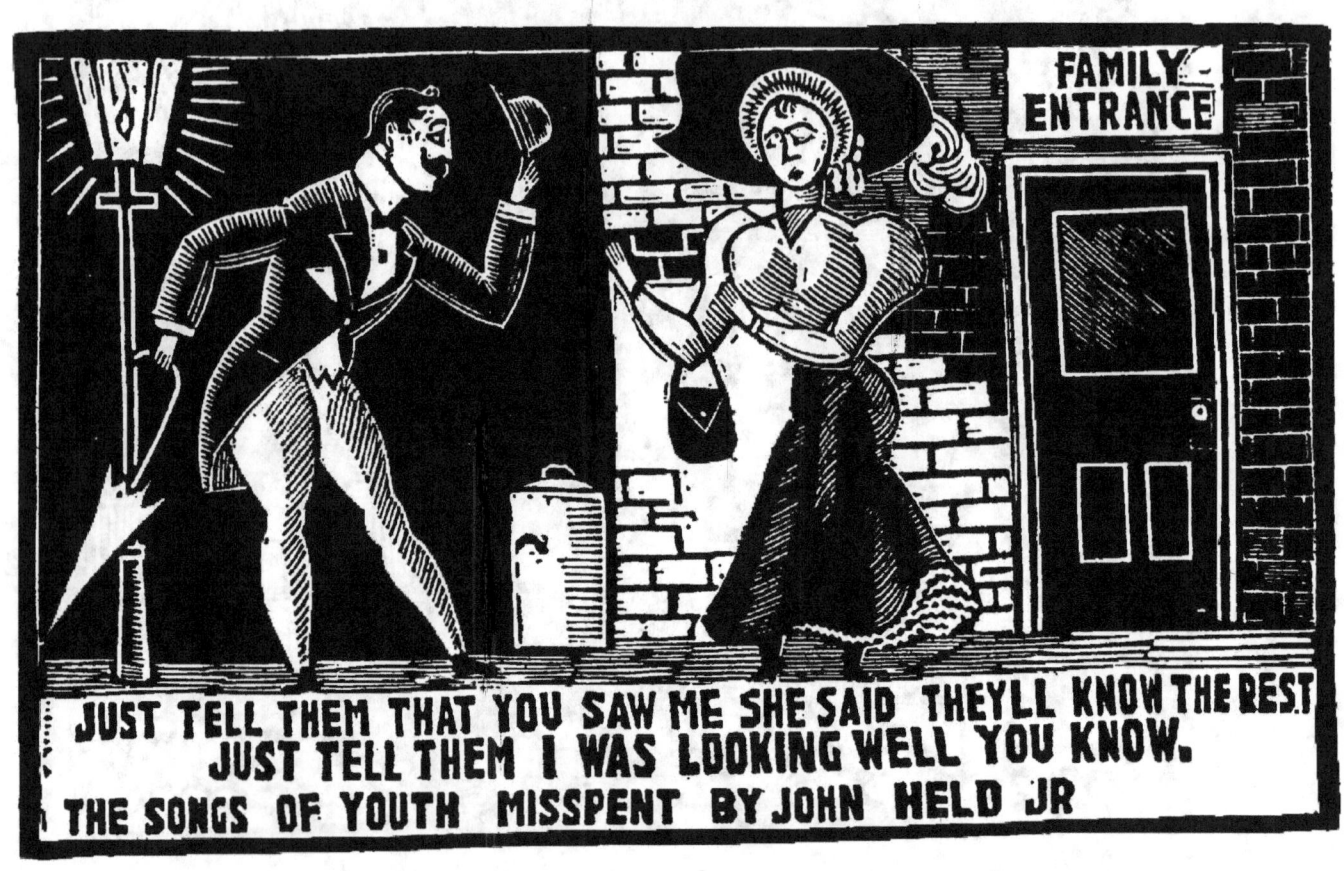

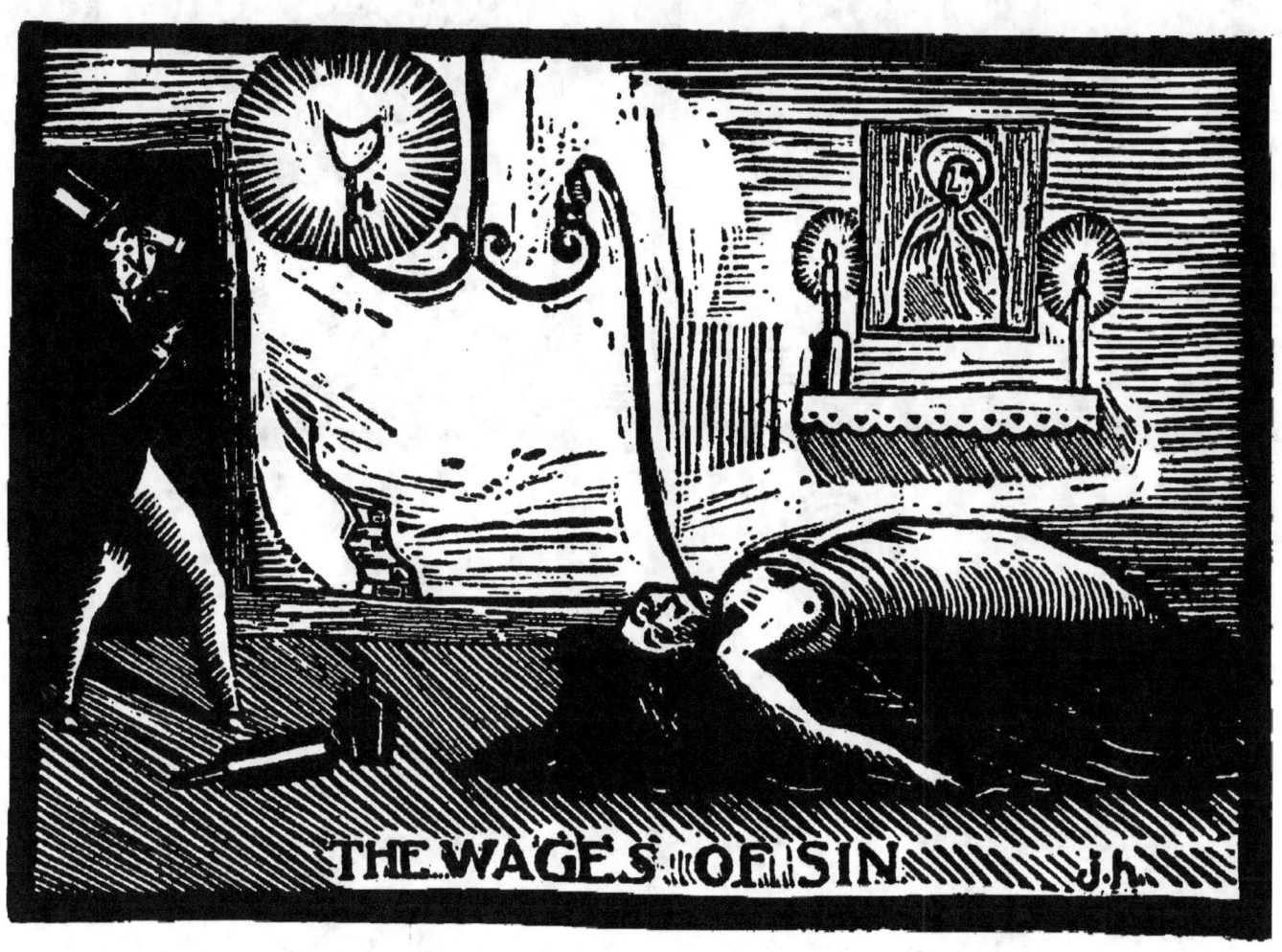

THE WAGES OF SIN   j.h.

THE FATE OF THE CIGARETTE FIEND
ENGRAVED BY JOHN HELD JR.

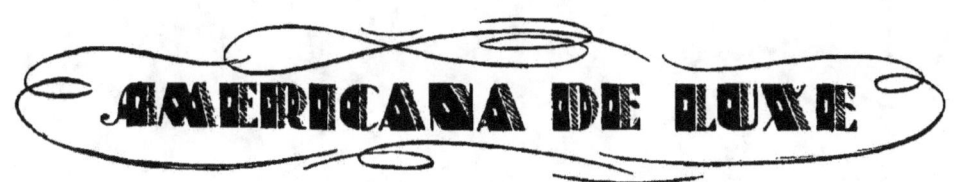

AMERICANA DE LUXE

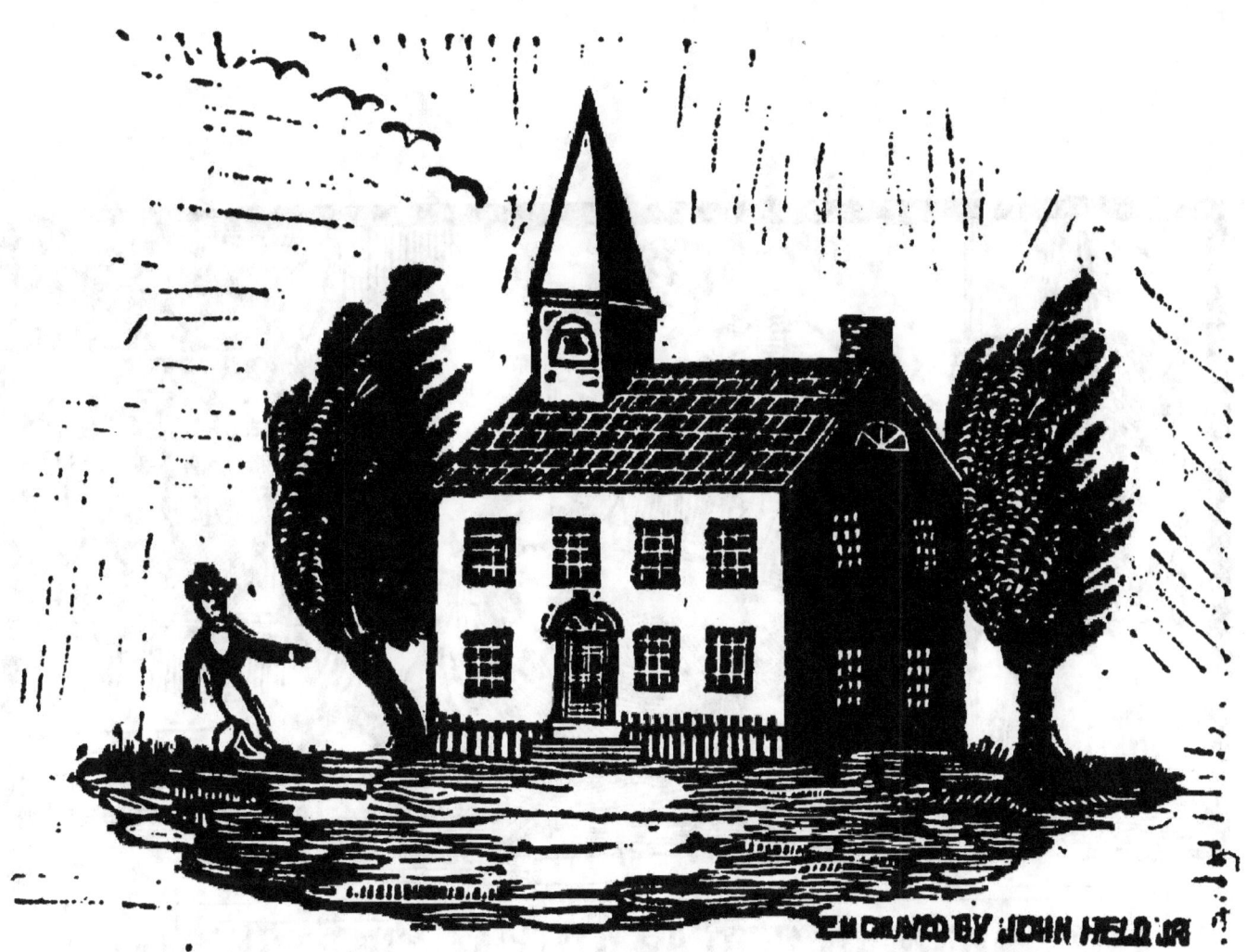

ENGRAVED BY JOHN HELD JR

The CHURCH THAT GEORGE WASHINGTON, SLEPT IN

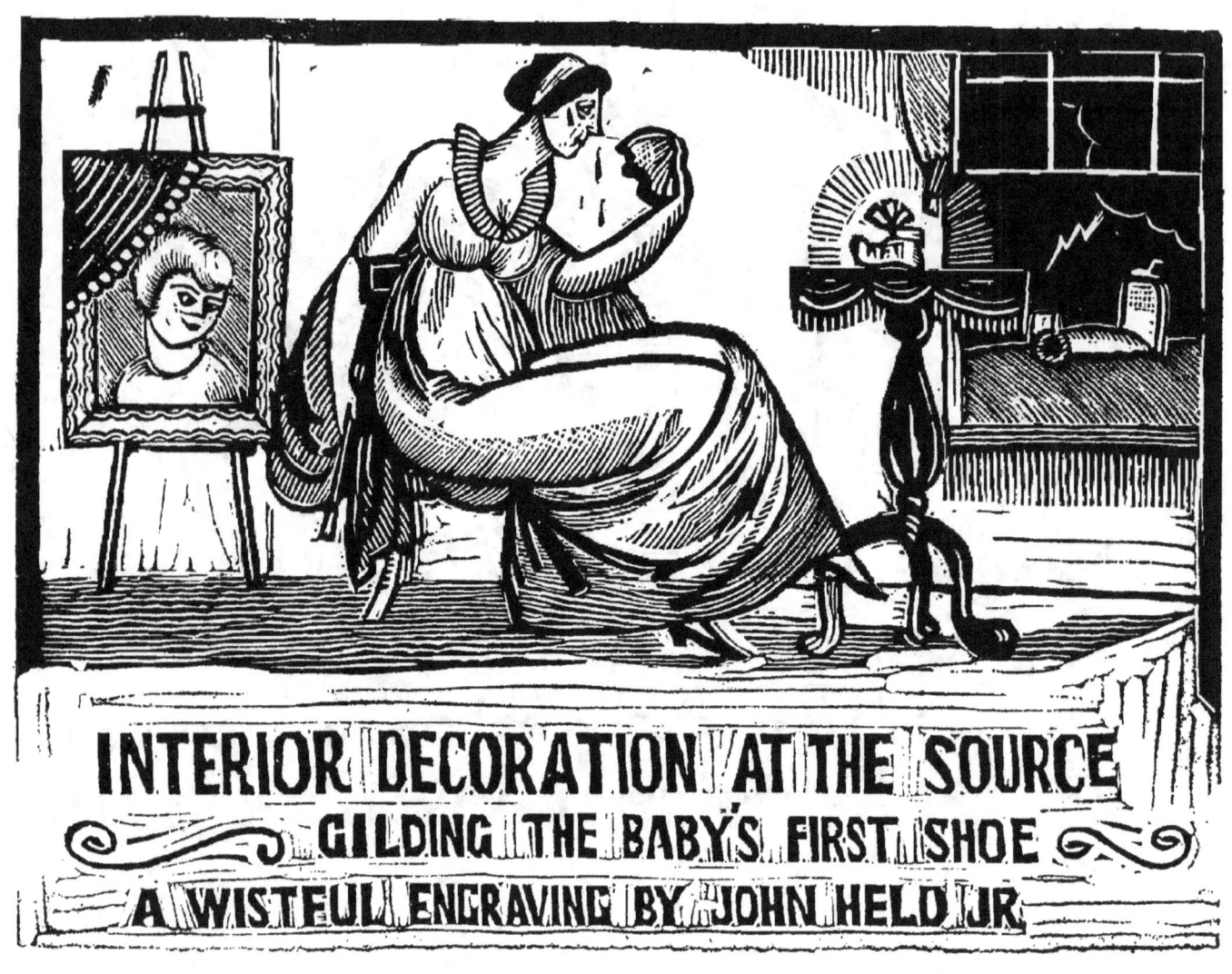

INTERIOR DECORATION AT THE SOURCE
GILDING THE BABY'S FIRST SHOE
A WISTFUL ENGRAVING BY JOHN HELD JR

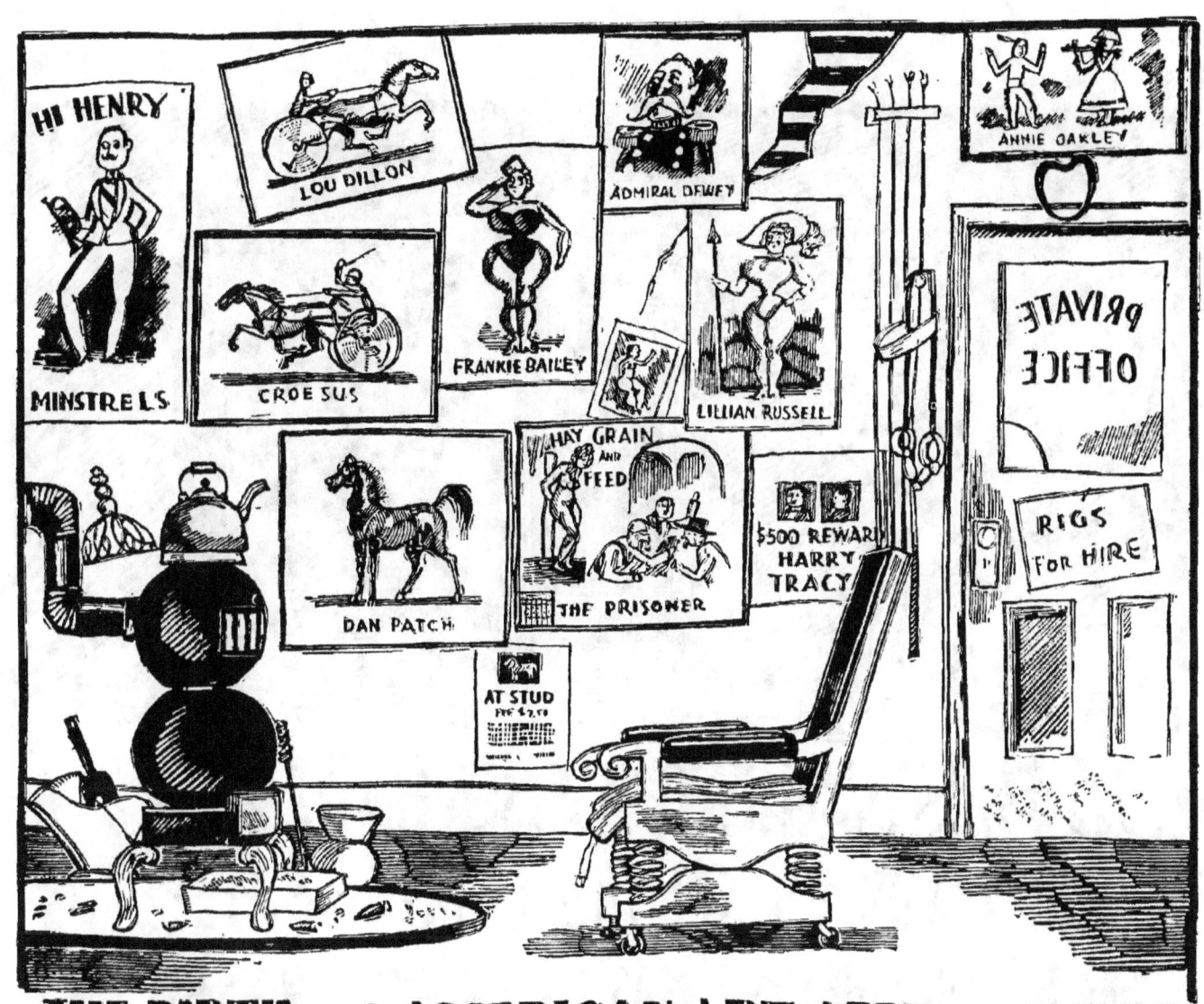

THE BIRTH of AMERICAN ART APPRECIATION
BY JOHN HELD JR. PIONEER ENGRAVER.
WHO RECALLS THE MAGIC ENCHANTMENT OF THE OFFICE OF the LIVERY BARN

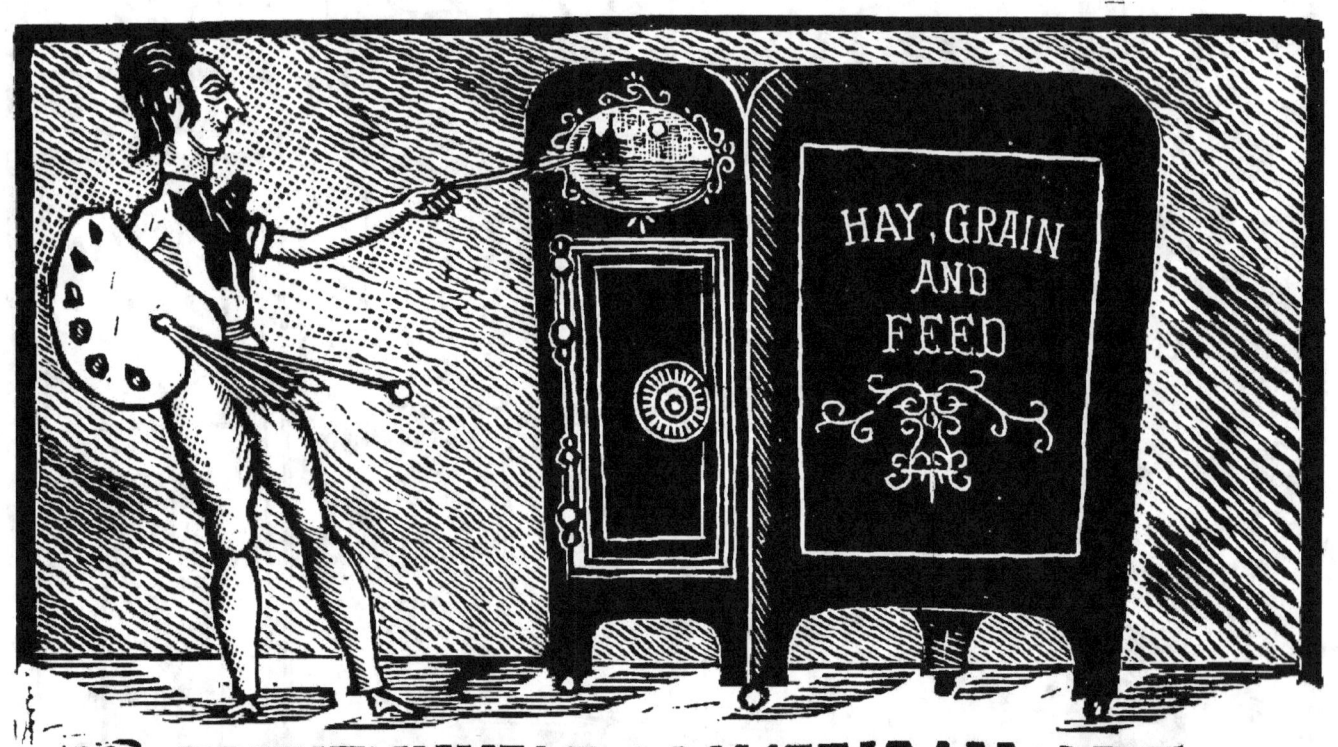

The FOUNTAINHEAD of AMERICAN ART
THE LANDSCAPE ON THE OFFICE SAFE
ENG BY JOHN HELD JR MASTER OF WIT AND SATIRE

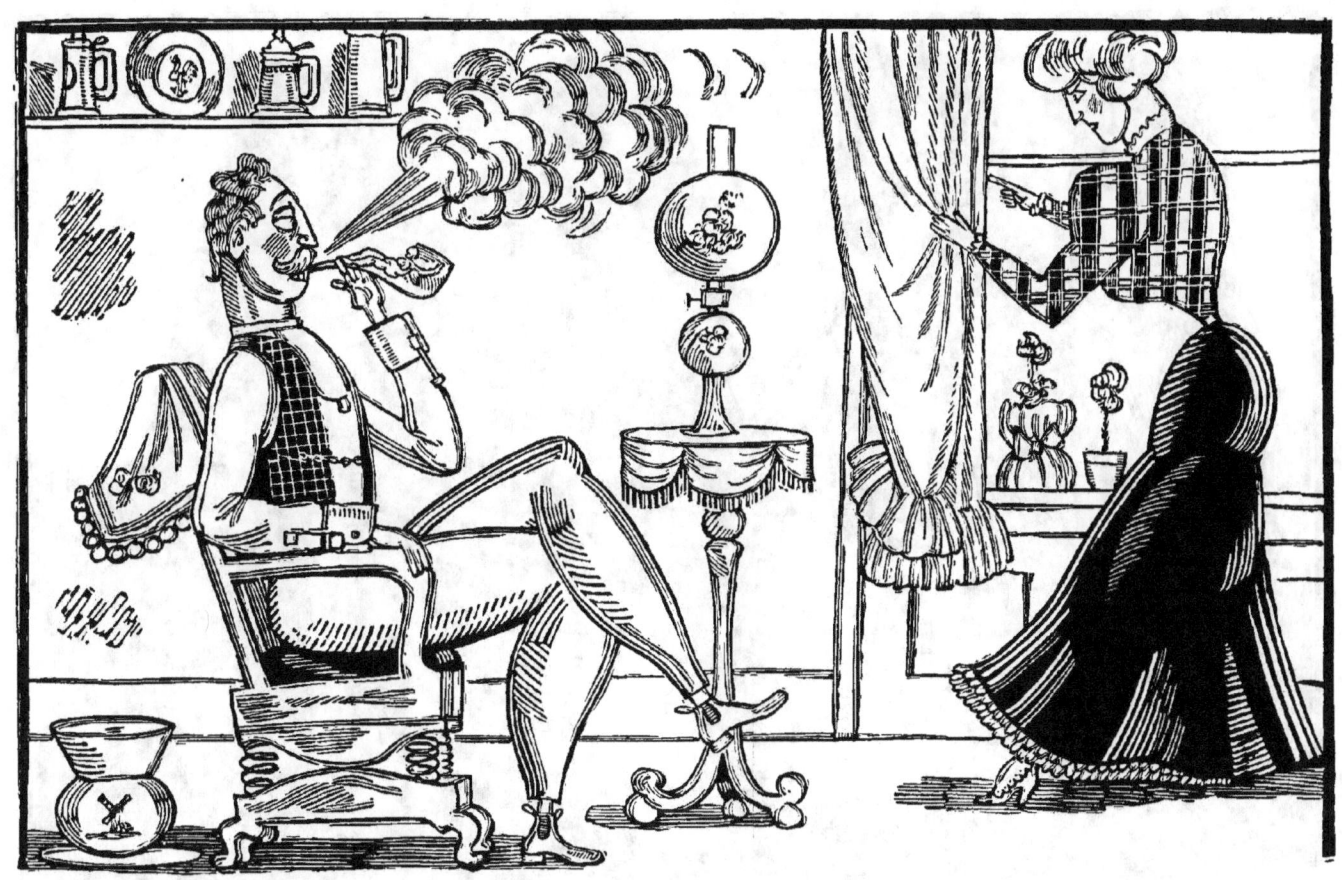

A Solemn Ceremony of Utmost Importance

COLORING the MEERSCHAUM PIPE

Engraved by **JOHN HELD JR** who is ever ready for a fight or a frolic

OH HEARTLESS MEMORY

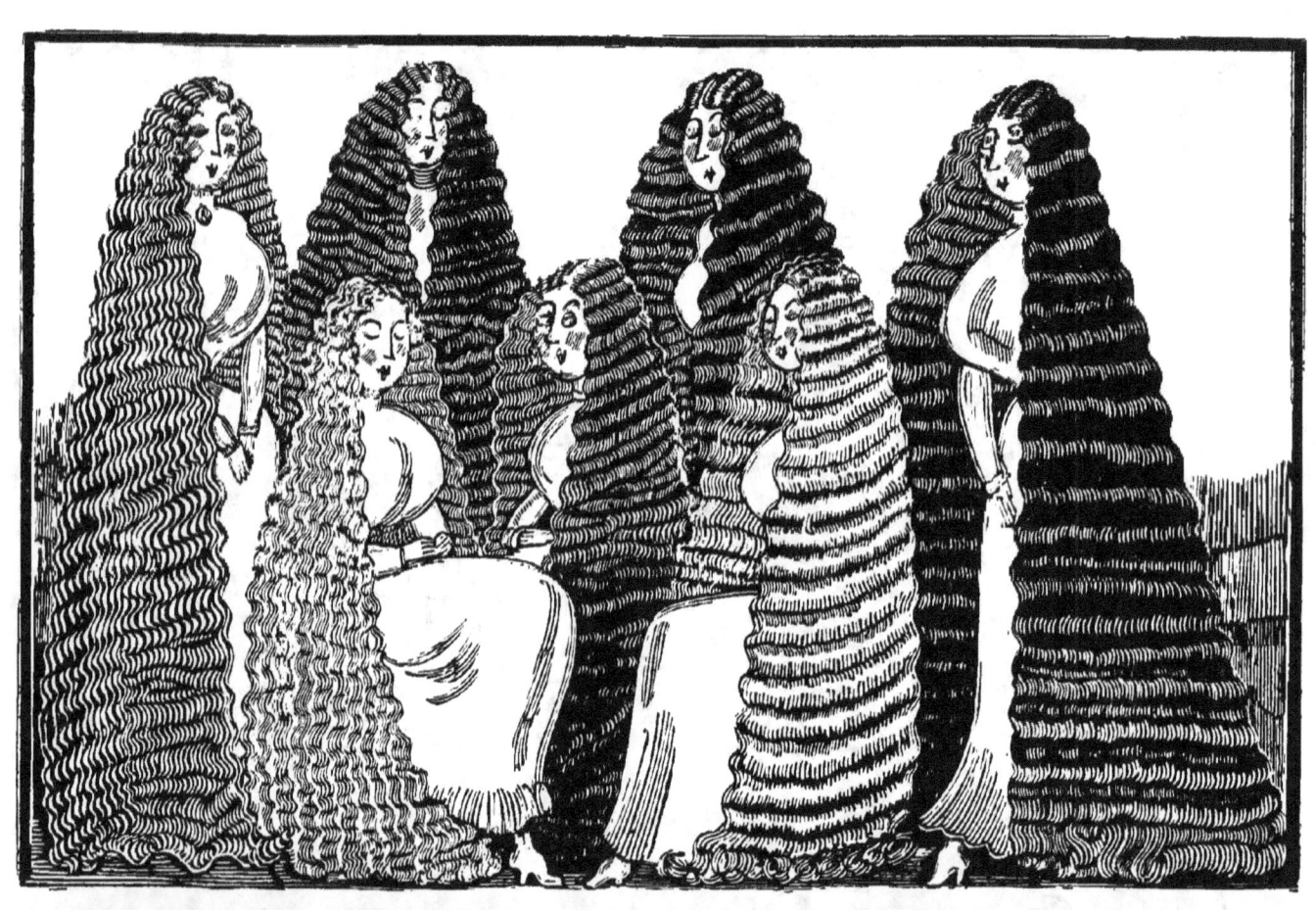

DREAM GIRLS of a DIM DECADE
SEVEN SUTHERLAND SISTERS
ENG. BY JOHN HELD JR SINGER OF OLD SONGS

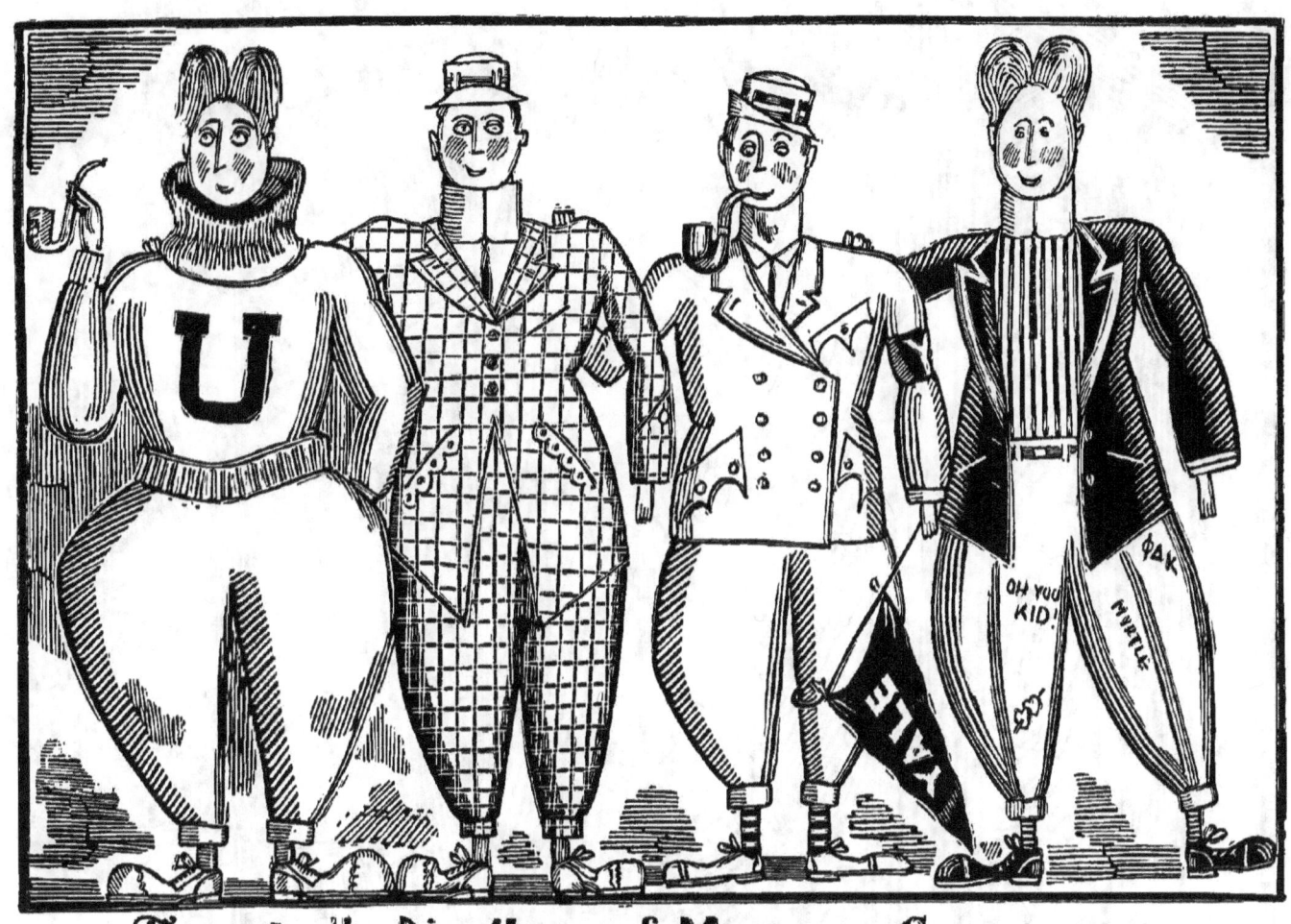

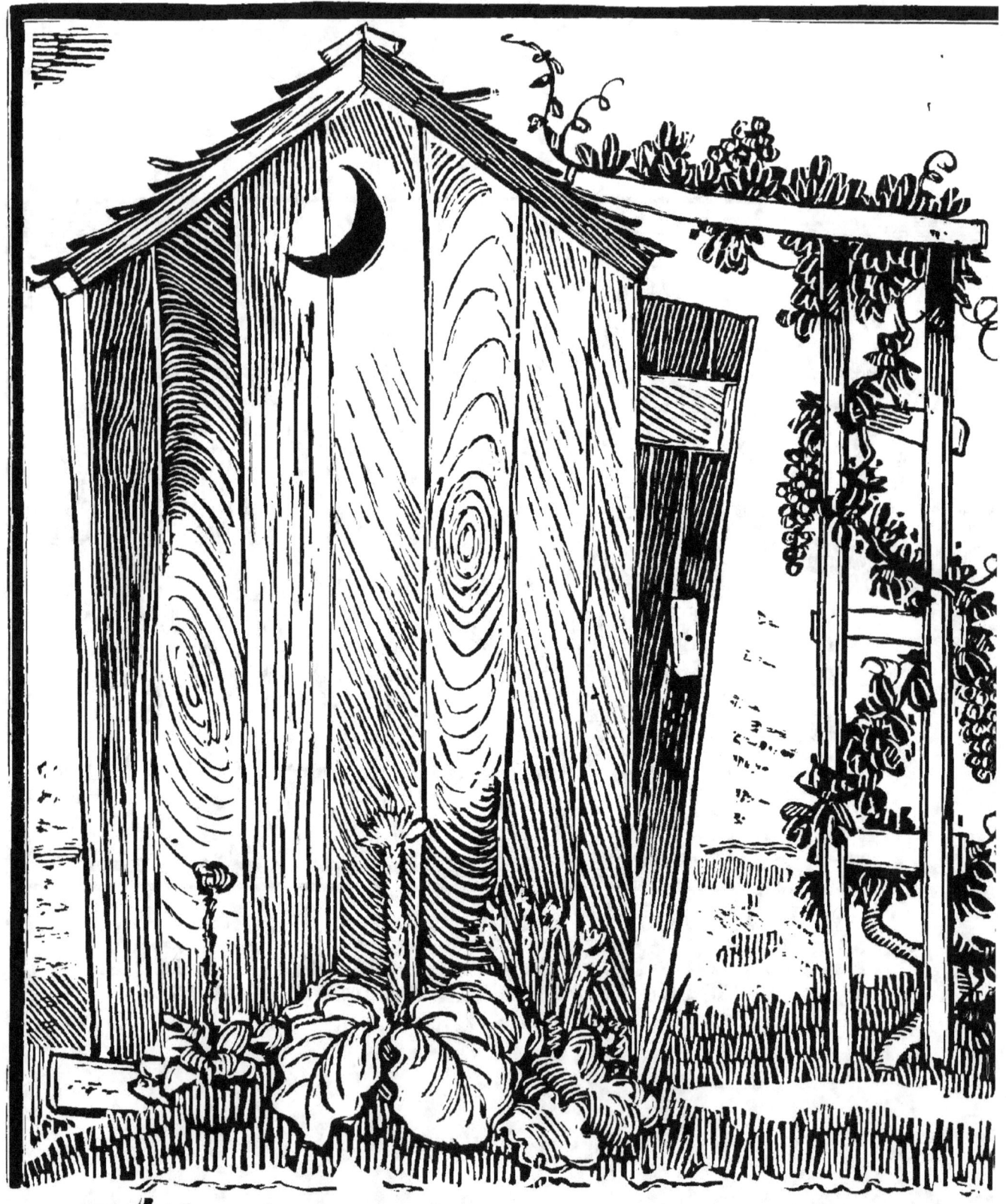

The FOUNT OF AMERICA

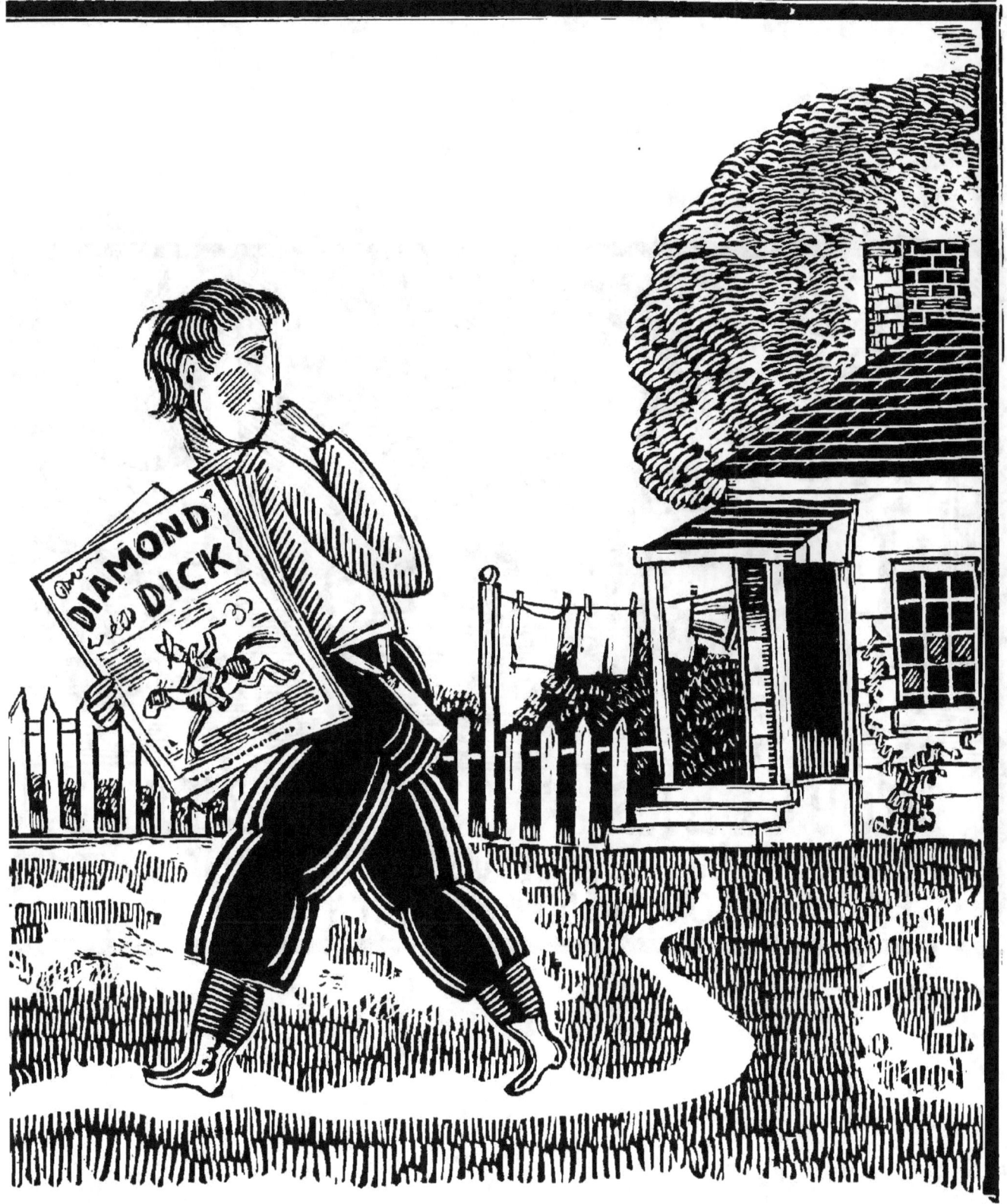

LITERARY APPRECIATION

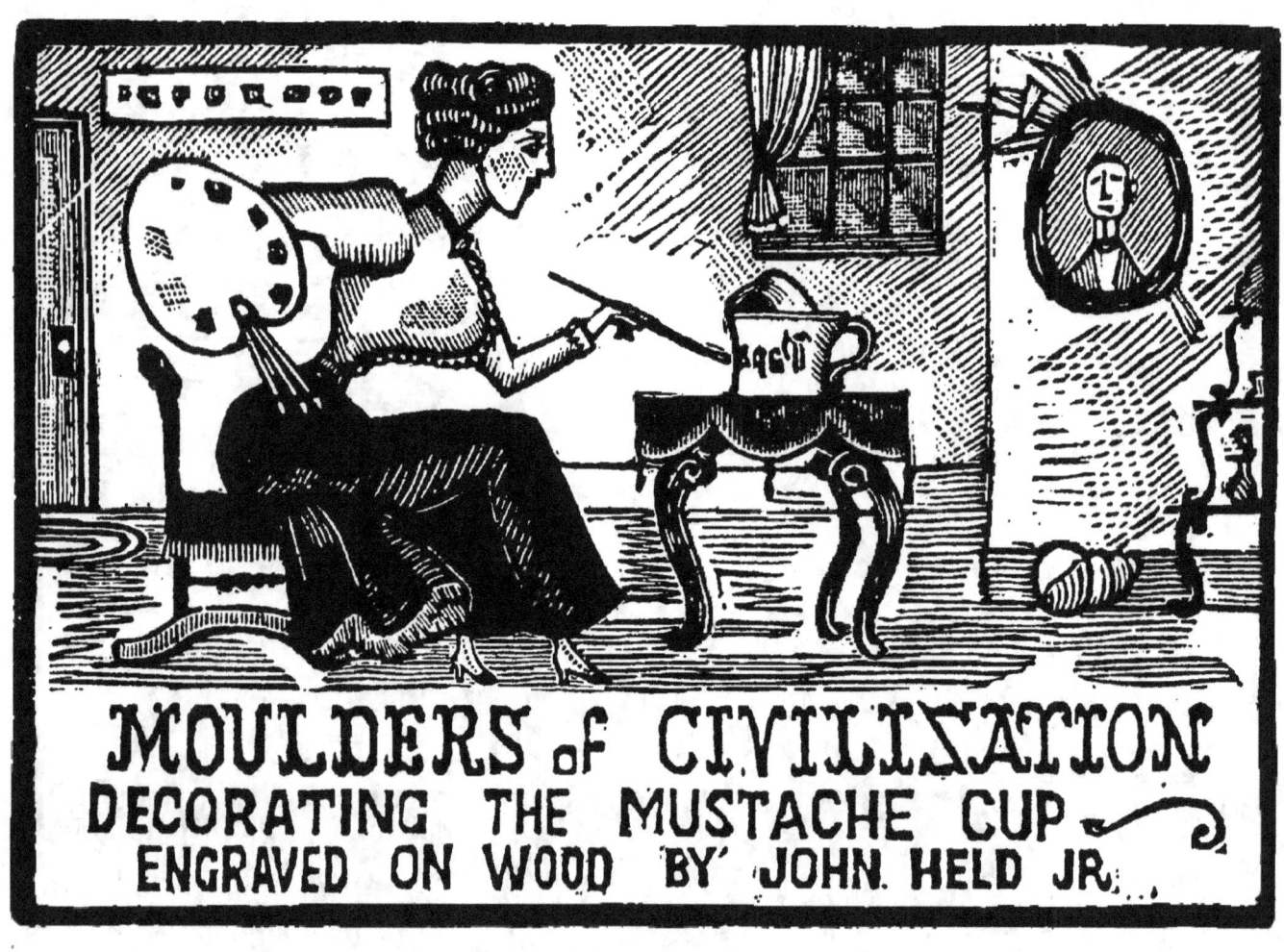

MOULDERS of CIVILISATION
DECORATING THE MUSTACHE CUP
ENGRAVED ON WOOD BY JOHN HELD JR.

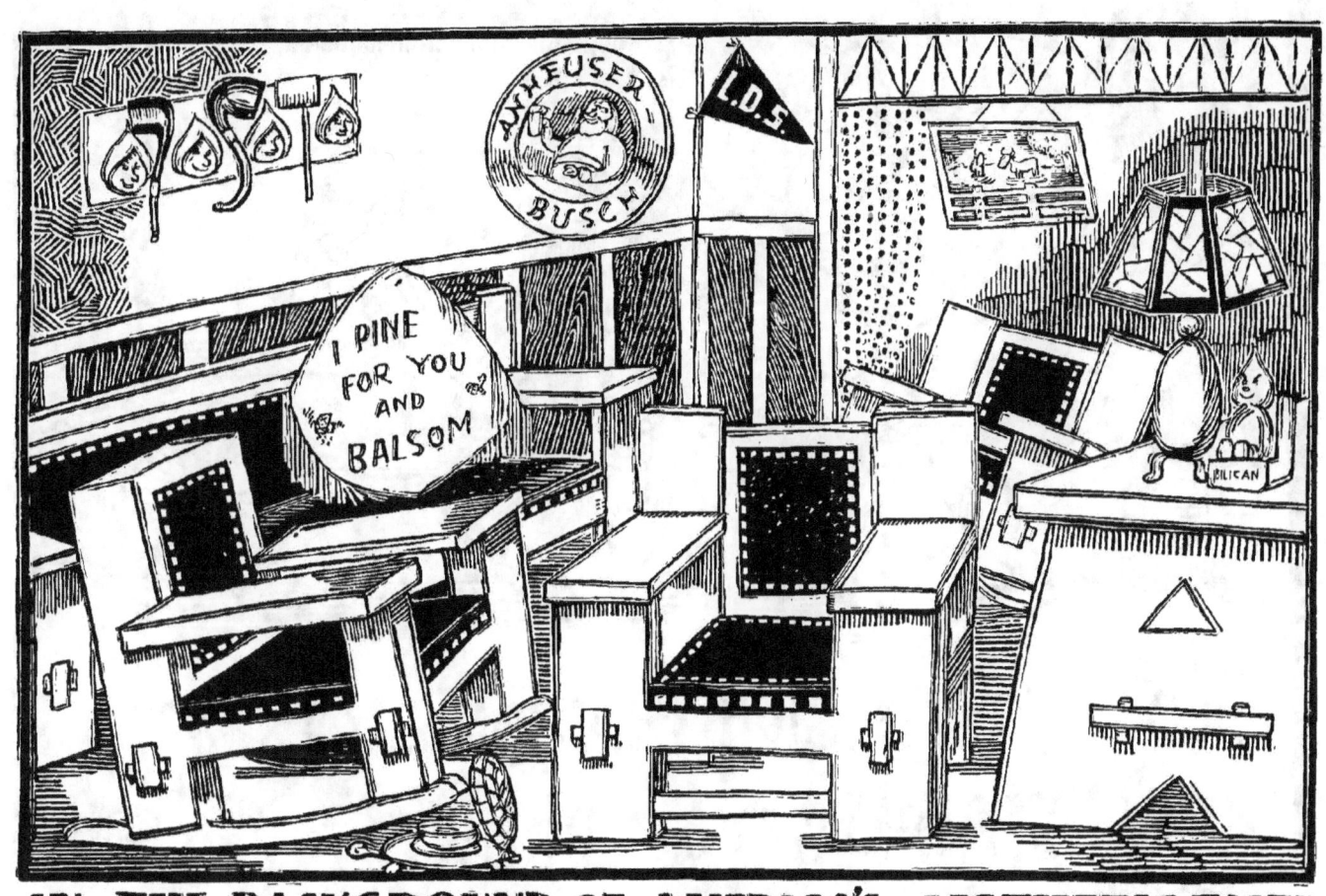

IN THE BACKGROUND OF AMERICA'S AESTHETIC TASTE
MISSION FURNITURE
ENGRAVED BY JOHN HELD JR PHILOSOPHER AND POET

43

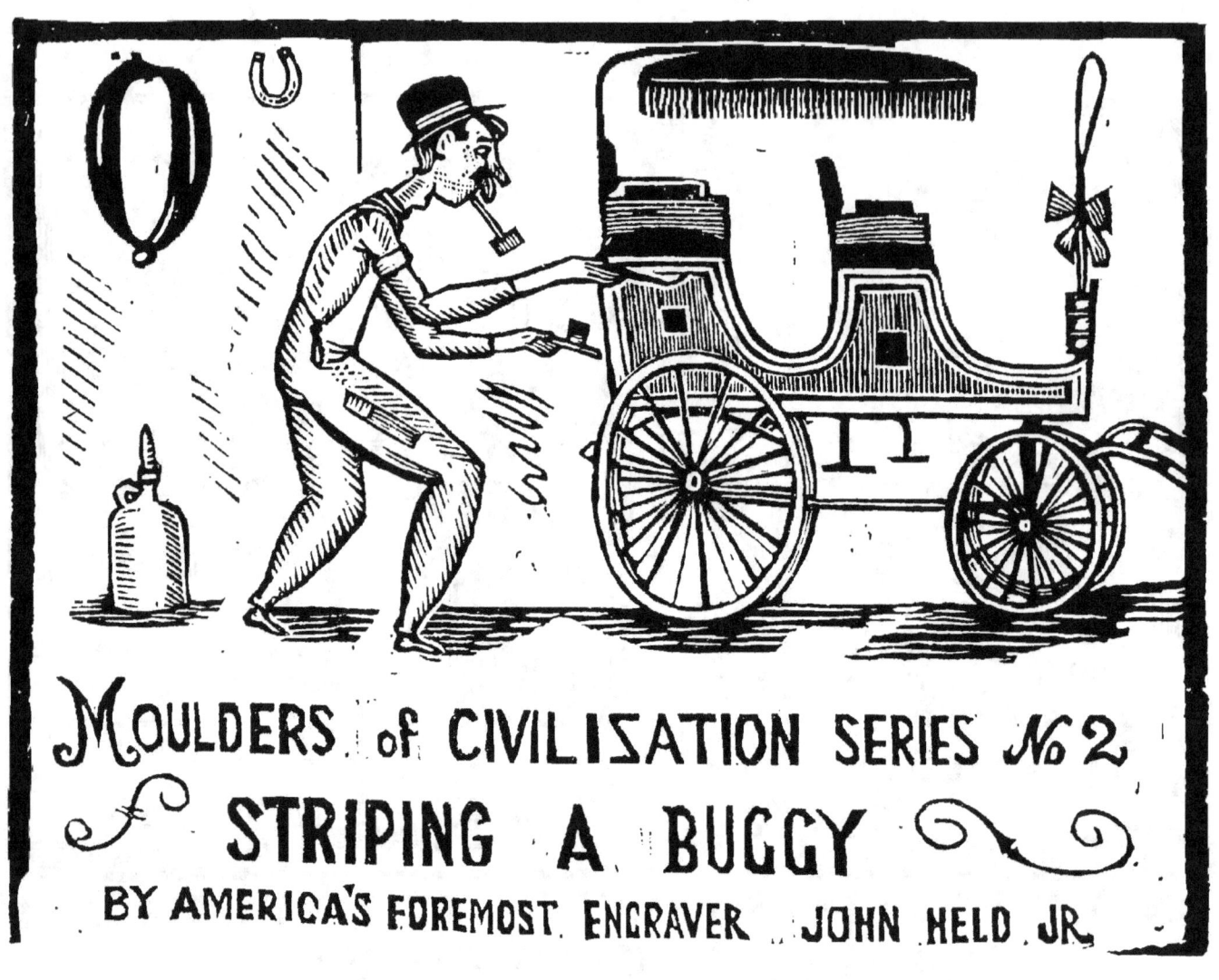

MOULDERS of CIVILISATION SERIES № 2
STRIPING A BUGGY
BY AMERICA'S FOREMOST ENGRAVER JOHN HELD JR.

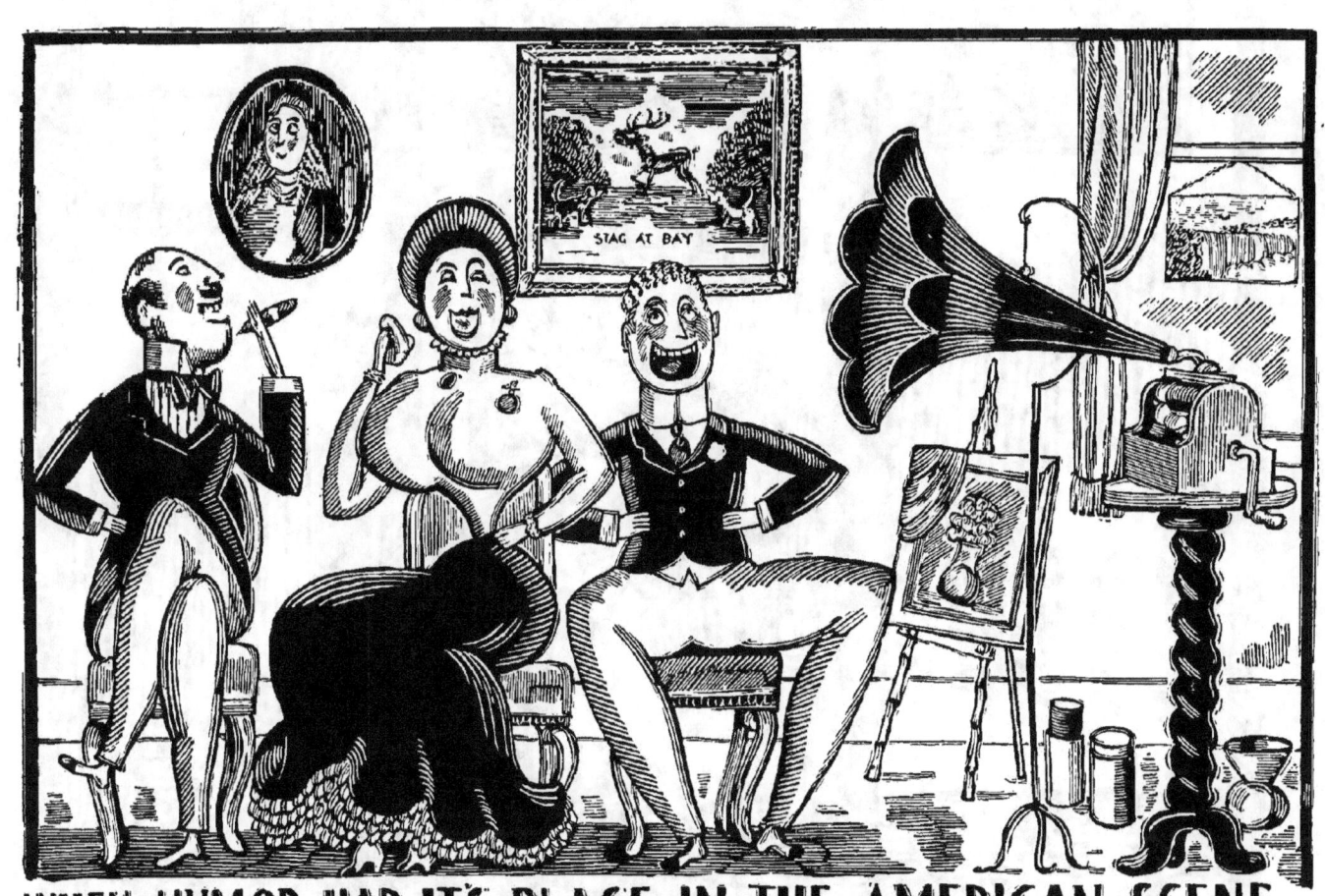

WHEN HUMOR HAD IT'S PLACE IN THE AMERICAN SCENE
Listening to "COHEN ON THE TELEPHONE"
ENG BY JOHN HELD JR THE GHOUL WHO DIGS IN THE GRAVES OF THE PAST

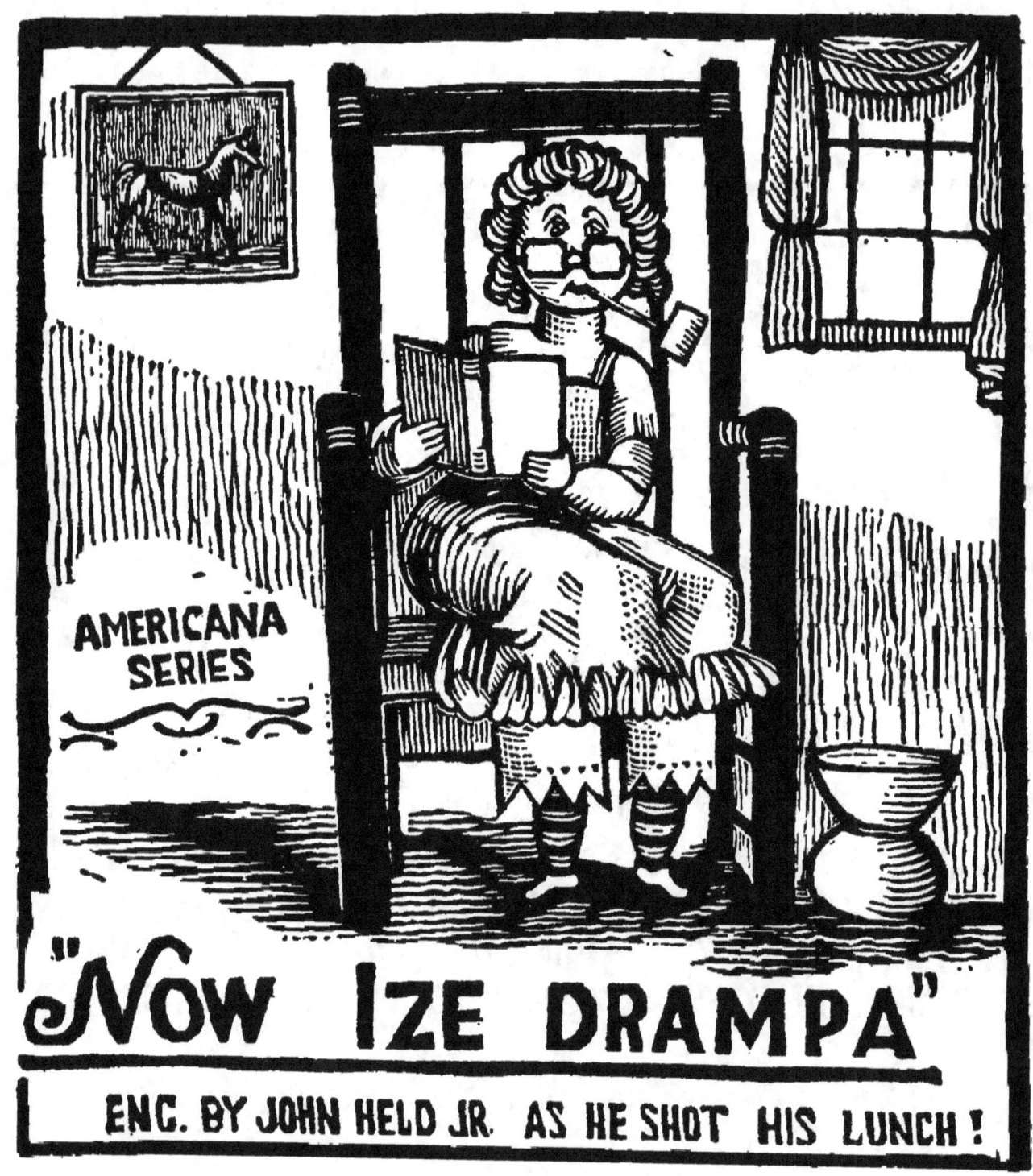

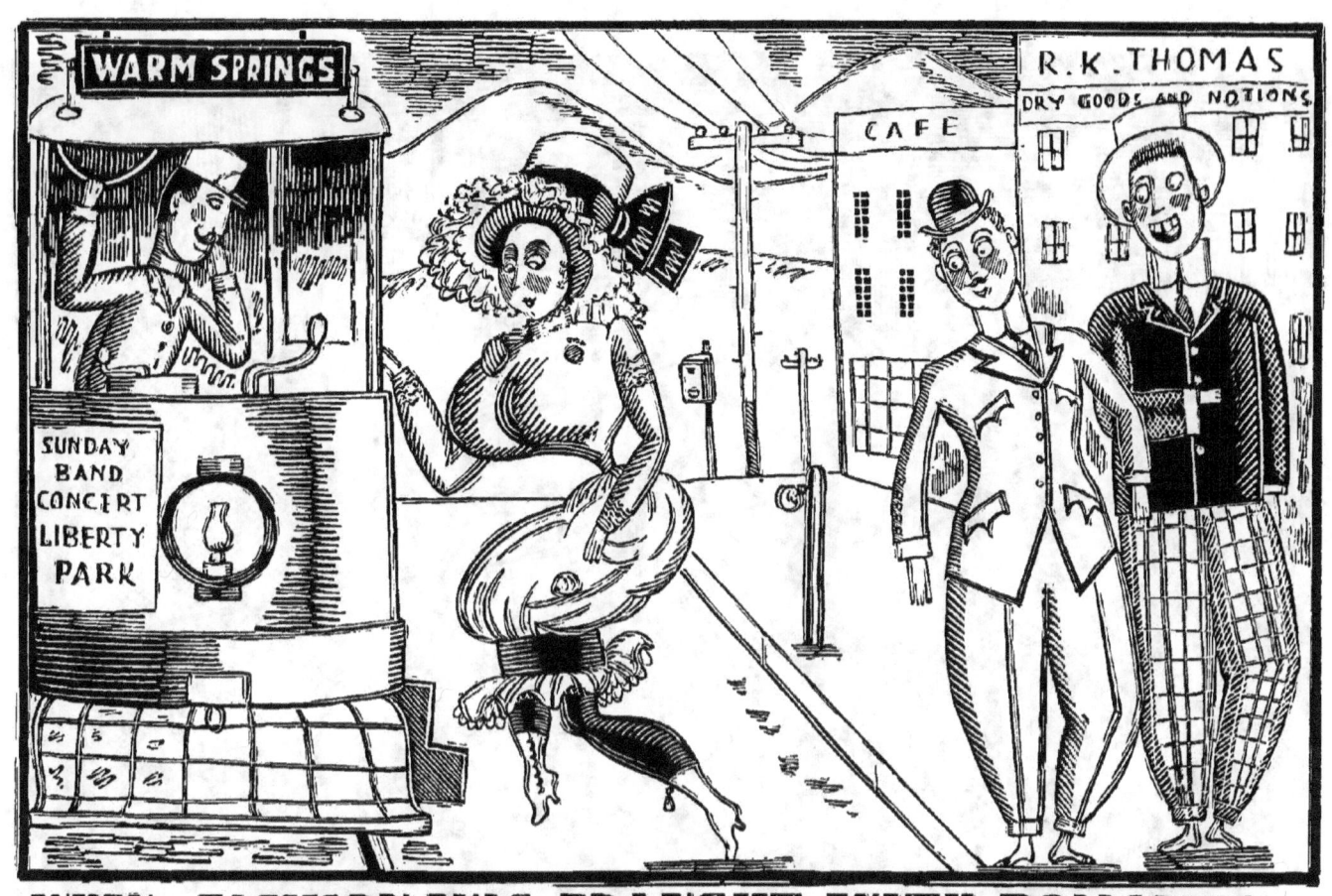

WHEN FASHION WAS FRAUGHT WITH ROMANCE
The HOBBLE SKIRT
ENG. BY JOHN HELD JR A SCAMP IF THERE EVER WAS ONE.

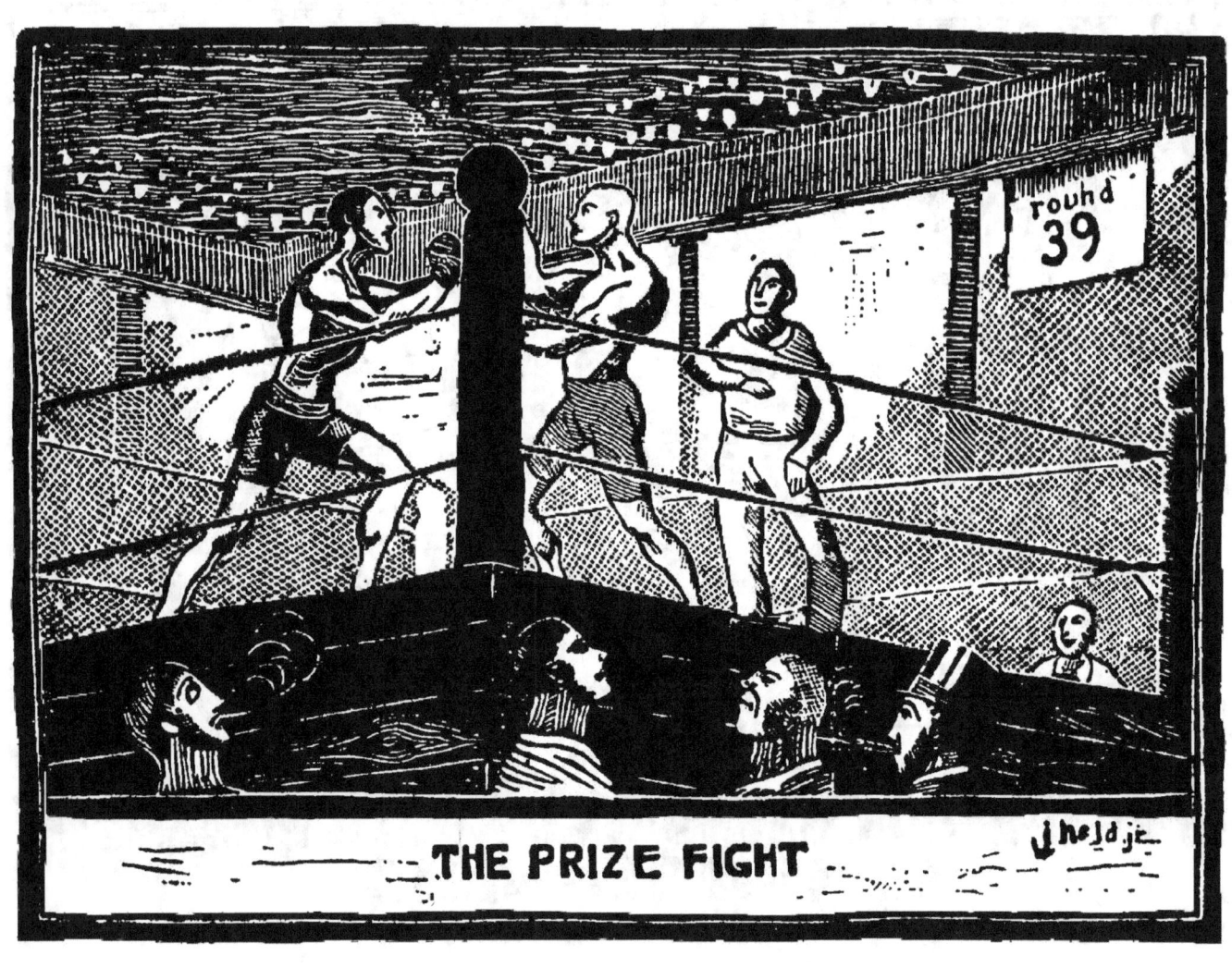

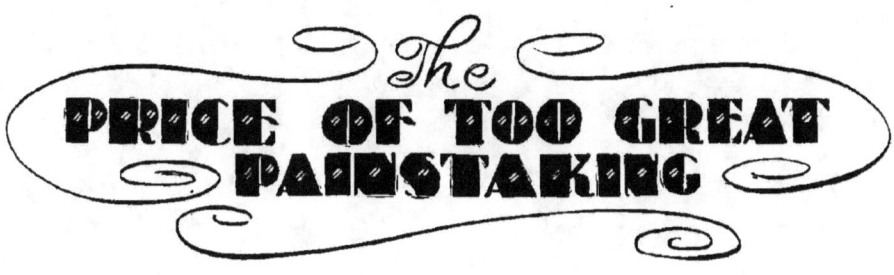

The PRICE OF TOO GREAT PAINSTAKING

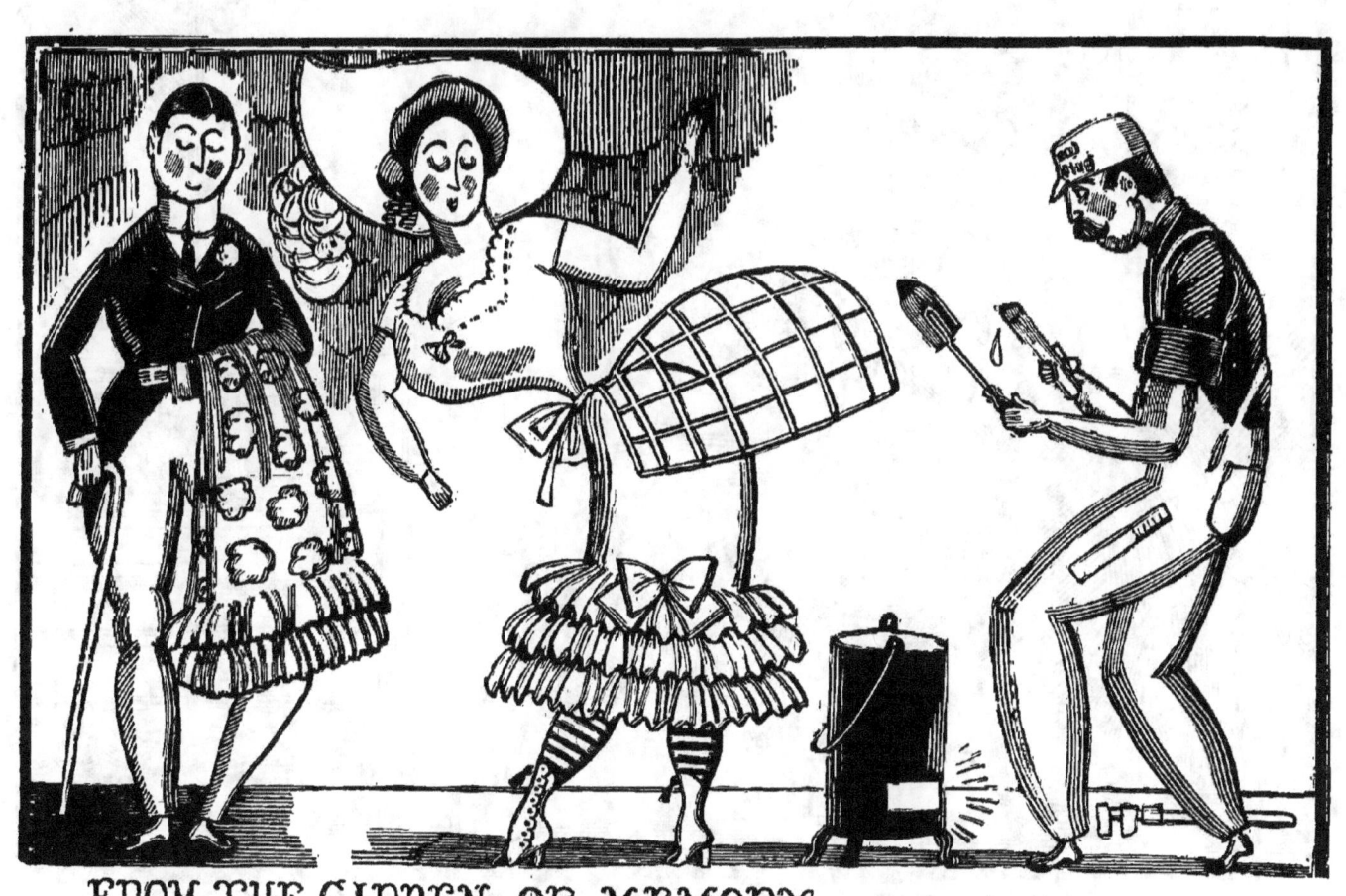

FROM THE GARDEN OF MEMORY

SOLDERING the BUSTLE

ENG BY JOHN HELD JR. BY ARRANGEMENT WITH JOHN HELD JR

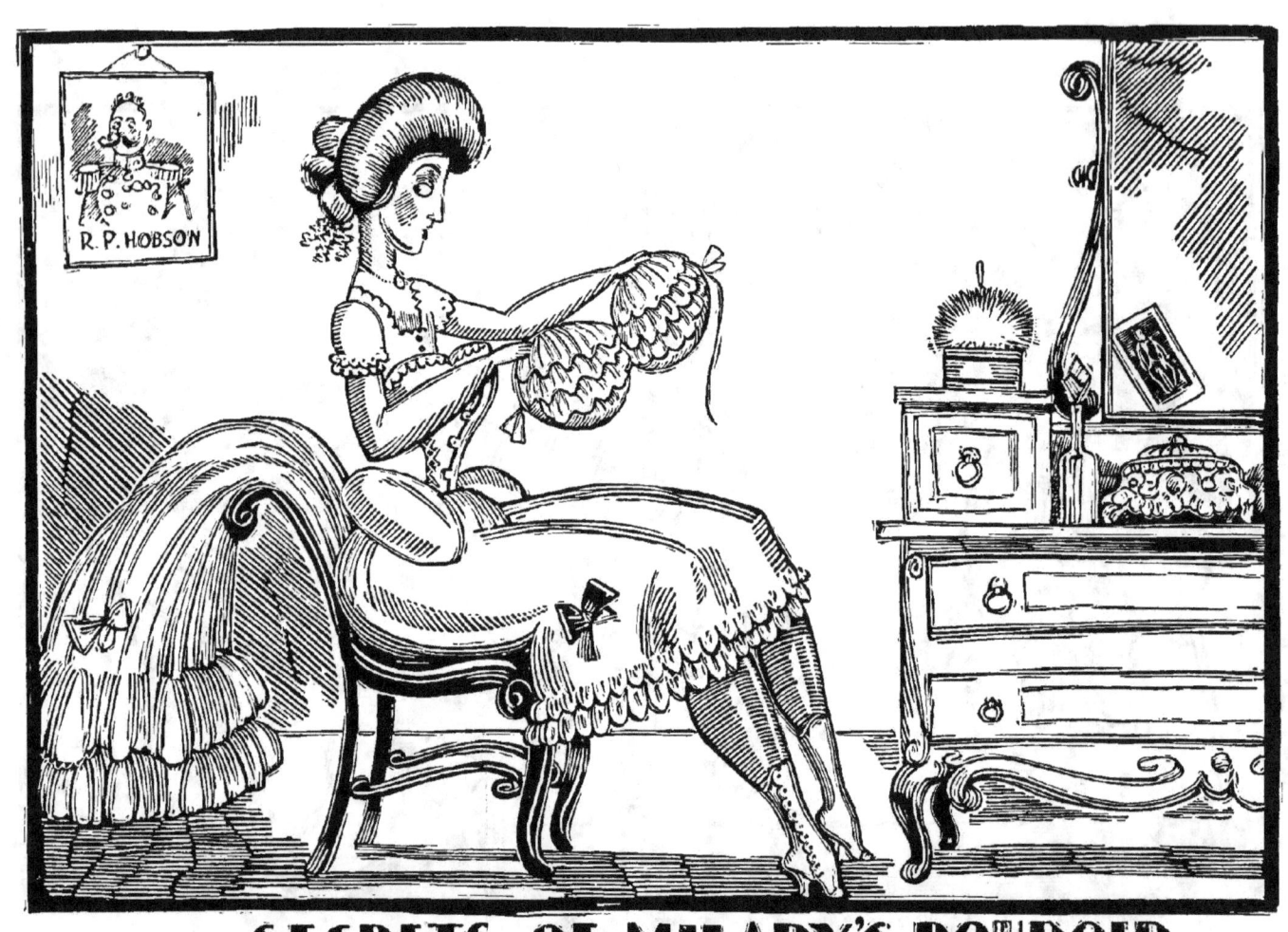

SECRETS OF MILADY'S BOUDOIR
The STRATEGIC RUFFLES
ENGRAVED BY JOHN HELD JR. THE OLD SPANISH CAVALIER

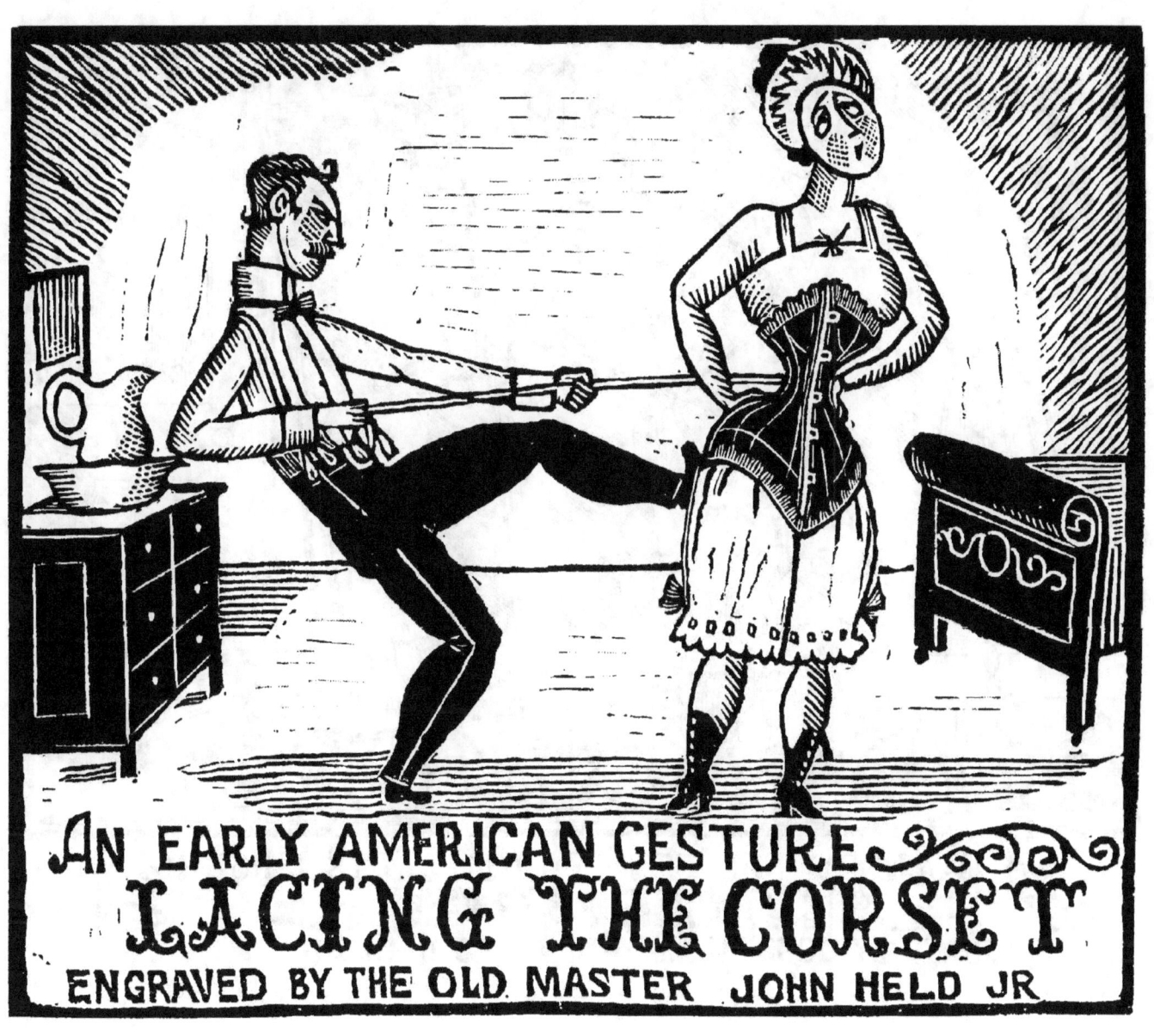

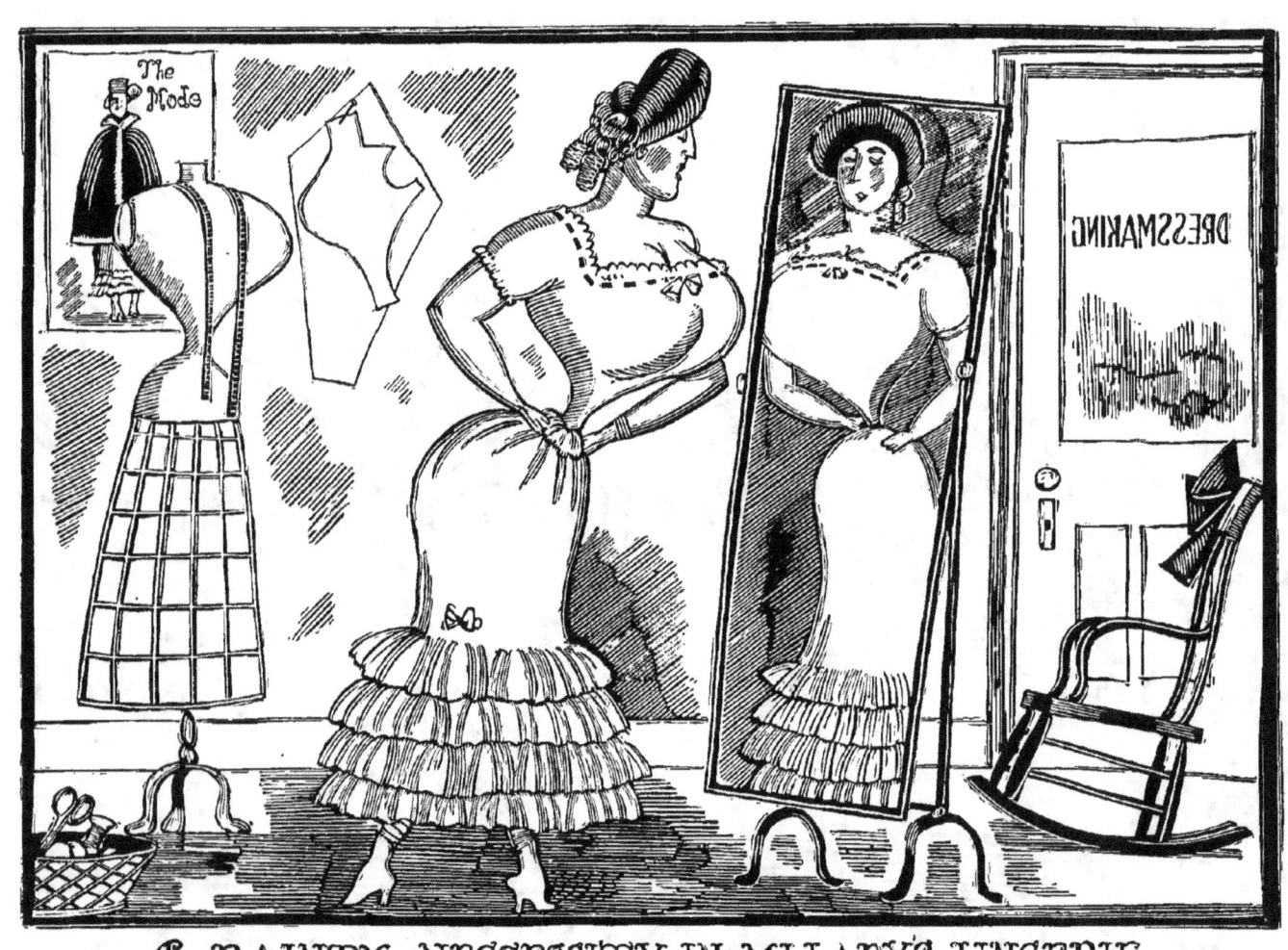

A DAINTY NECCESSITY IN MI·LADY'S LINGERIE
The **CORSET COVER**
ENGRAVED BY JOHN HELD JR WITH A TOSS OF HEAD

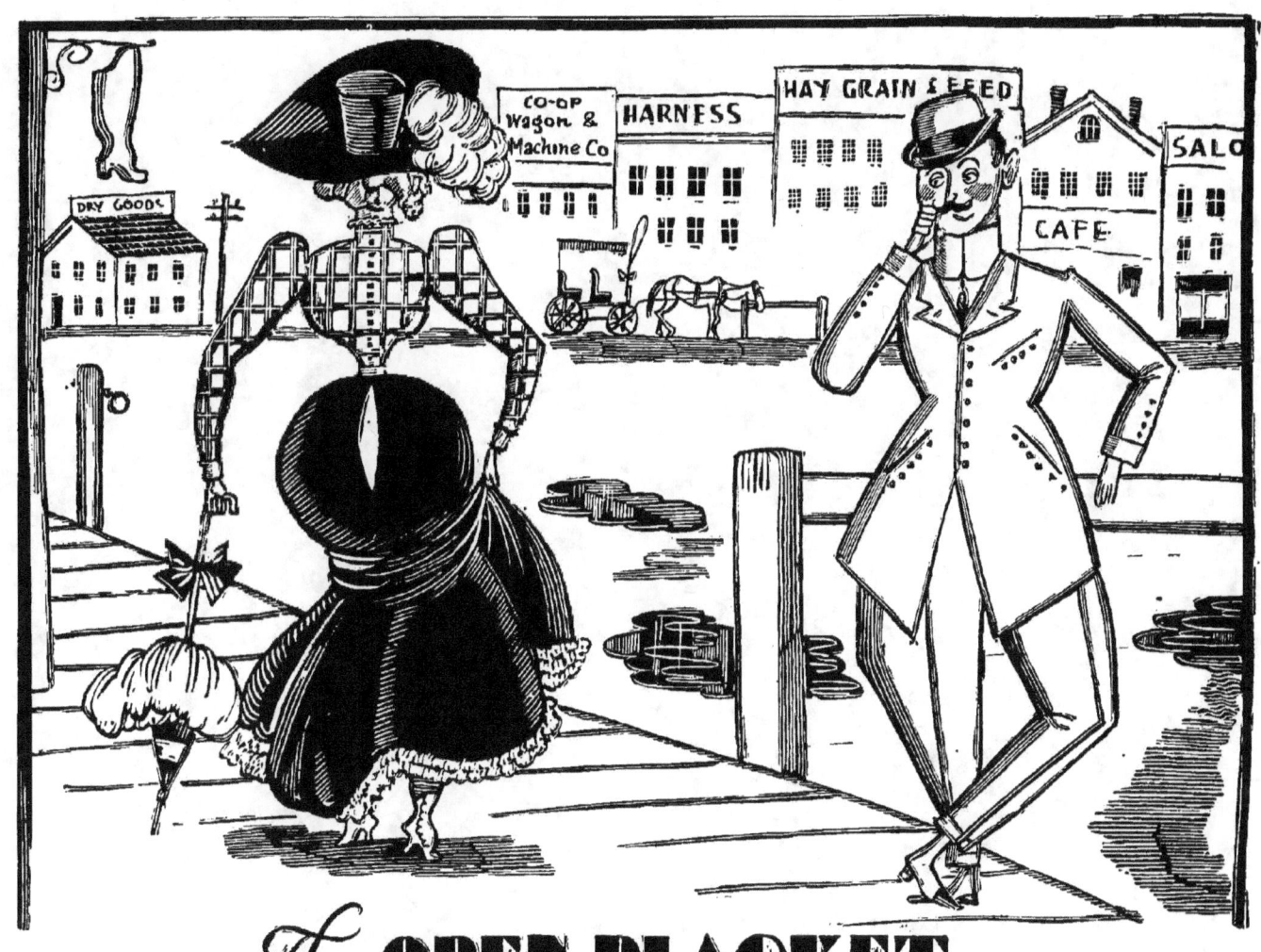

The OPEN PLACKET

from the Memoirs of John Held Jr the Engraver

BIG MOMENTS IN THE FAINT ROSY PAST

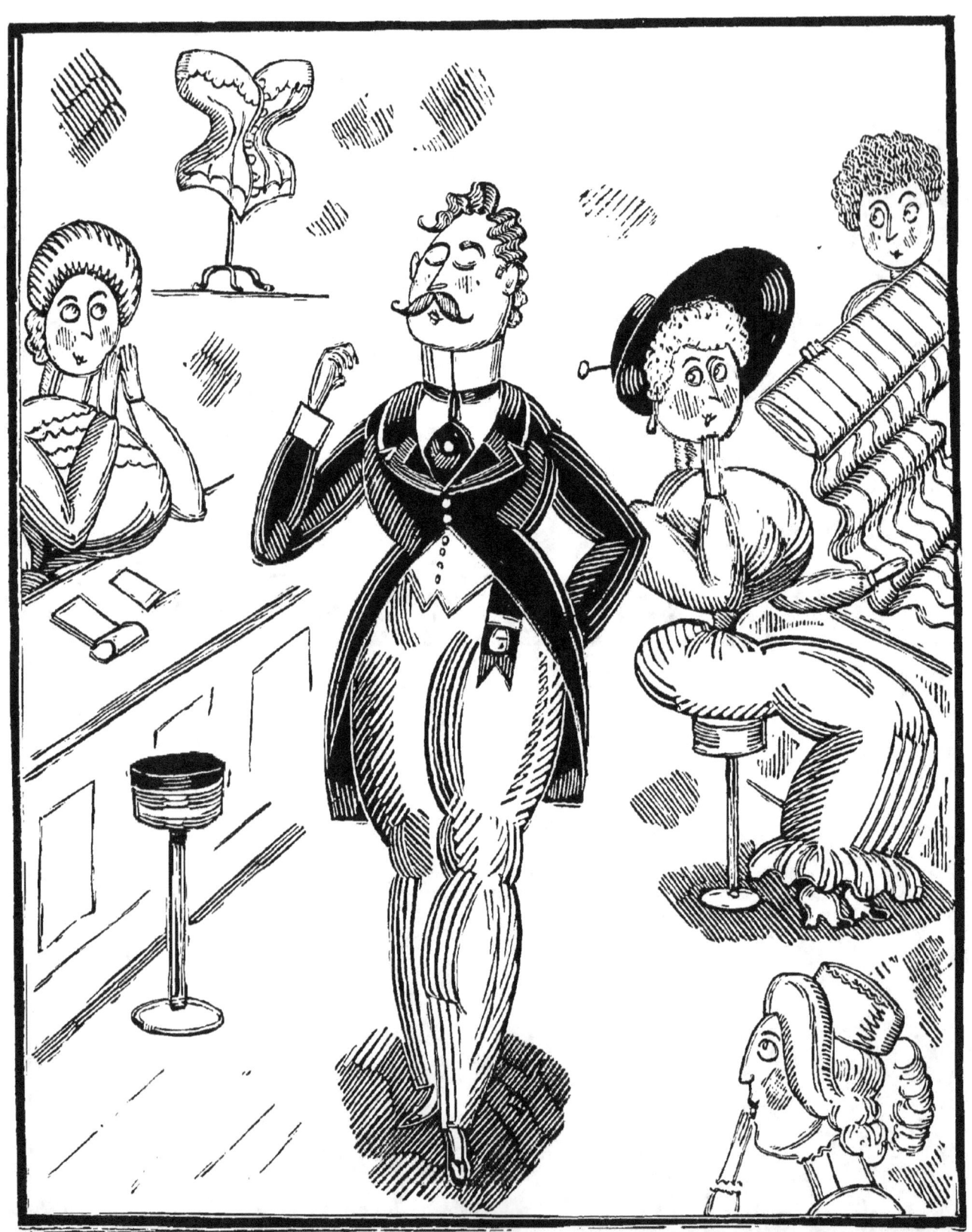

HIS MAJESTY *The* FLOOR WALKER

A SMASH ENGRAVING BY THAT POPULAR FAVORITE JOHN HELD JR READ WHAT THE CRITICS SAY

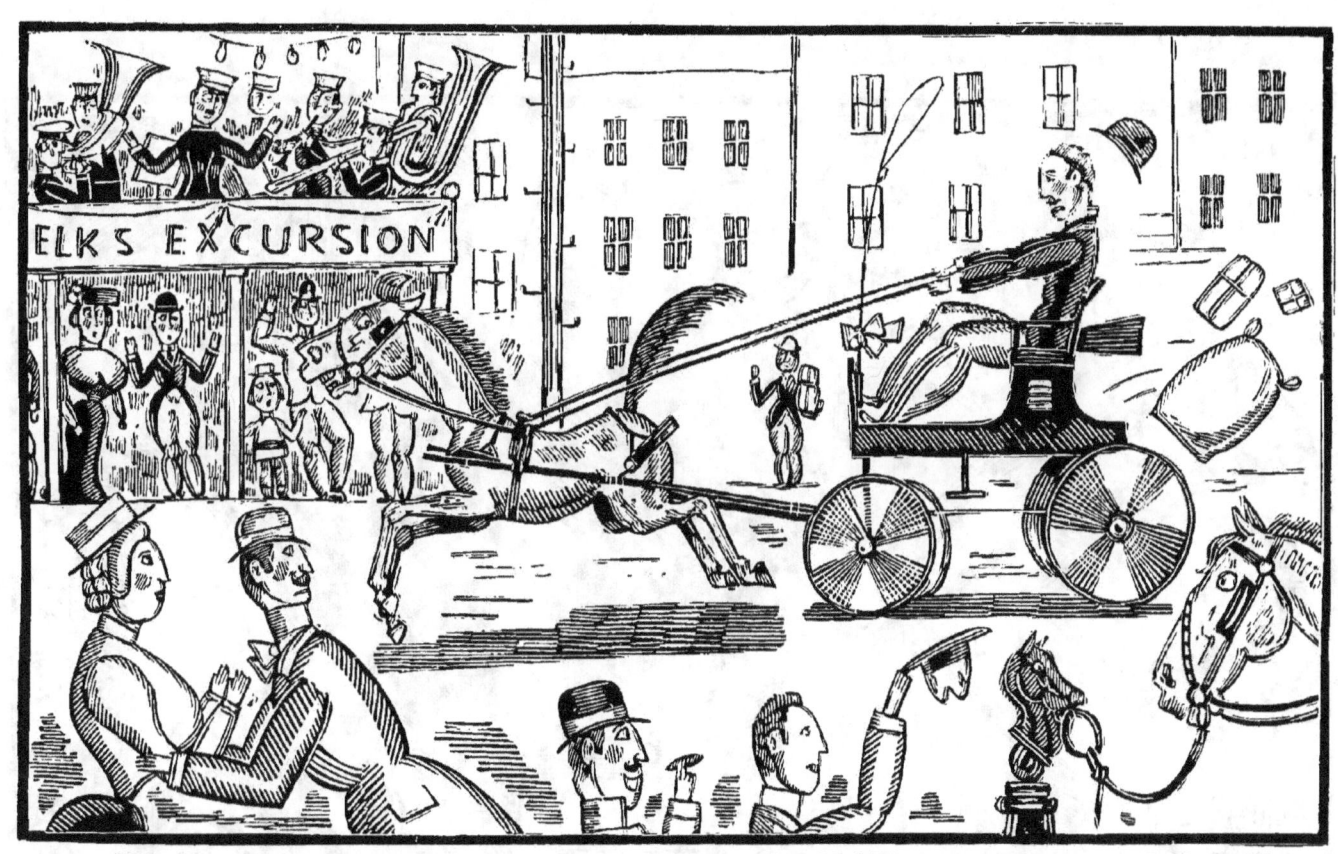

BIG MOMENTS IN THE FAINT ROSY PAST

THE RUNAWAY DURING THE SATURDAY NIGHT BAND CONCERT

ENGRAVED BY JOHN HELD JR WHO IS A WOLF IN SHEEP'S CLOTHING

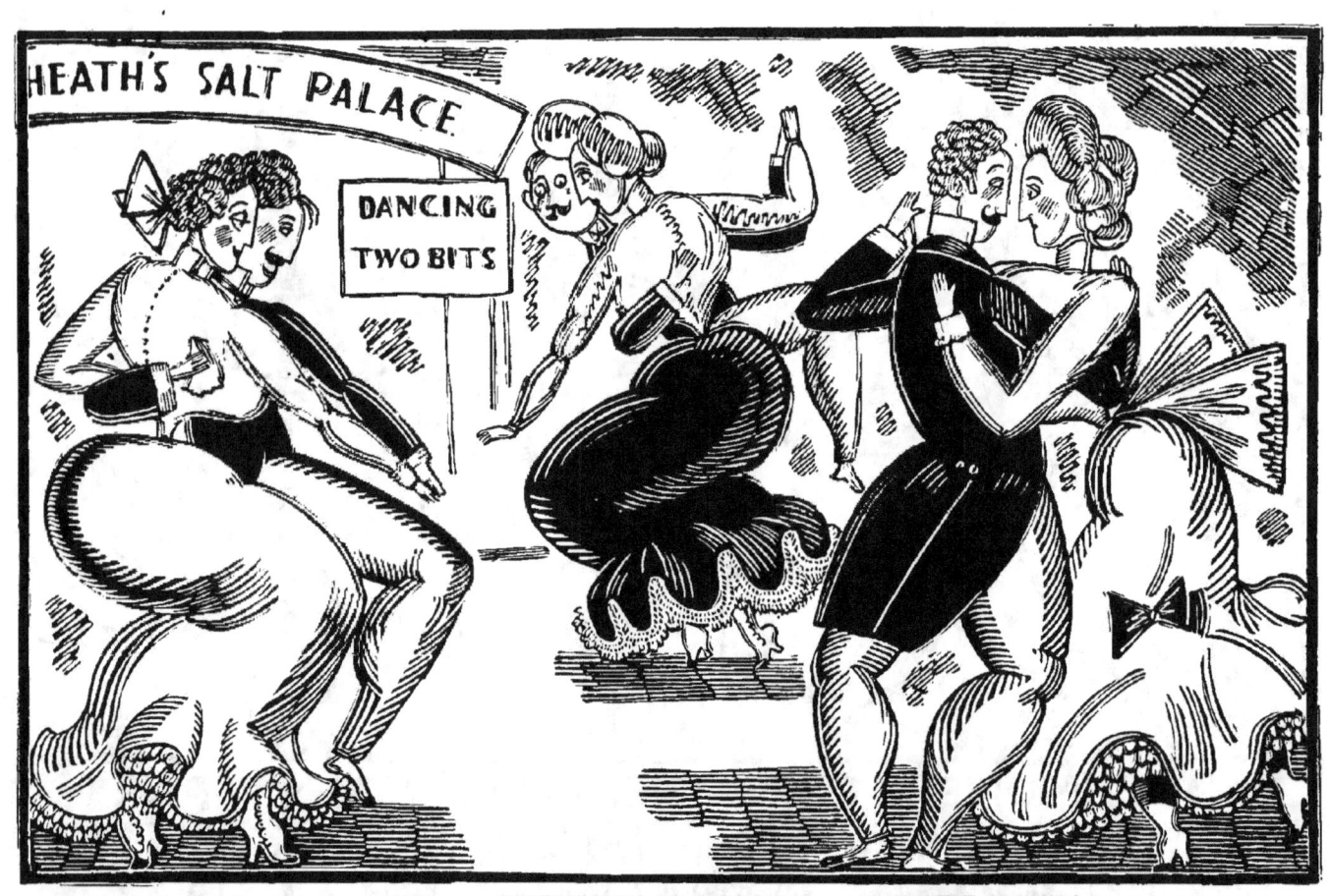

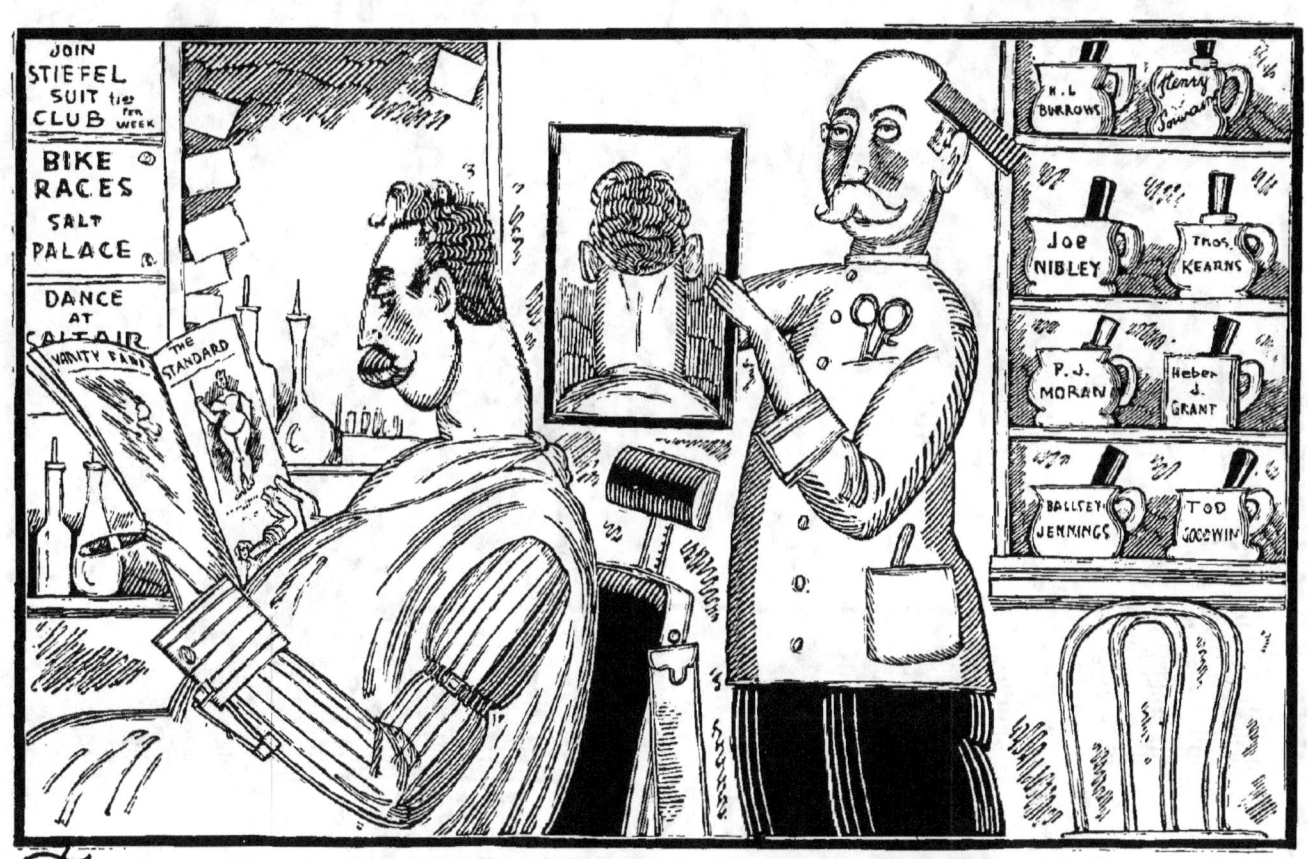

The DAYS WHEN CULTURE AND REFINEMENT WERE UPPERMOST AND CHIC.

THE SHAVING OF THE NECK

ENGRAVED BY **JOHN HELD JR** SON OF A FAMOUS CORNETIST

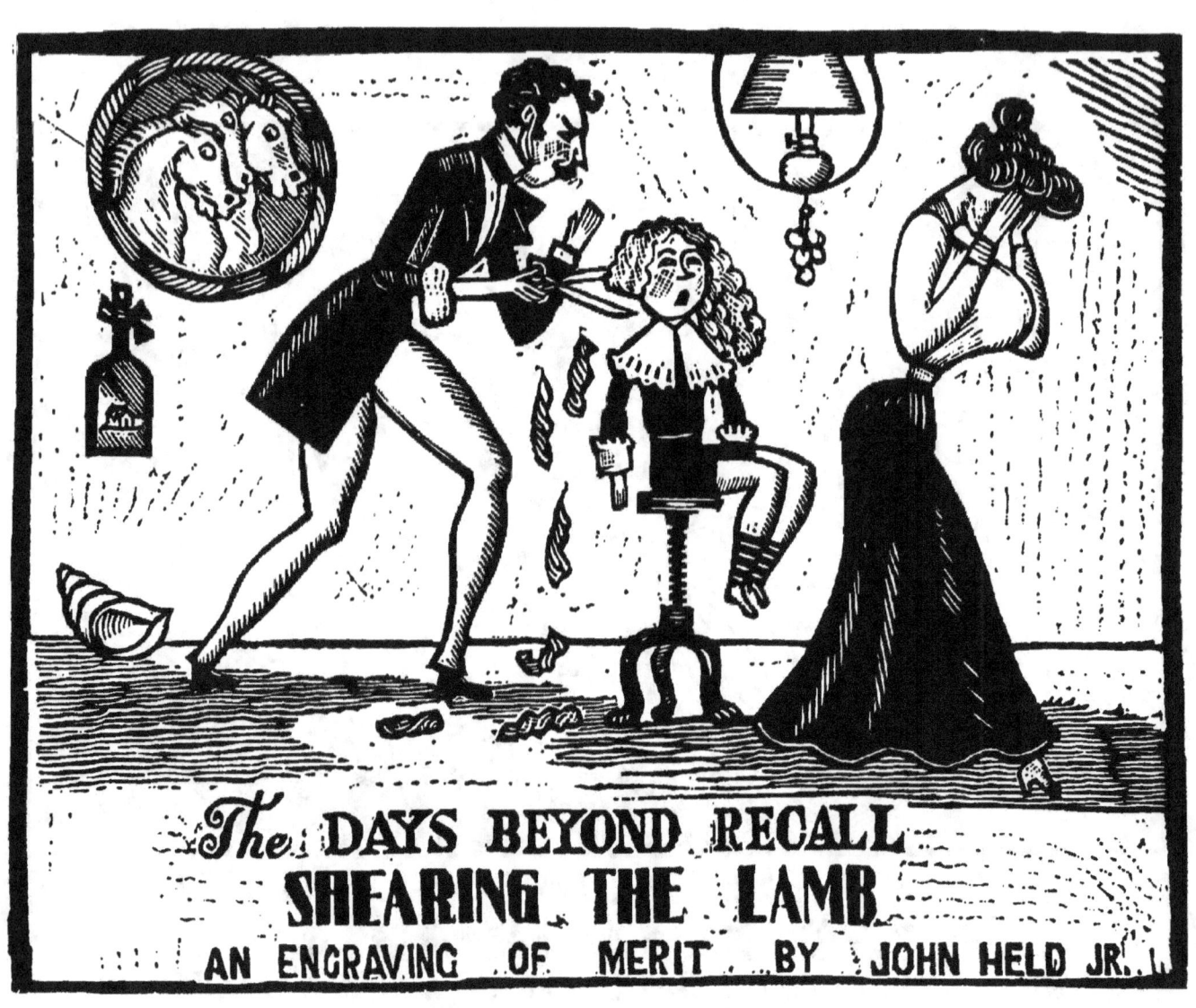

THE DAYS BEYOND RECALL
SHEARING THE LAMB
AN ENGRAVING OF MERIT BY JOHN HELD JR.

58

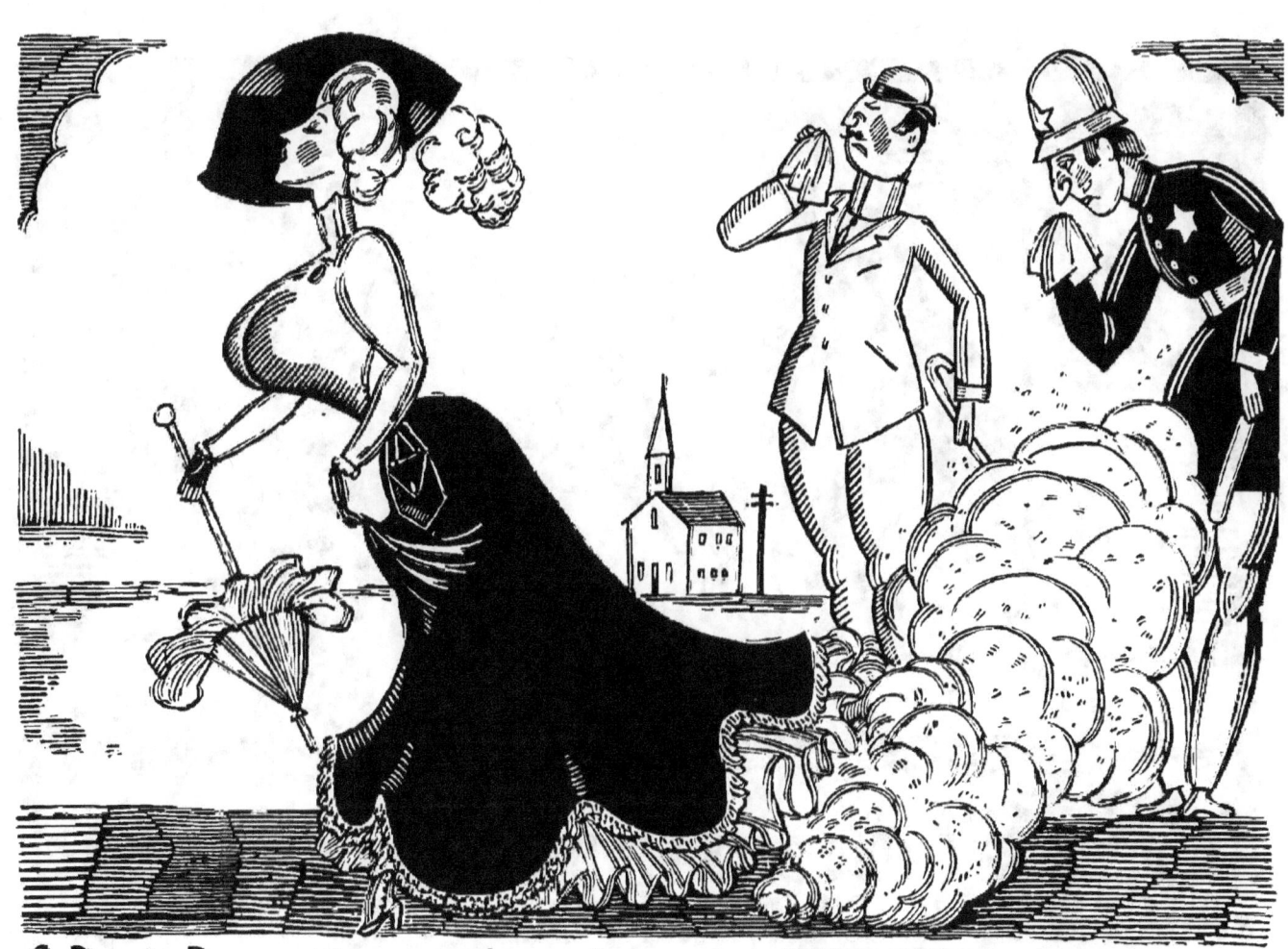

A Dainty Requisite of Milady's Lingerie **THE DUST RUFFLE**
Eng. by **JOHN HELD JR** and there is no fool like an old fool.

59

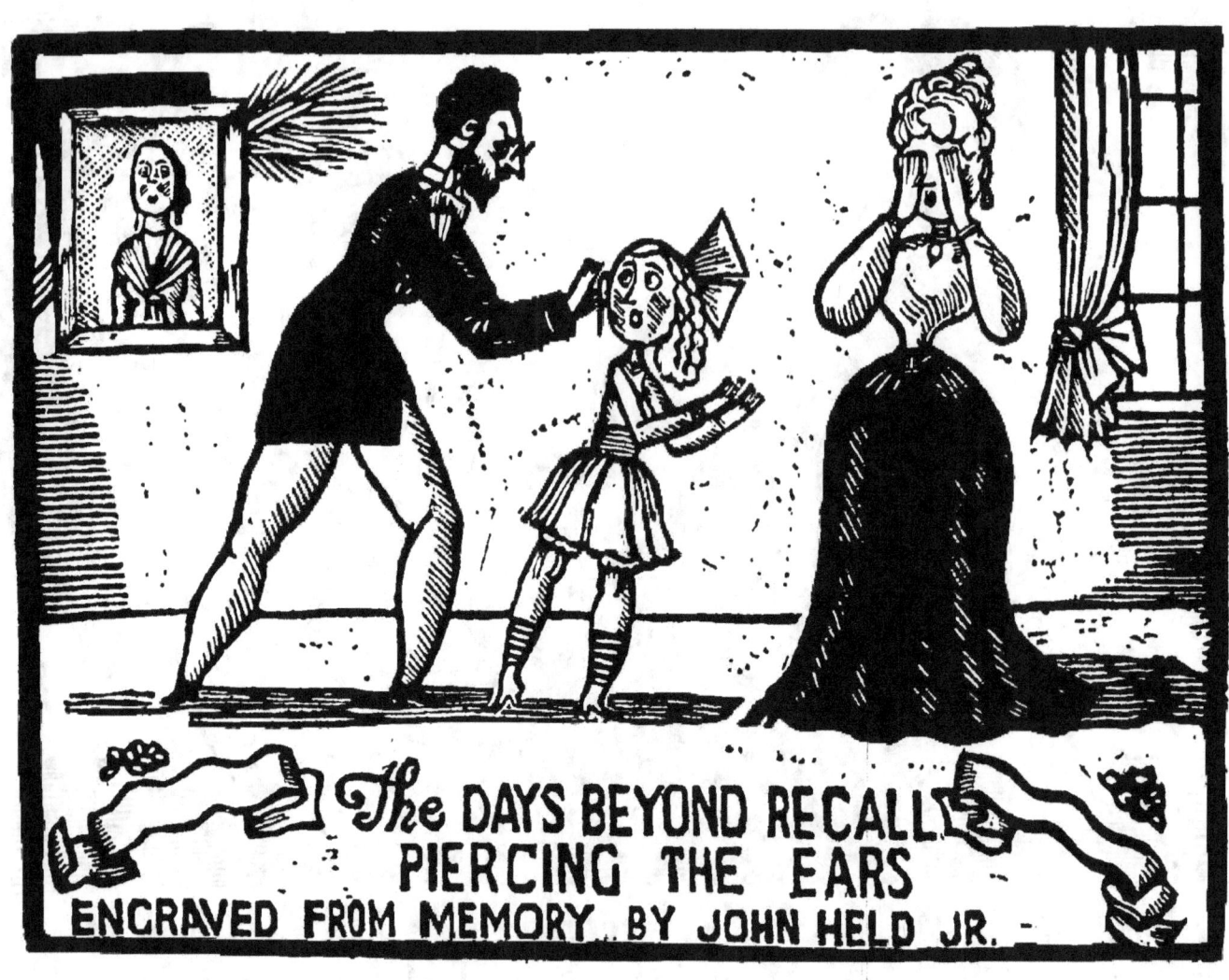

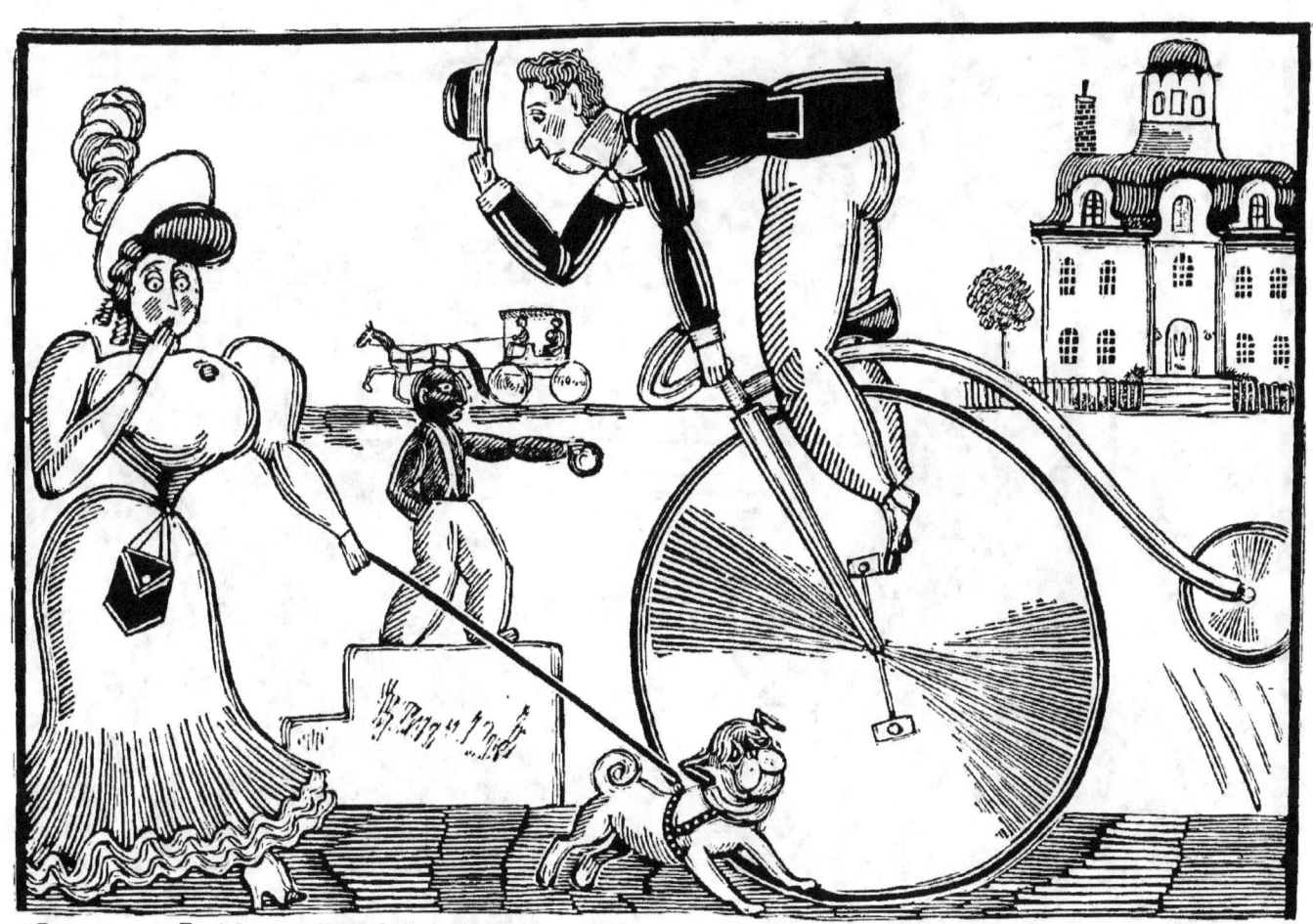

One of the DANGERS of riding a WHEEL on the Sidewalk. Eng. by JOHN HELD JR in a moment of whimsey

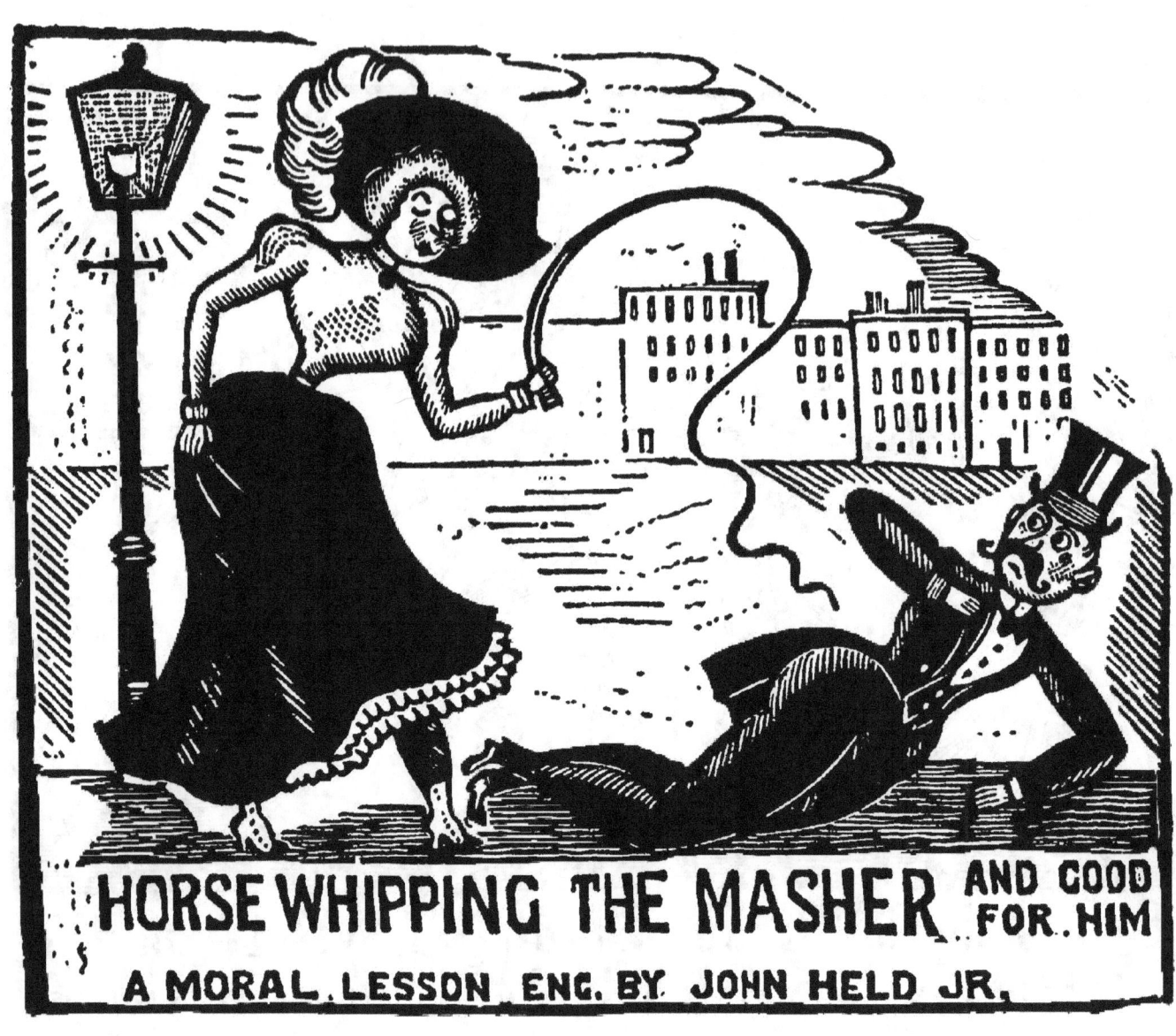

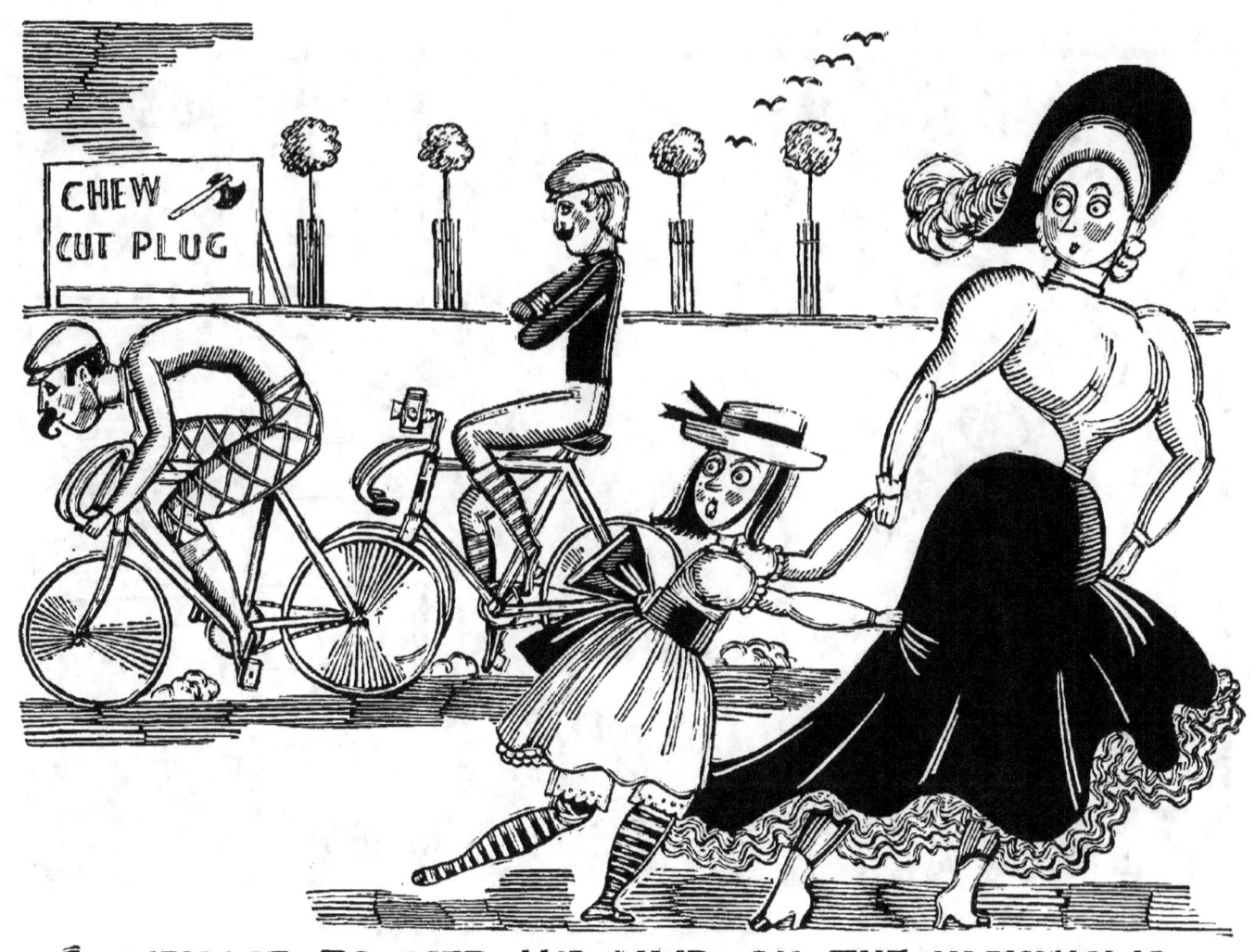

A MENACE TO LIFE AND LIMB ON THE HIGHWAYS
The SCORCHERS
Eng By JOHN HELD JR - Who is the toast of the town

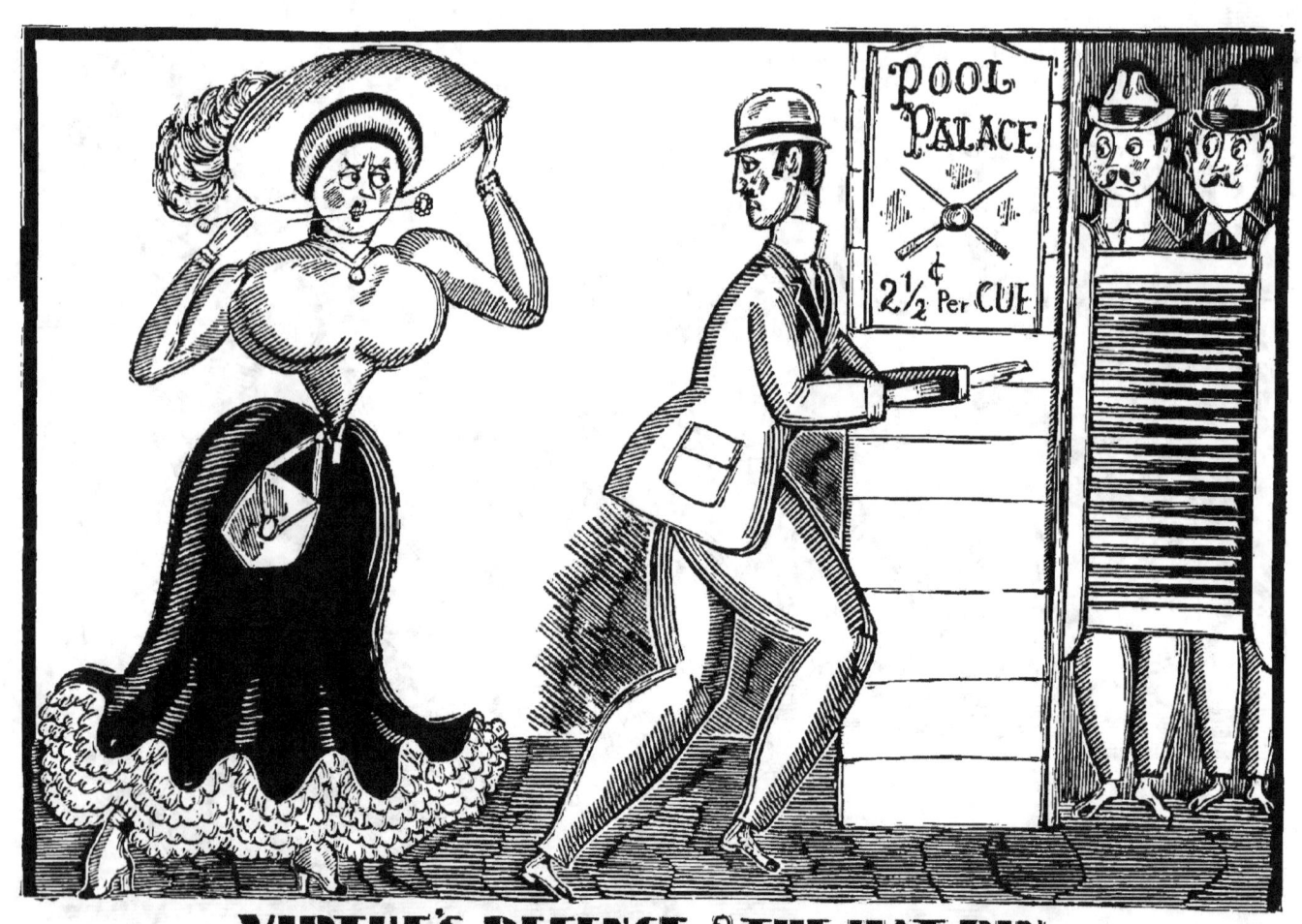

VIRTUE'S DEFENCE & THE HAT PIN
ENG BY JOHN HELD JR AS HE CHOKES BACK HIS TRUE FEELINGS

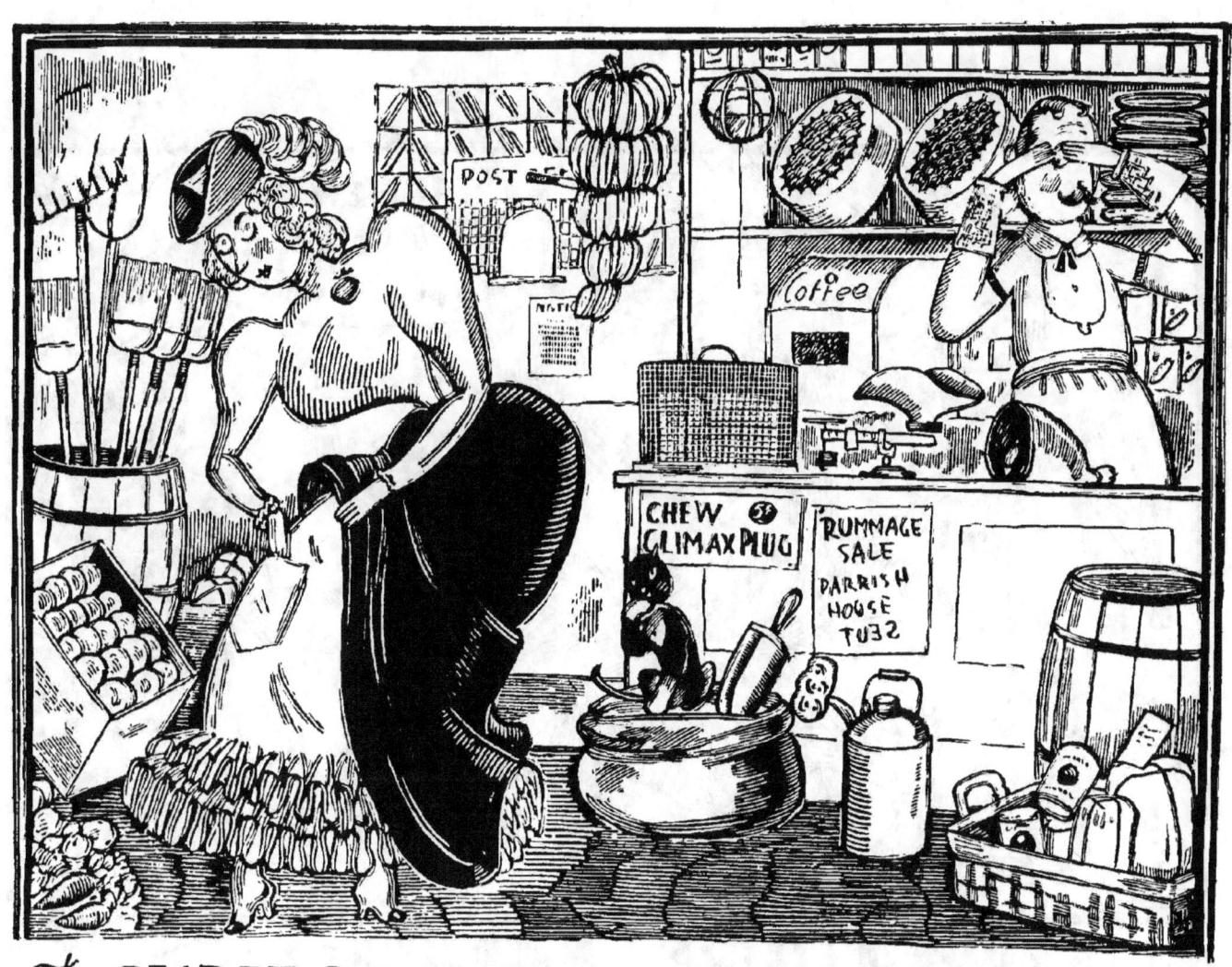

The SECRET POCKET IN THE PETTISKIRT
OH MEMORY SO CRUEL, SO BITTER
ENG BY JOHN HELD JR WHO NEVER TOOK A LESSON IN HIS LIFE

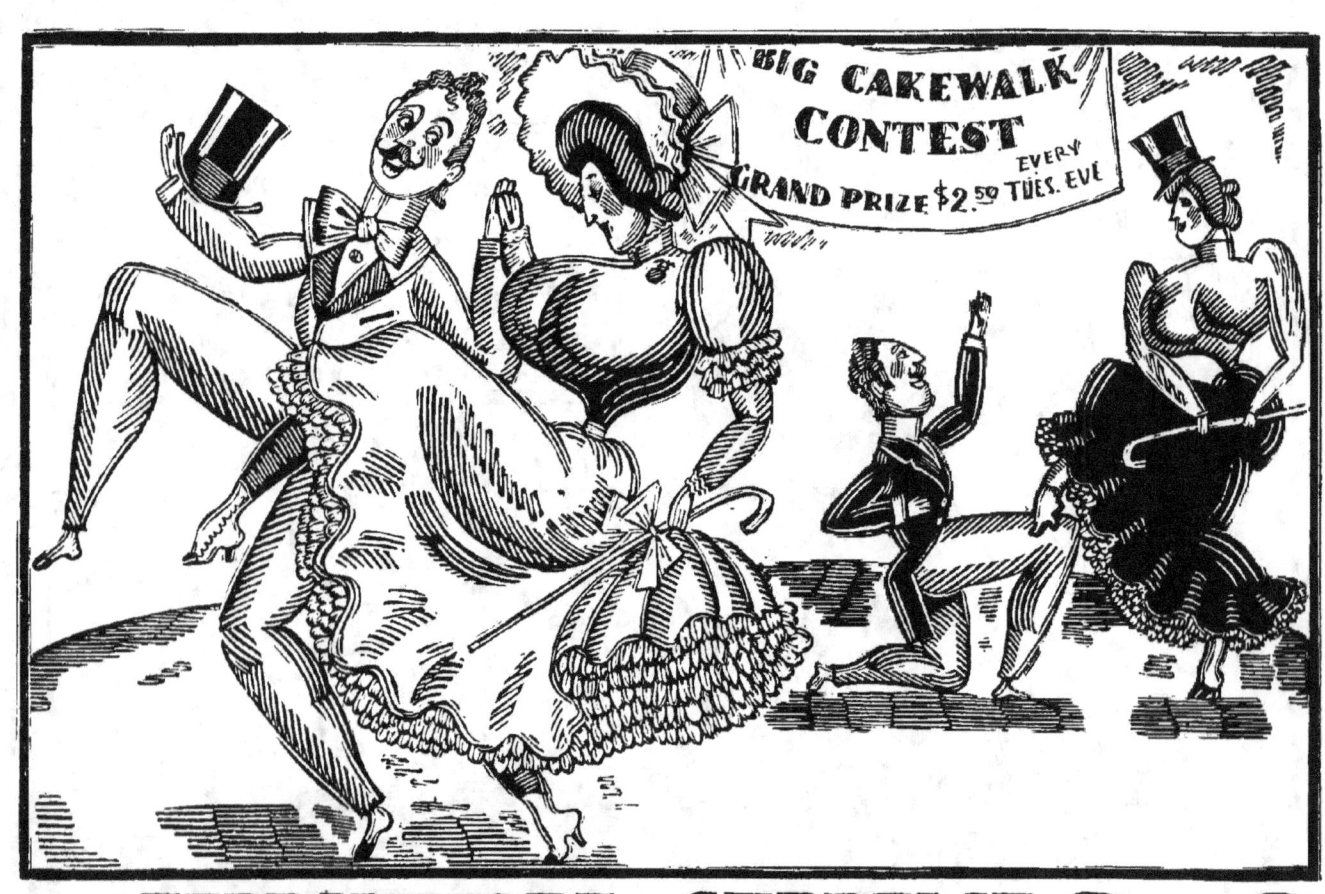

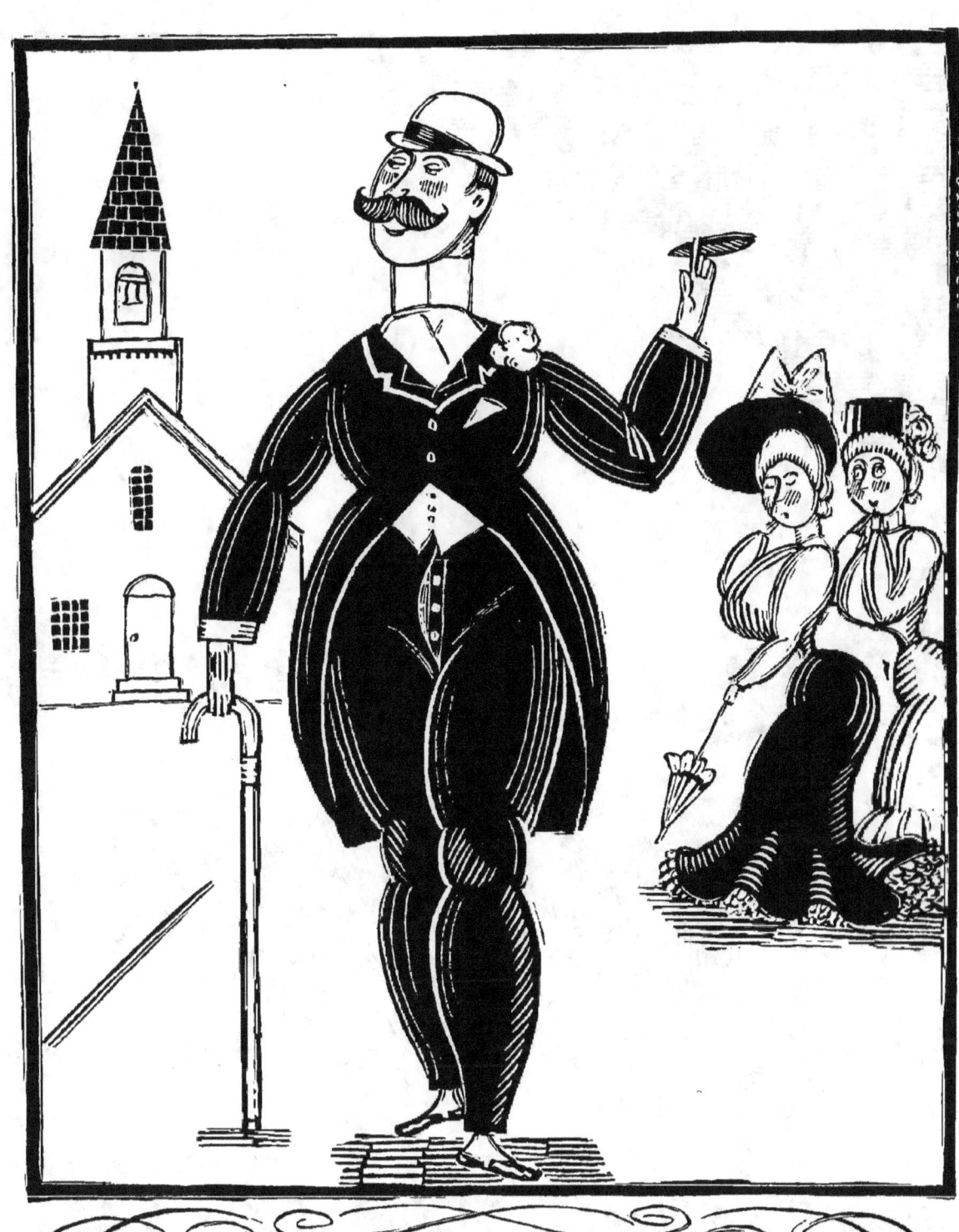

THE OPEN FLY

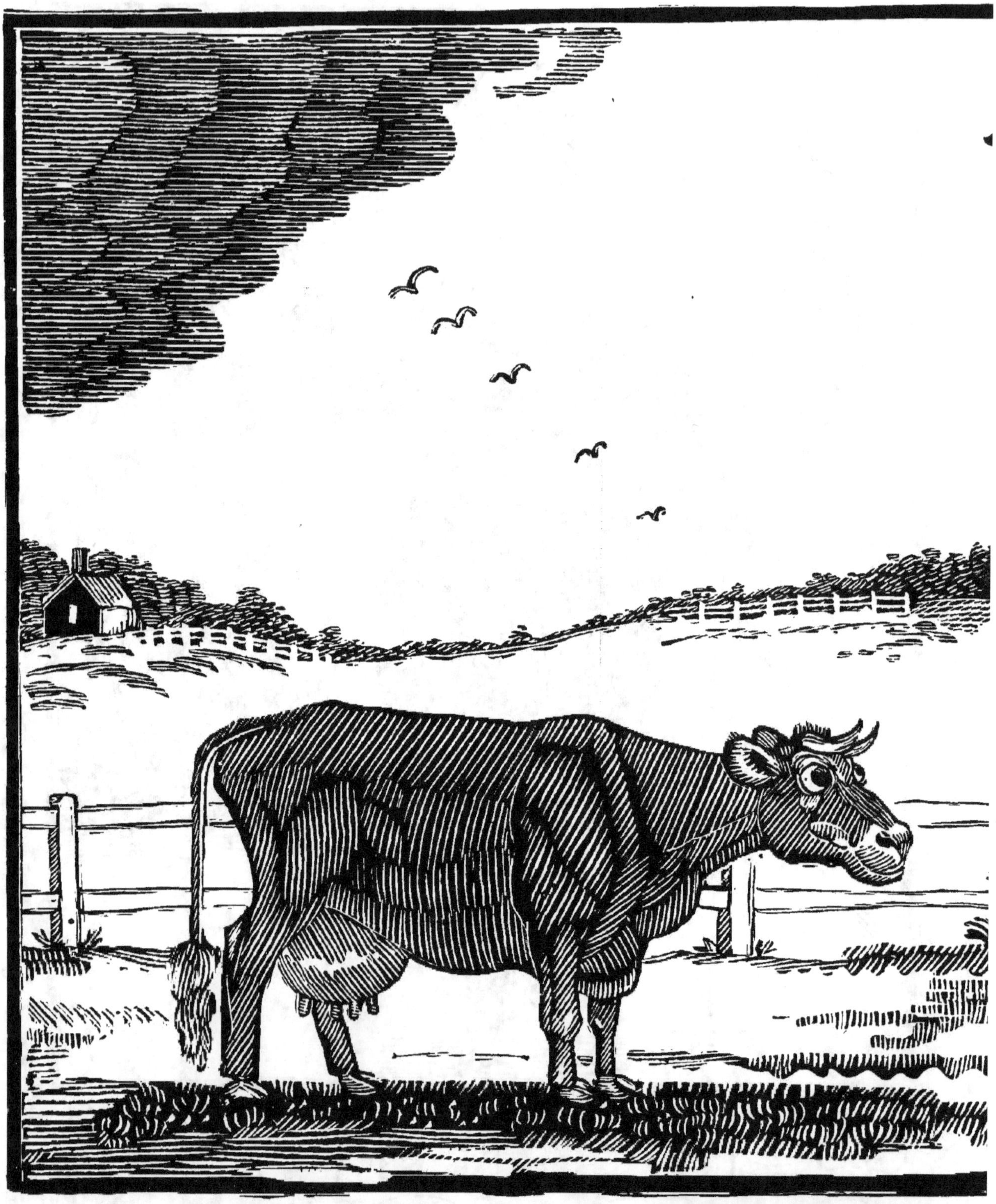

HER

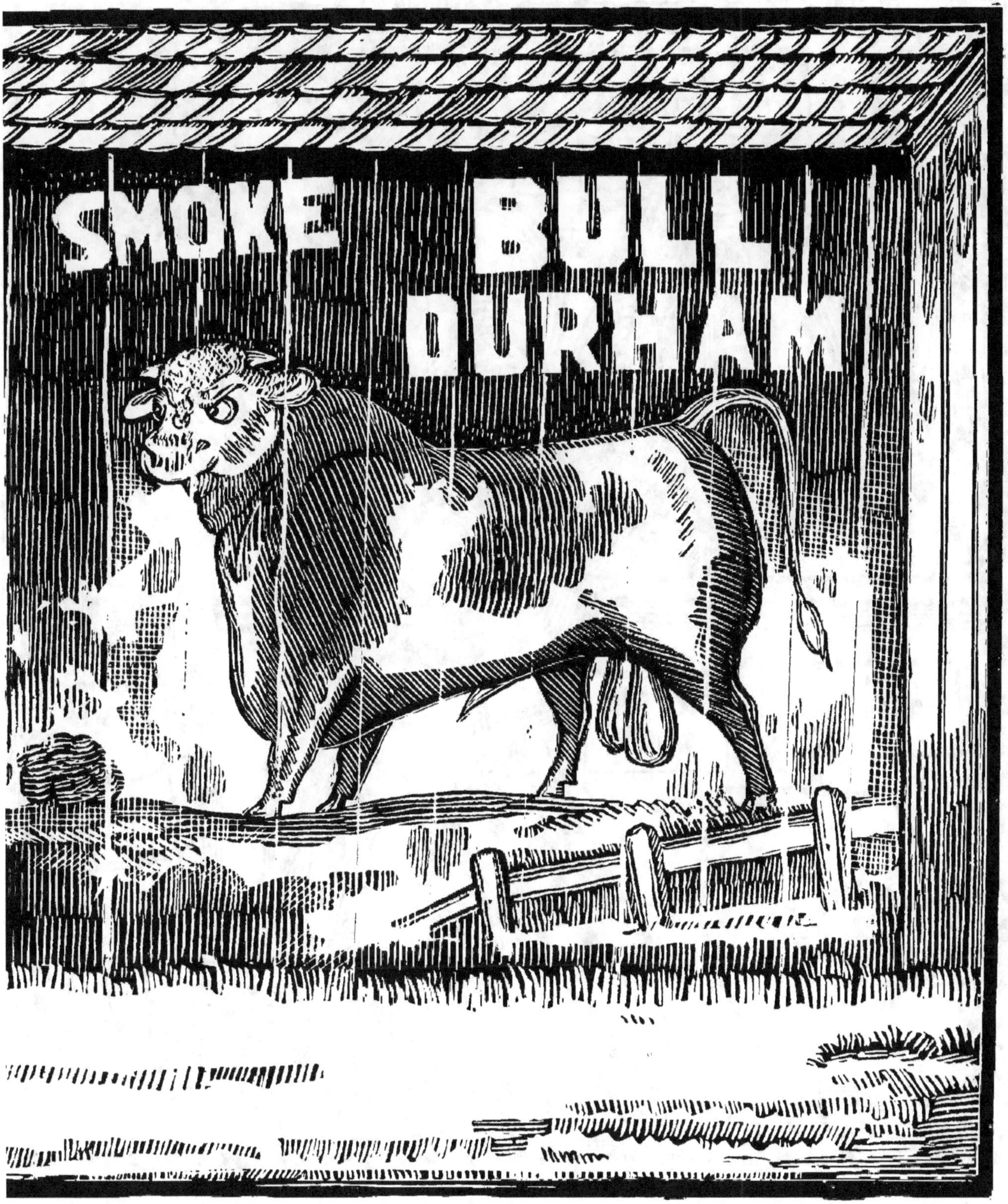

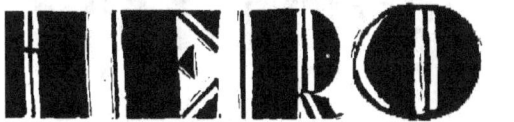

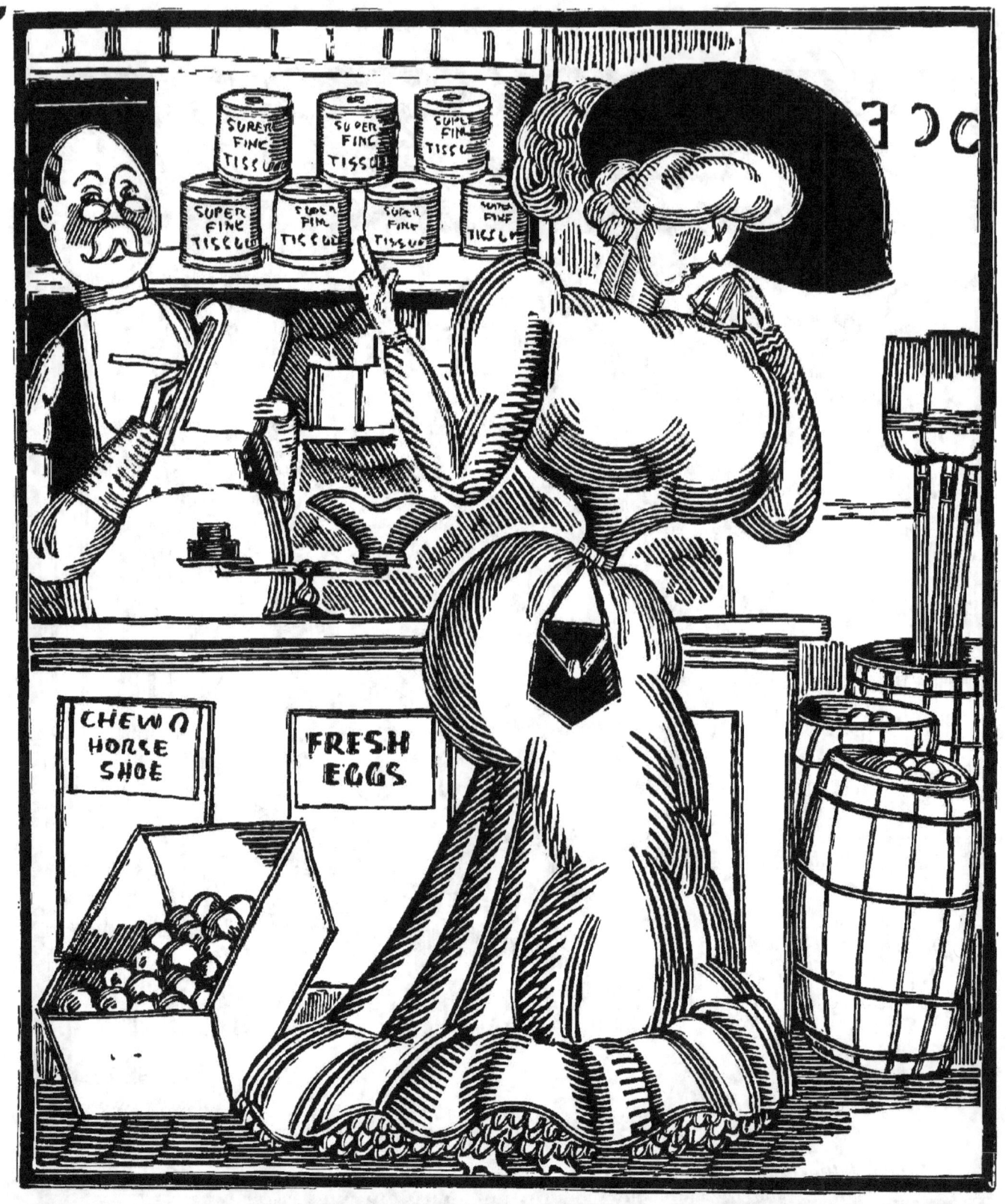

AN EMBARRASSING PURCHASE

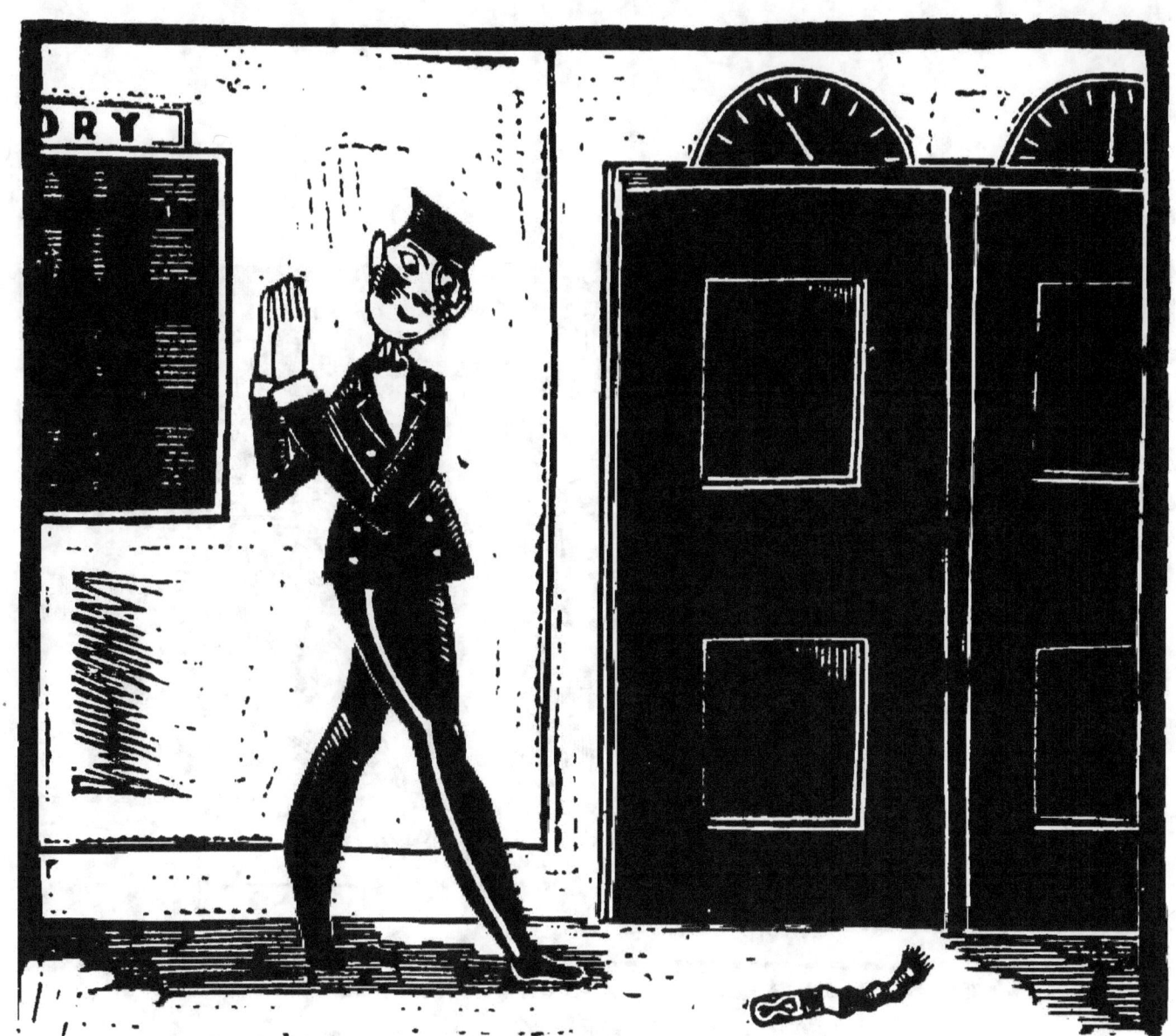

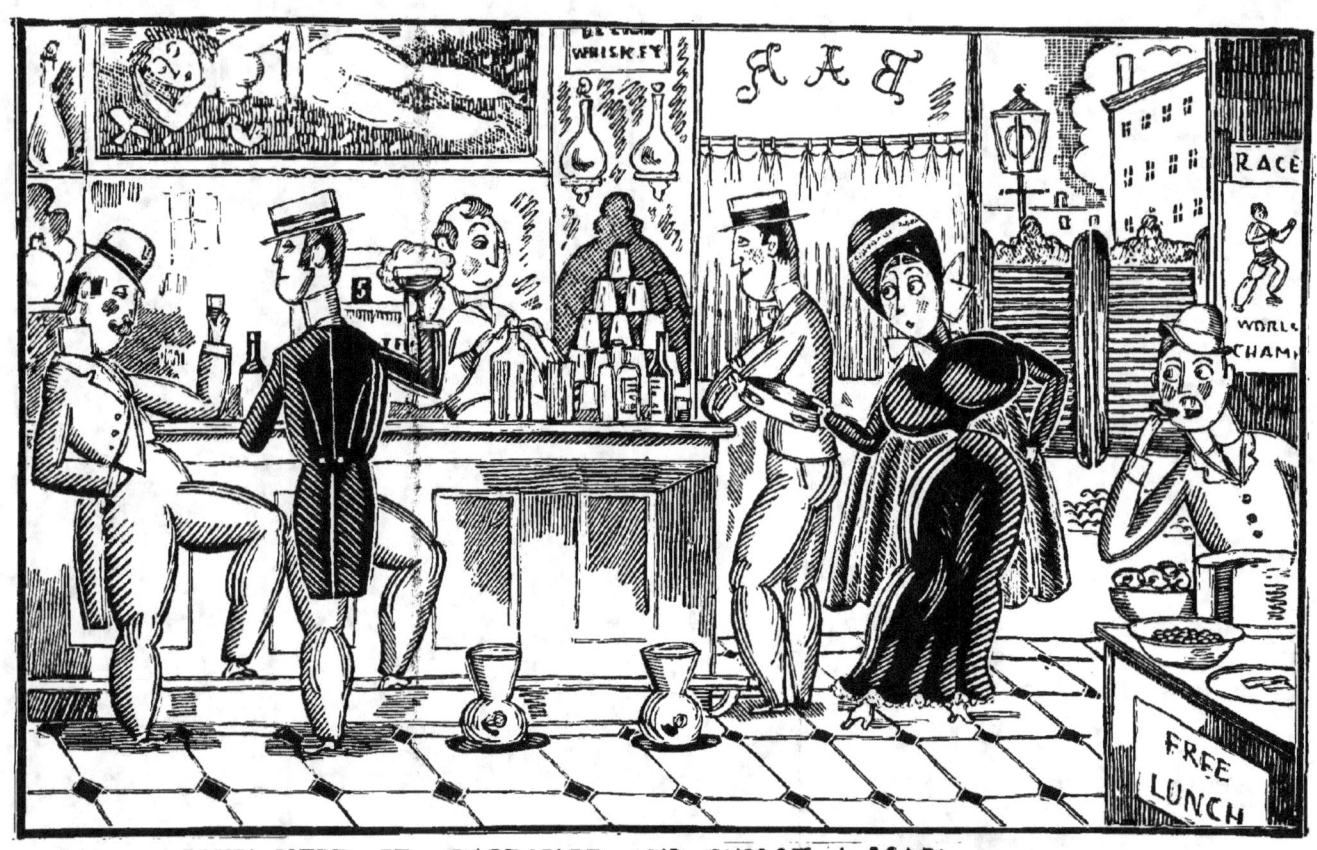

JOHN HELD JR ENGRAVER AND WHAT A MAN.

HAPPY DAYS

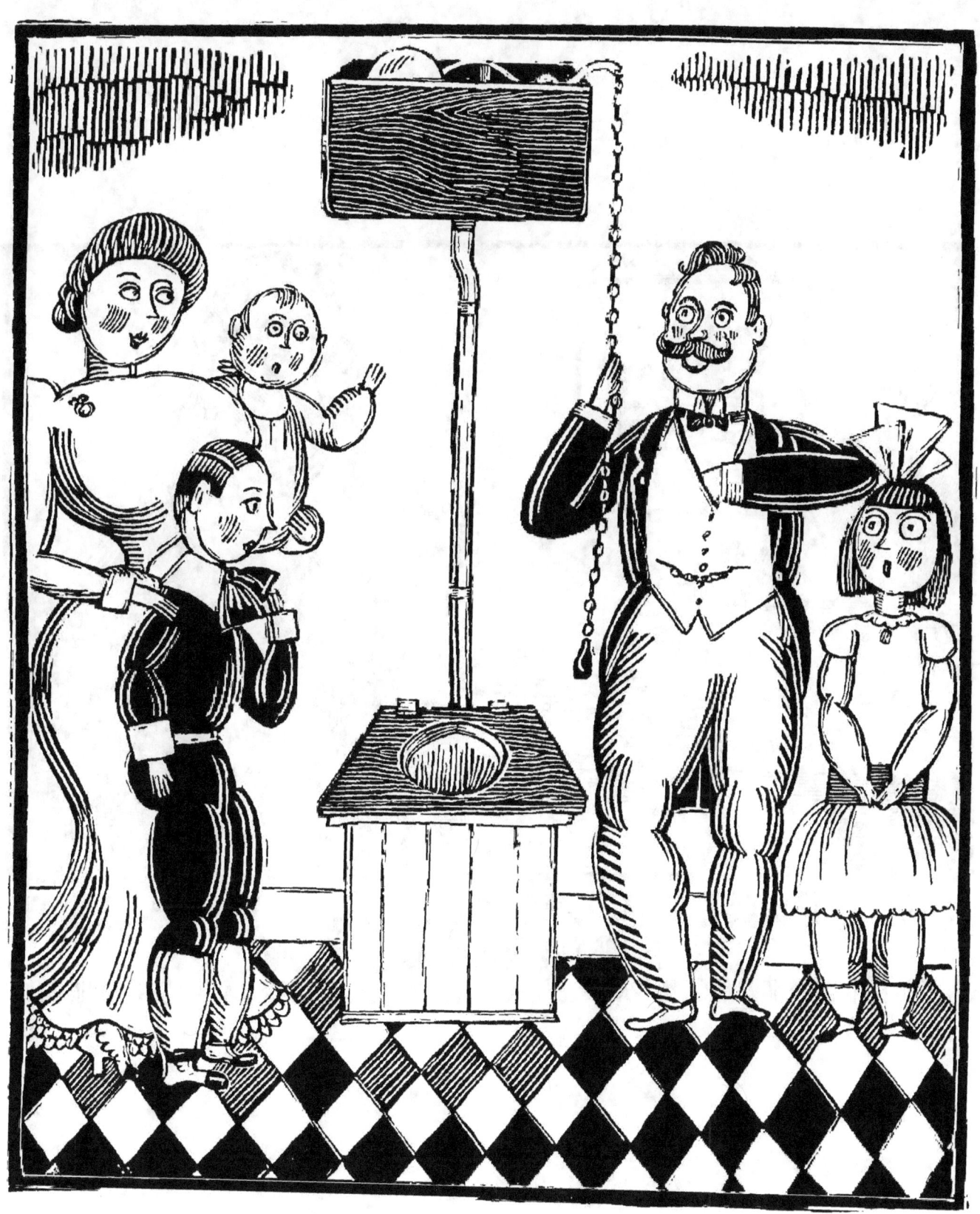

The **FIRST FLUSH**

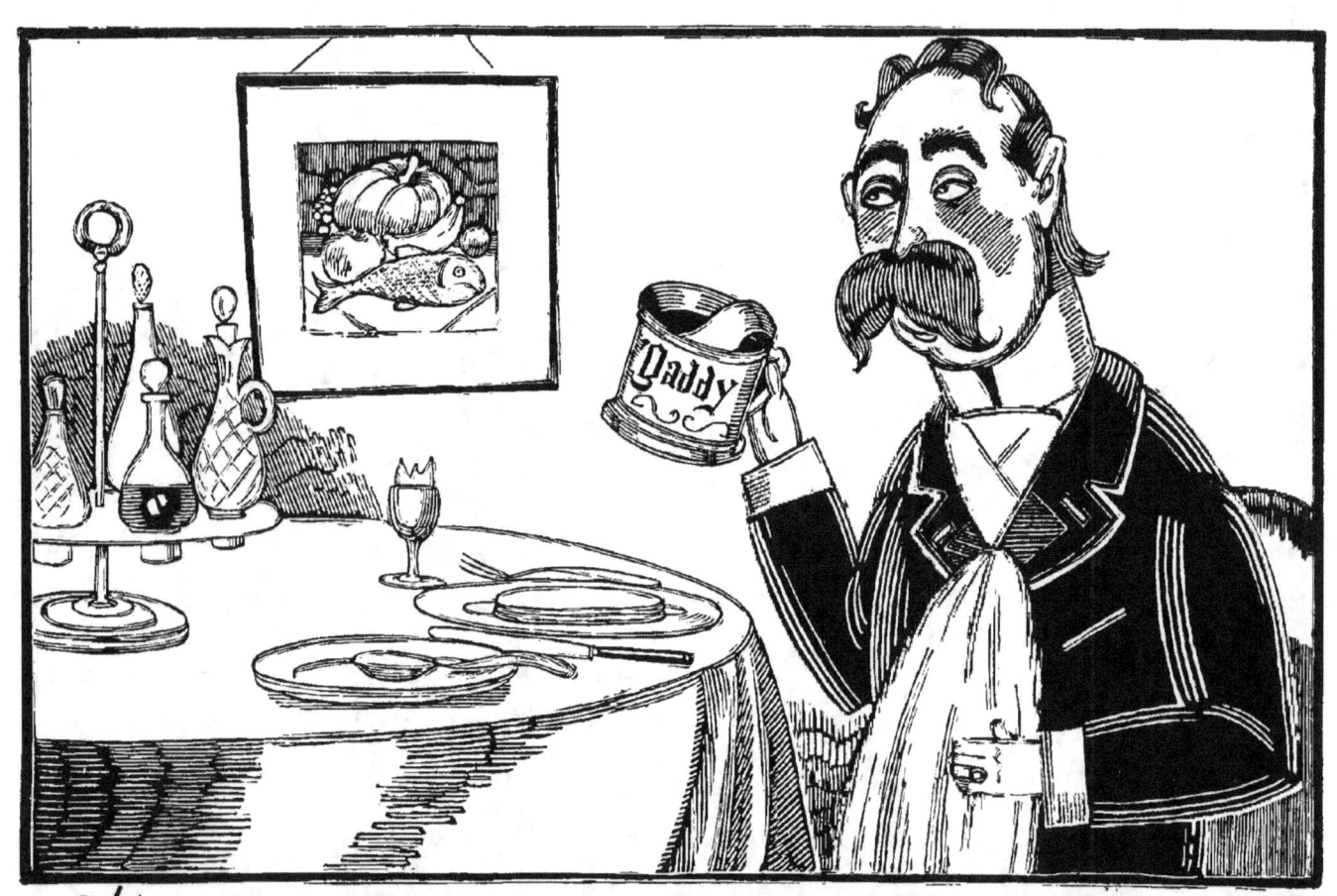

The ZENITH OF REFINED ELEGANCE
THE MOUSTACHE CUP

A JOHN HELD JR ENGRAVING, ENGRAVED BY JOHN HELD JR UNDER the PERSONAL SUPERVISON of JOHN HELD JR

THE WAY OF THE TRANSGRESSOR

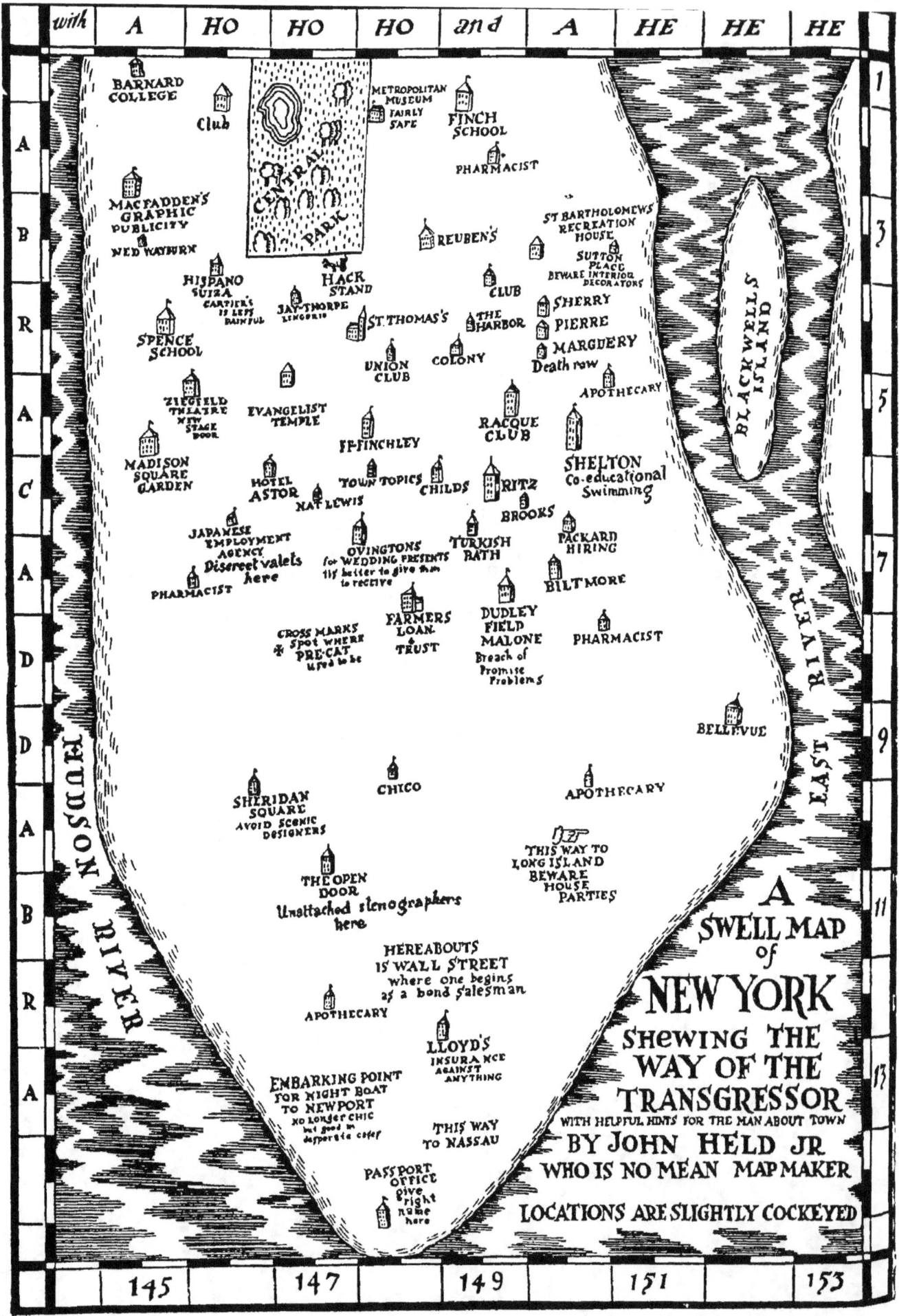

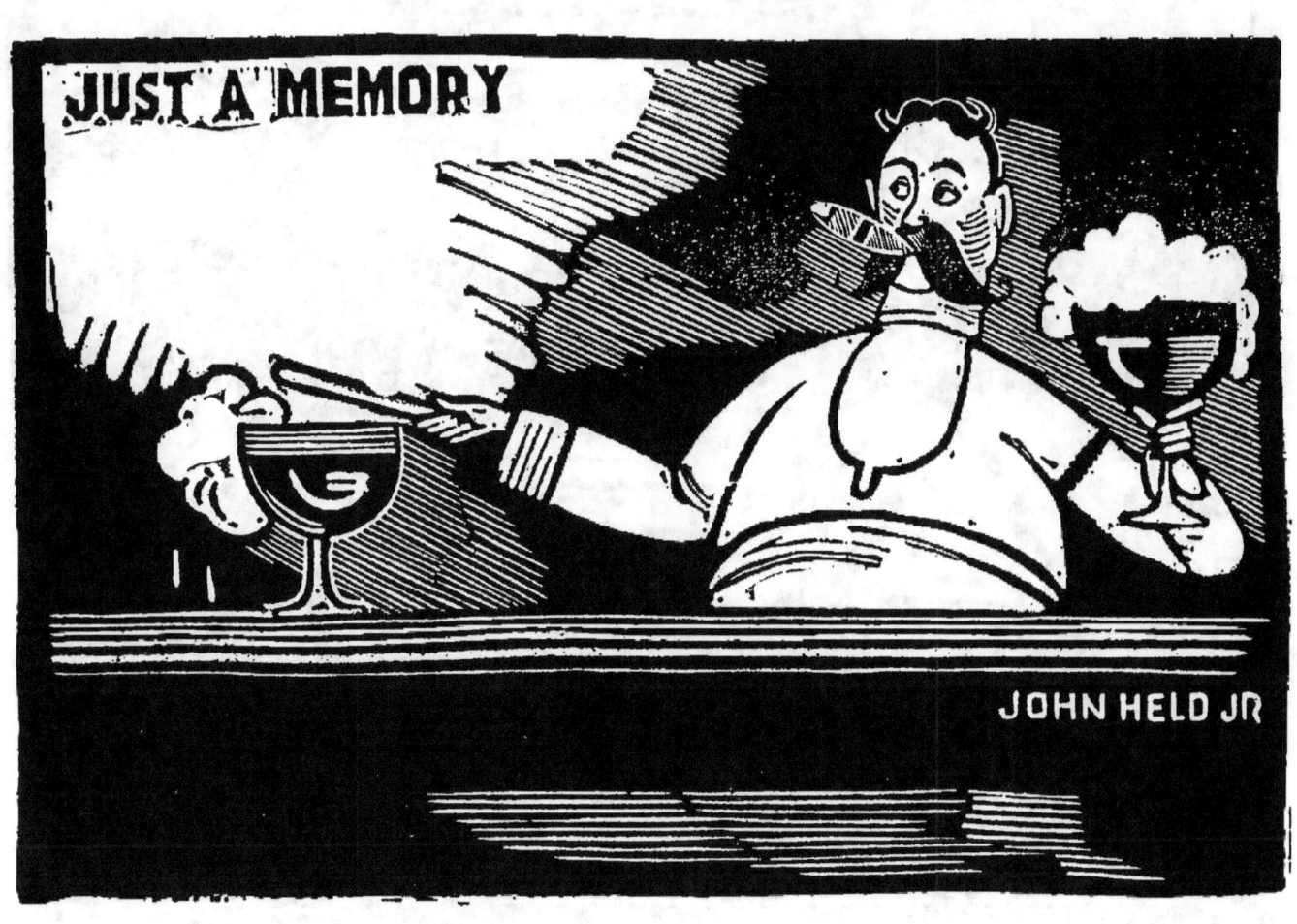

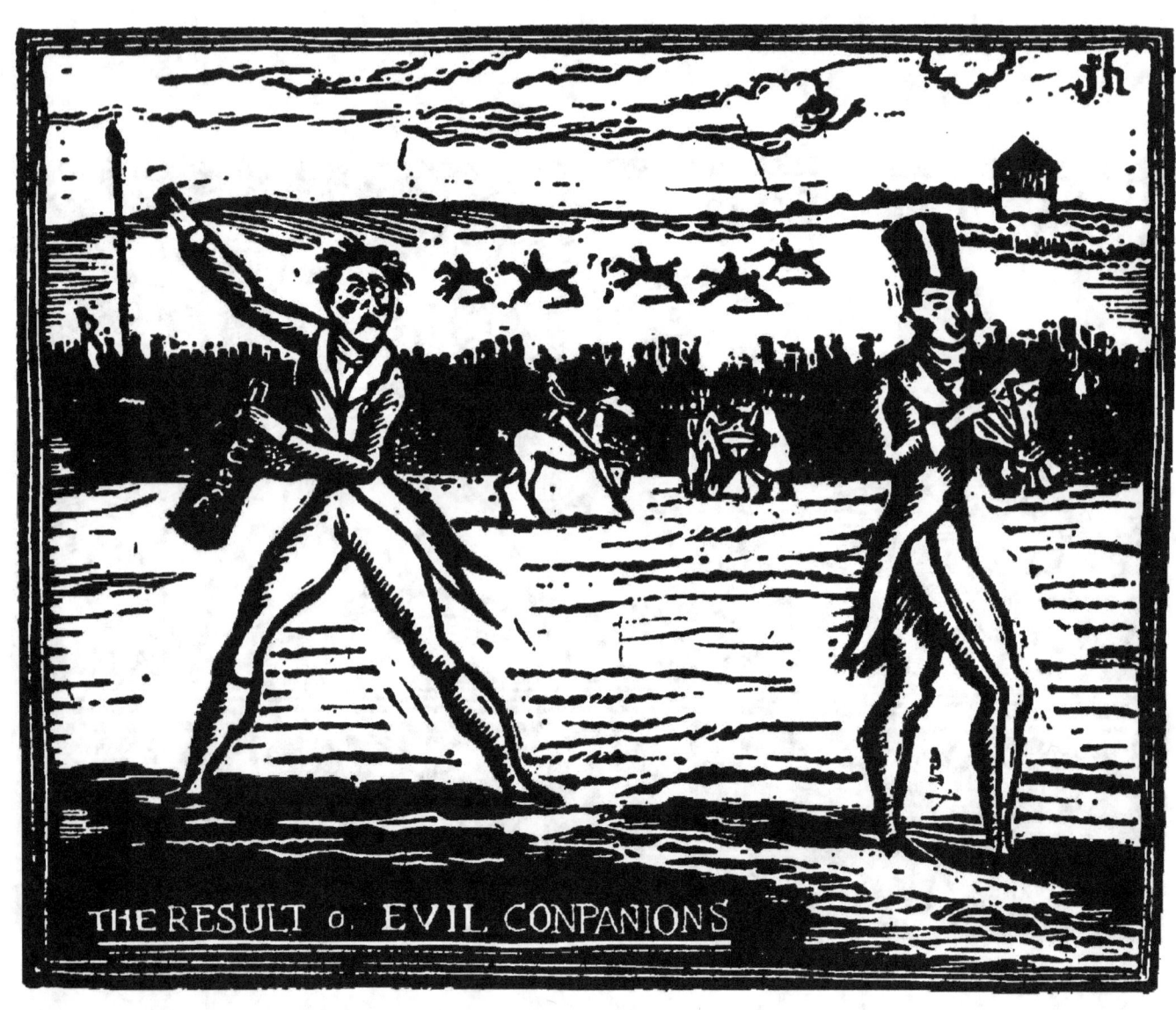

THE RESULT o. EVIL CONPANIONS

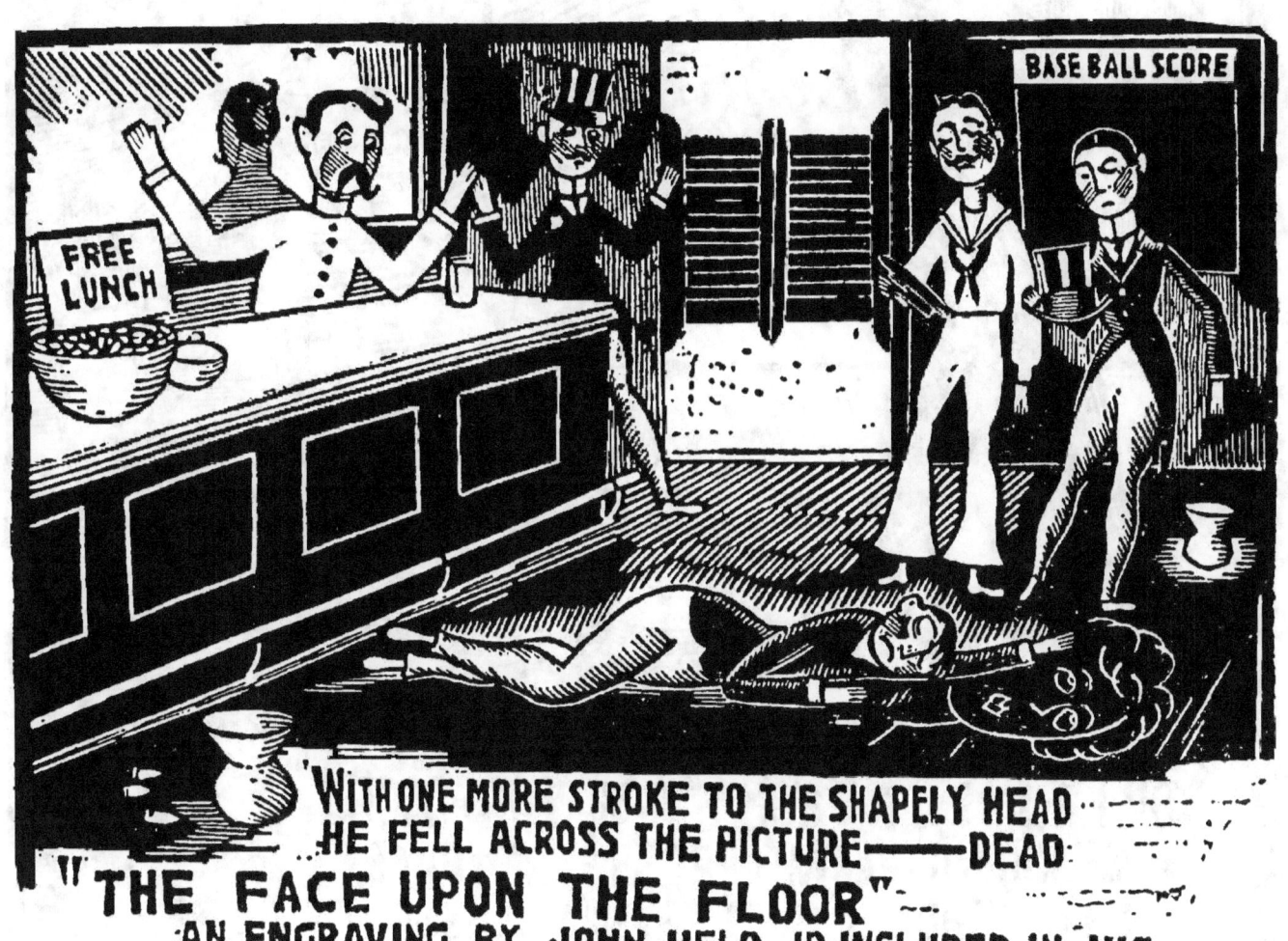

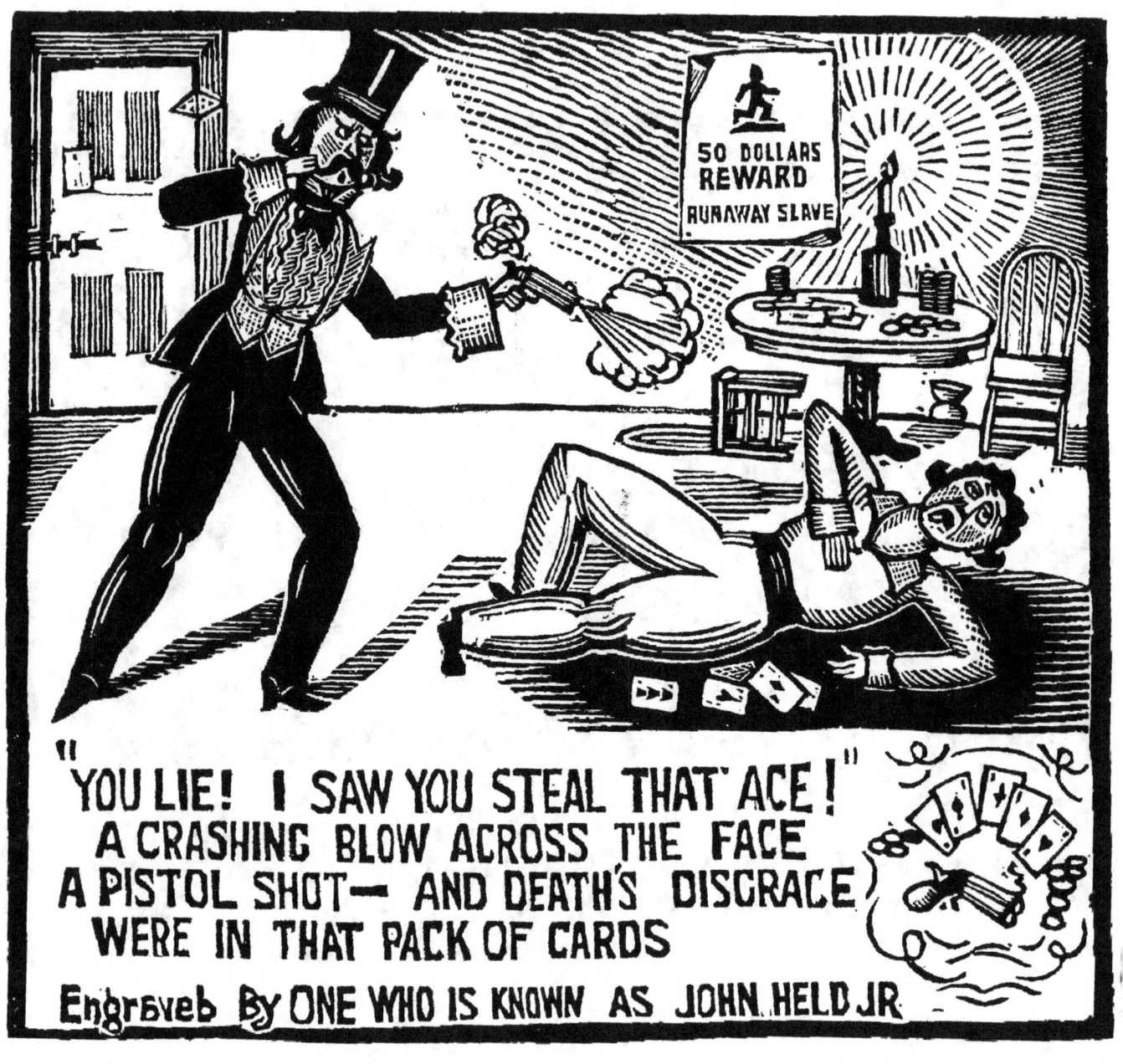

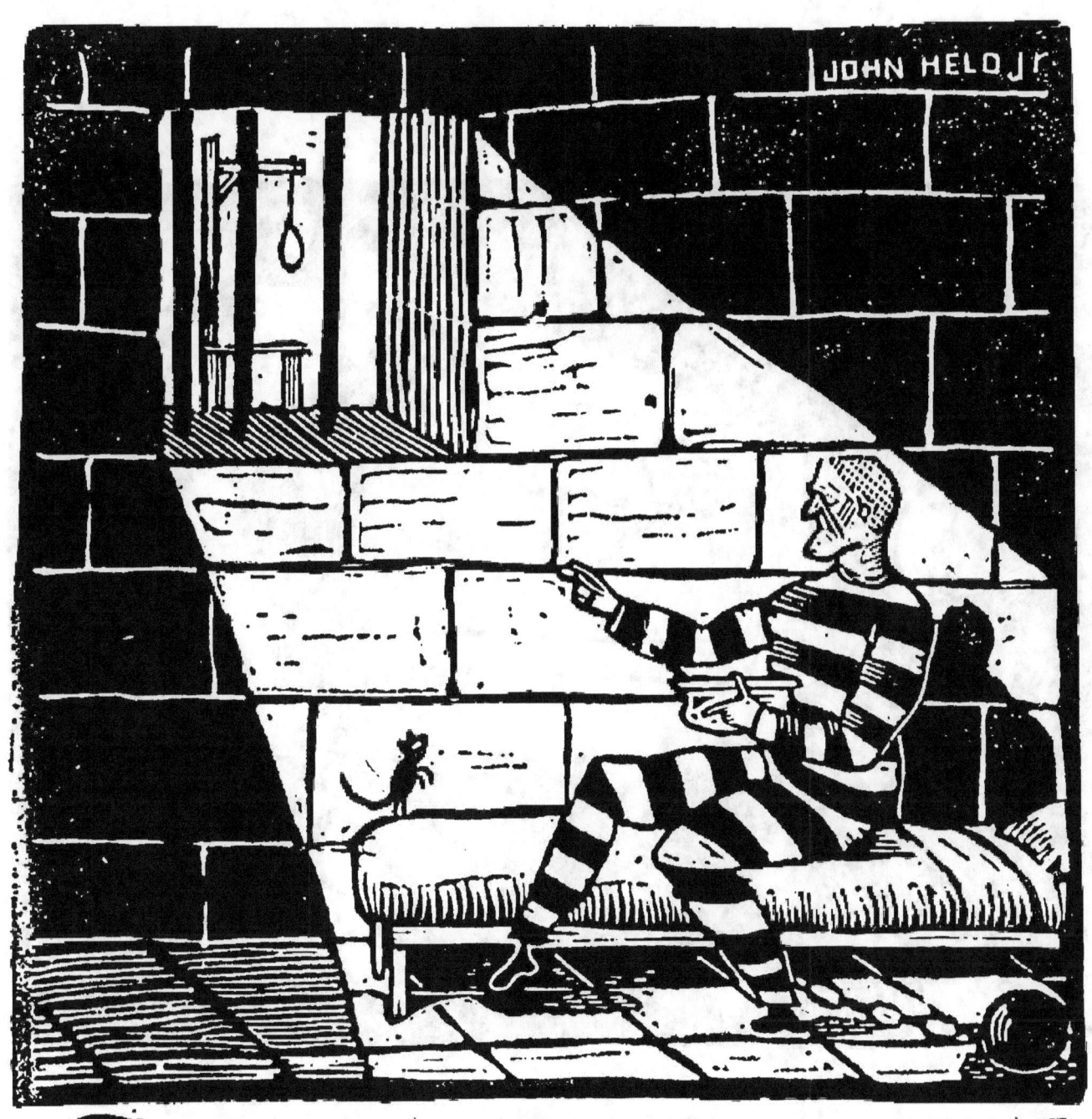

The CONVICT SHARES HIS CHRISTMAS DINNER

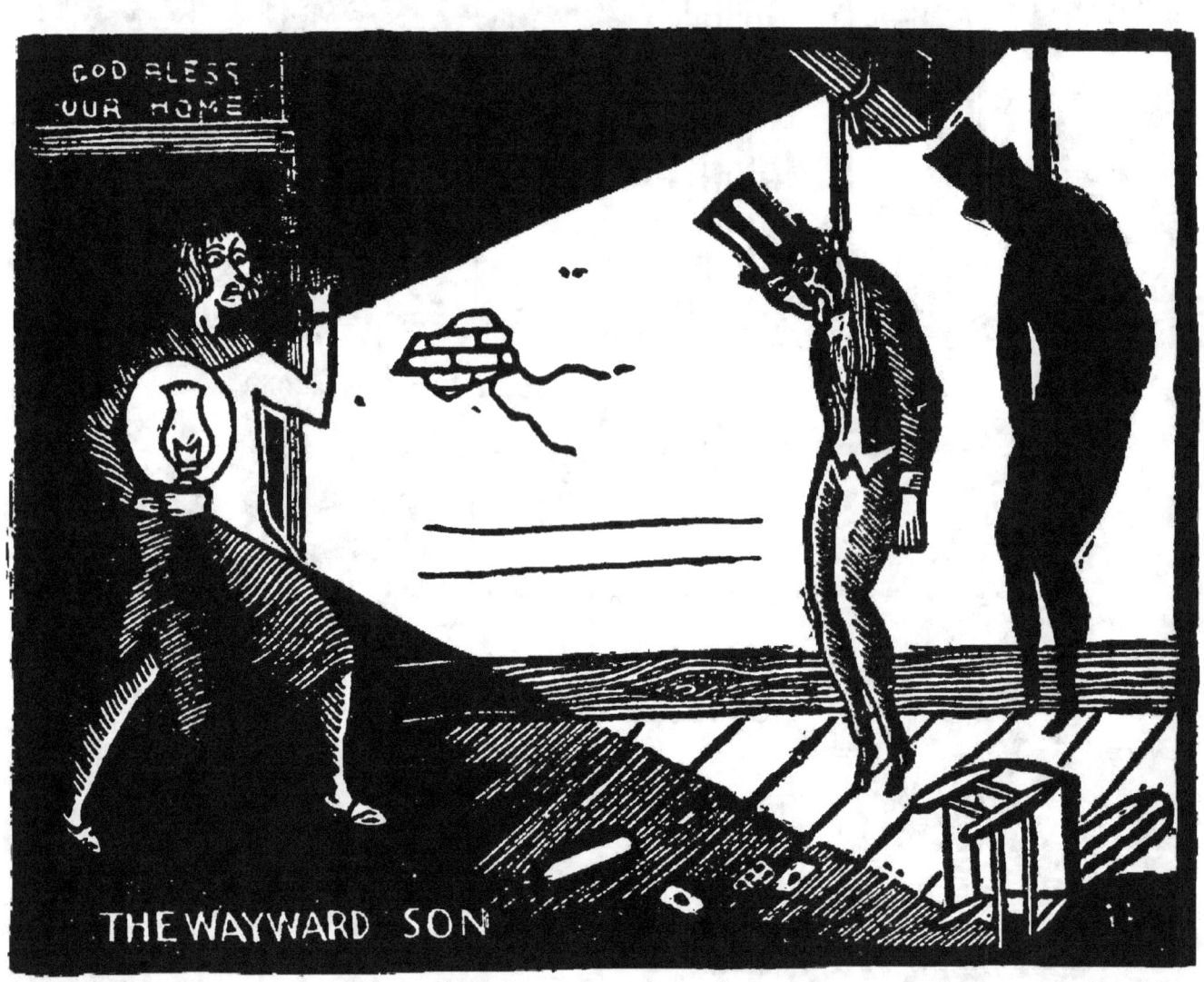

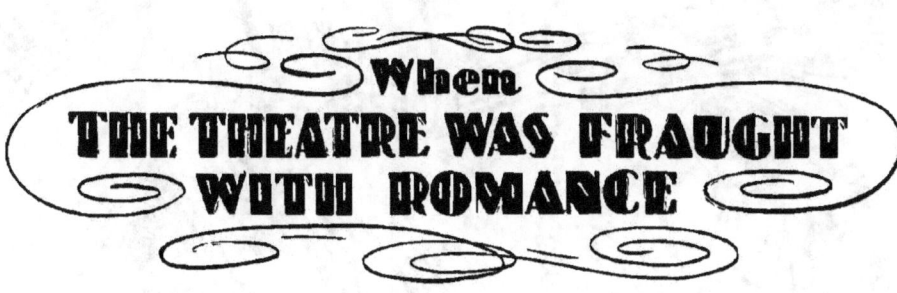

When THE THEATRE WAS FRAUGHT WITH ROMANCE

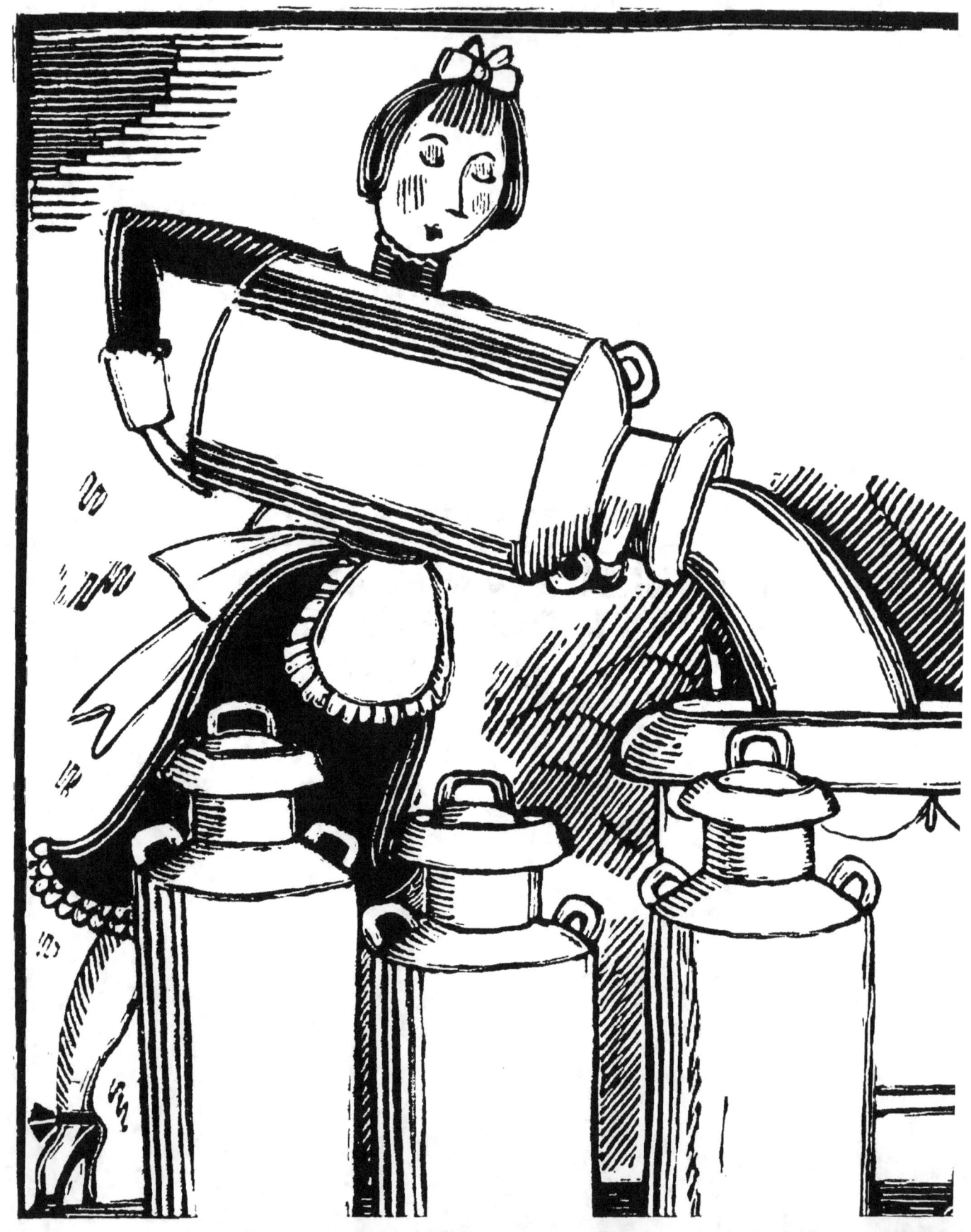

WHEN THE THEATRE WAS FRAUGHT WITH

ENGRAVED BY JOHN HELD

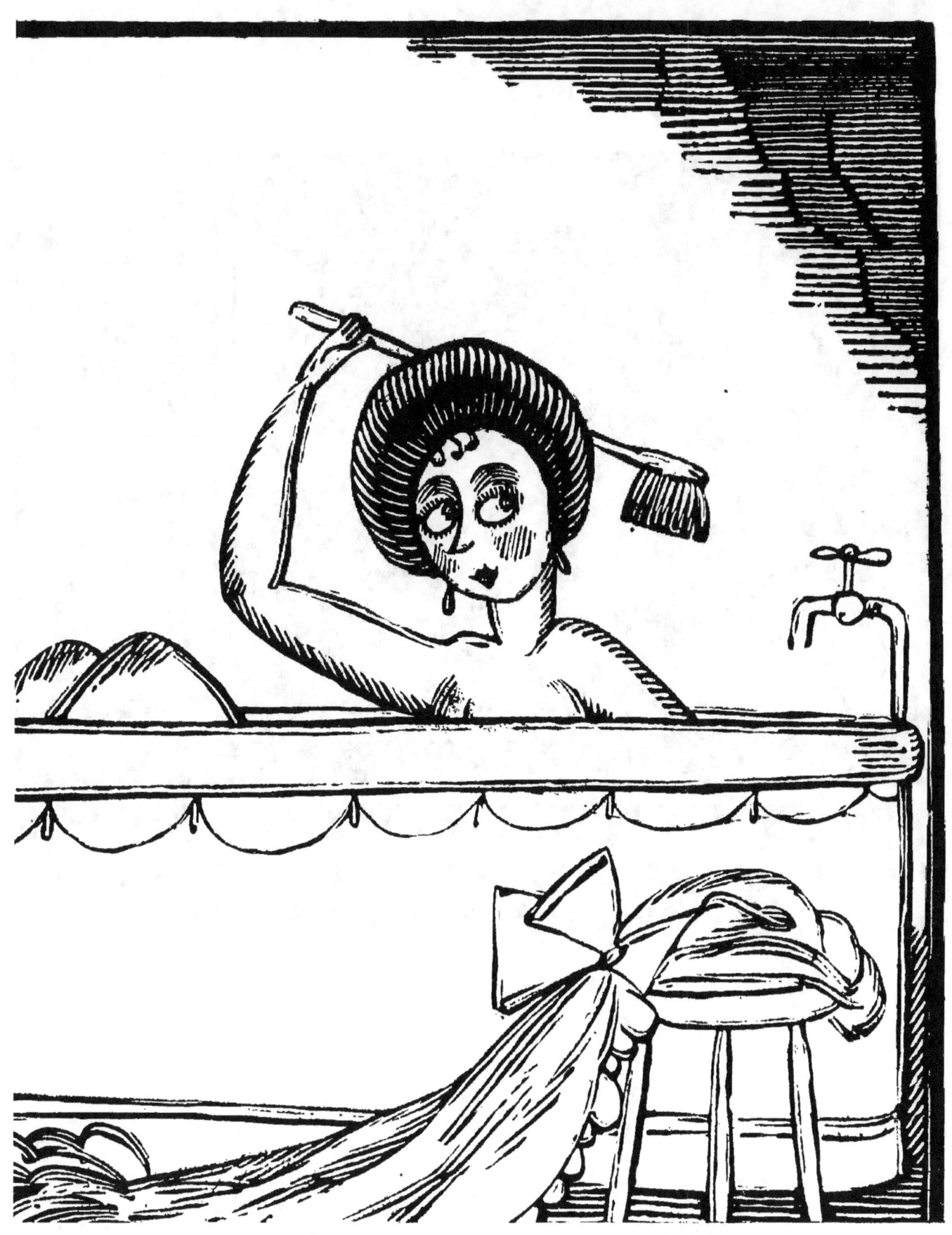

[N]ANCE ANNA HELD'S MILK BATH

WHO IS NO RELATION

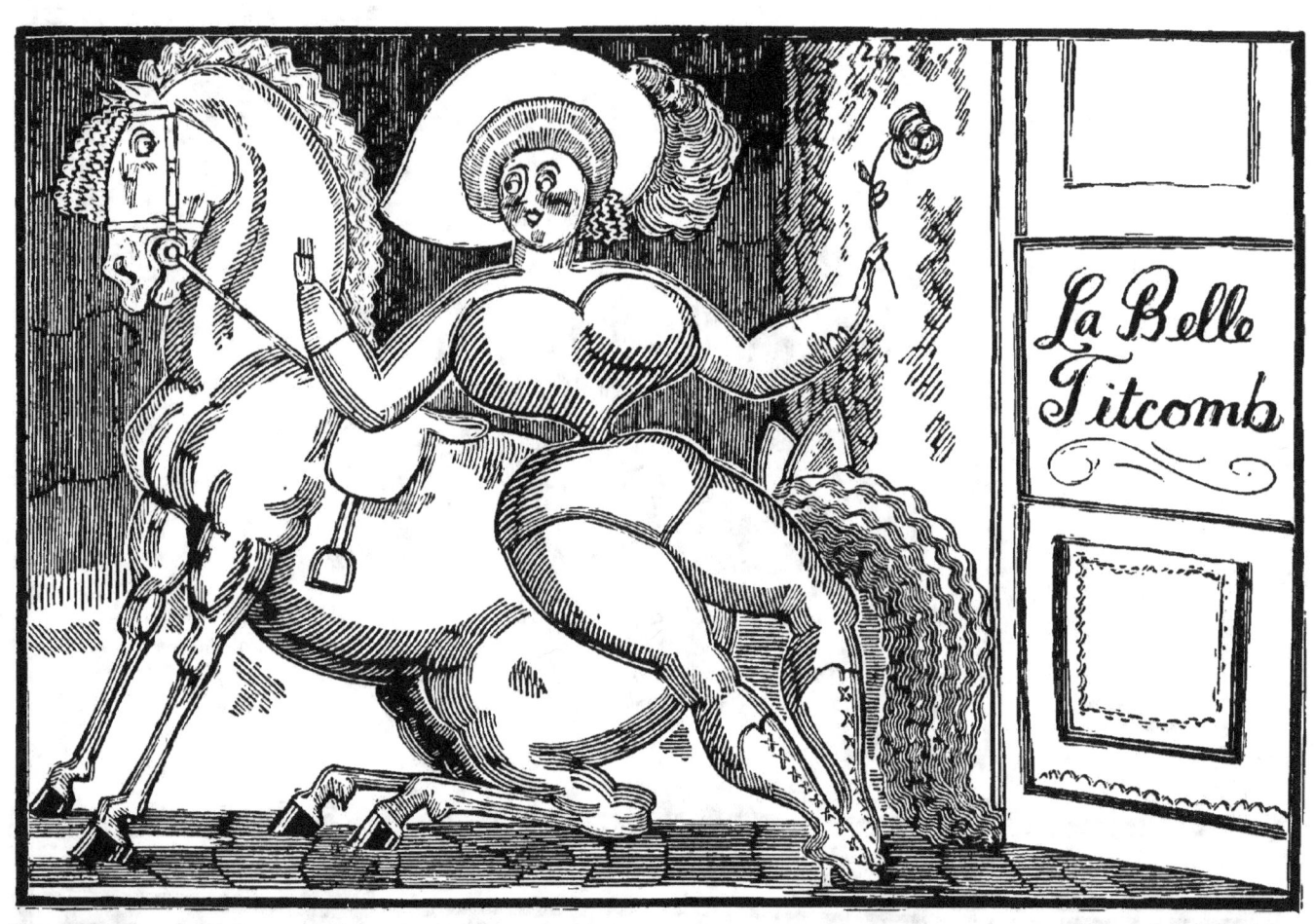

La Belle Titcomb

WHEN THE THEATRE WAS FRAUGHT with ROMANCE
A SCENE FROM YOUTH'S MEMORY ～ ENGRAVED BY THAT
OLD HUMANIST JOHN HELD JR

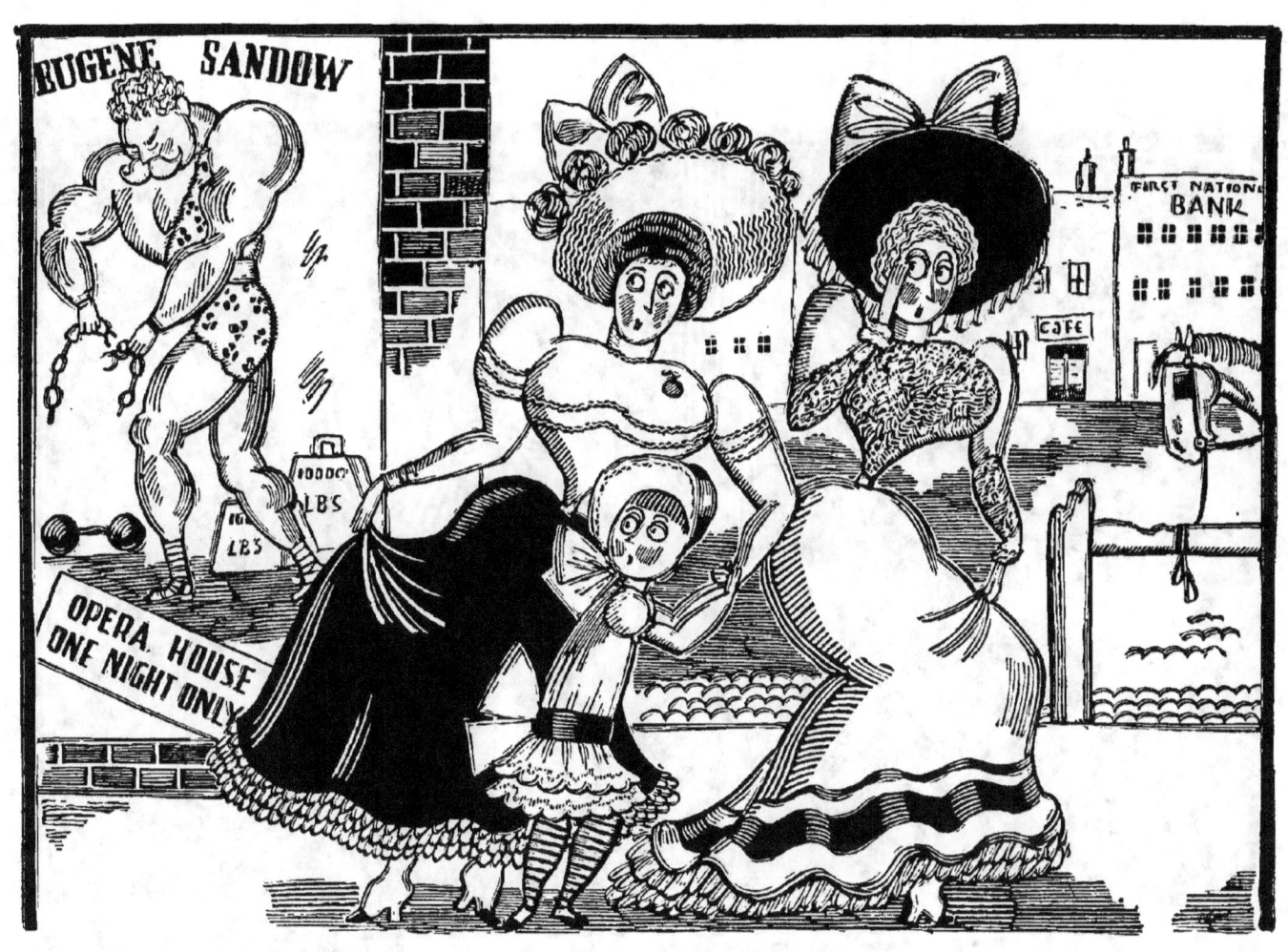

WHEN THE THEATRE WAS FRAUGHT with ROMANCE

The Thought is born of the FORM DIVINE

ENGRAVED BY JOHN HELD JR ADELVING INTO YESTERYEAR

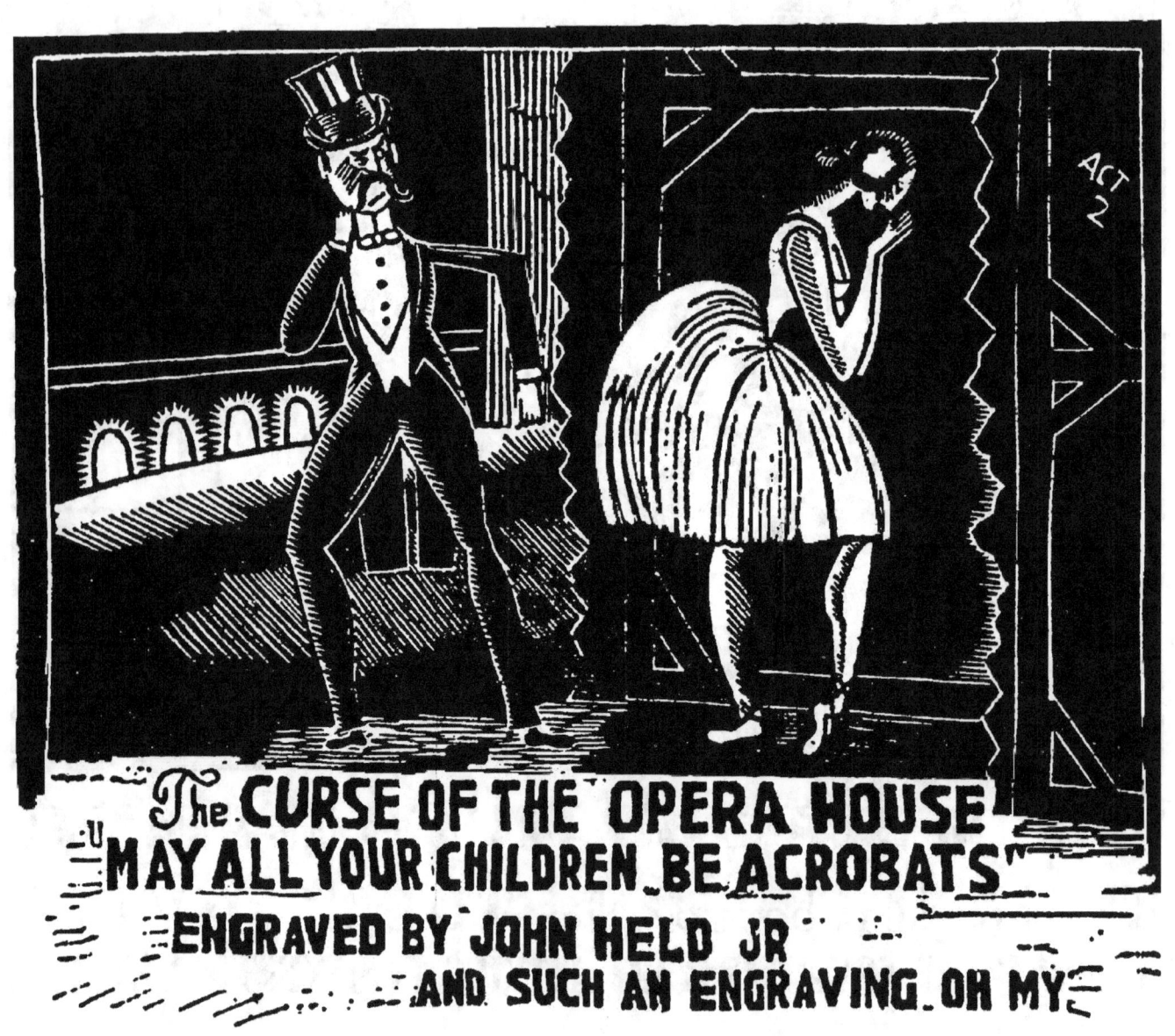

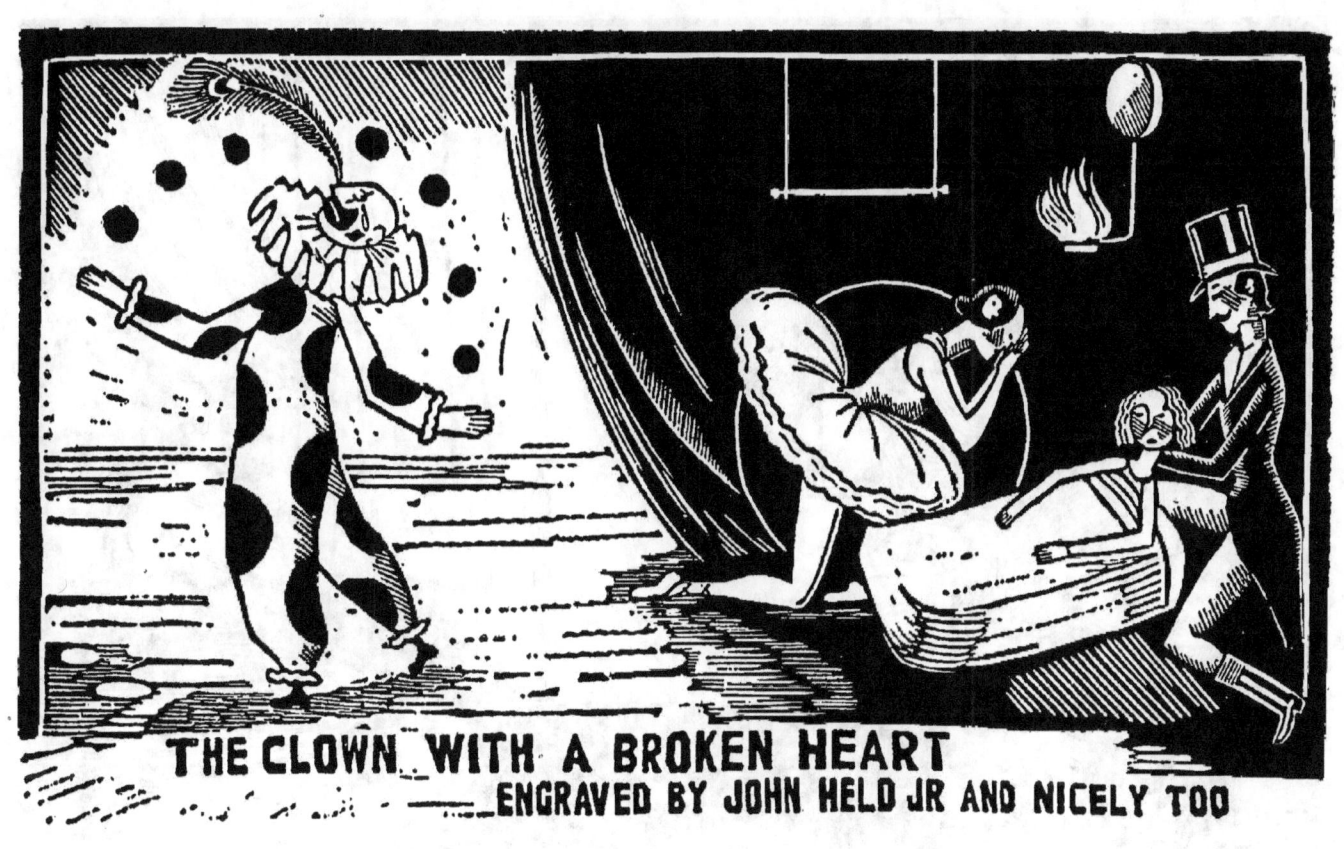

THE CLOWN WITH A BROKEN HEART
——ENGRAVED BY JOHN HELD JR AND NICELY TOO

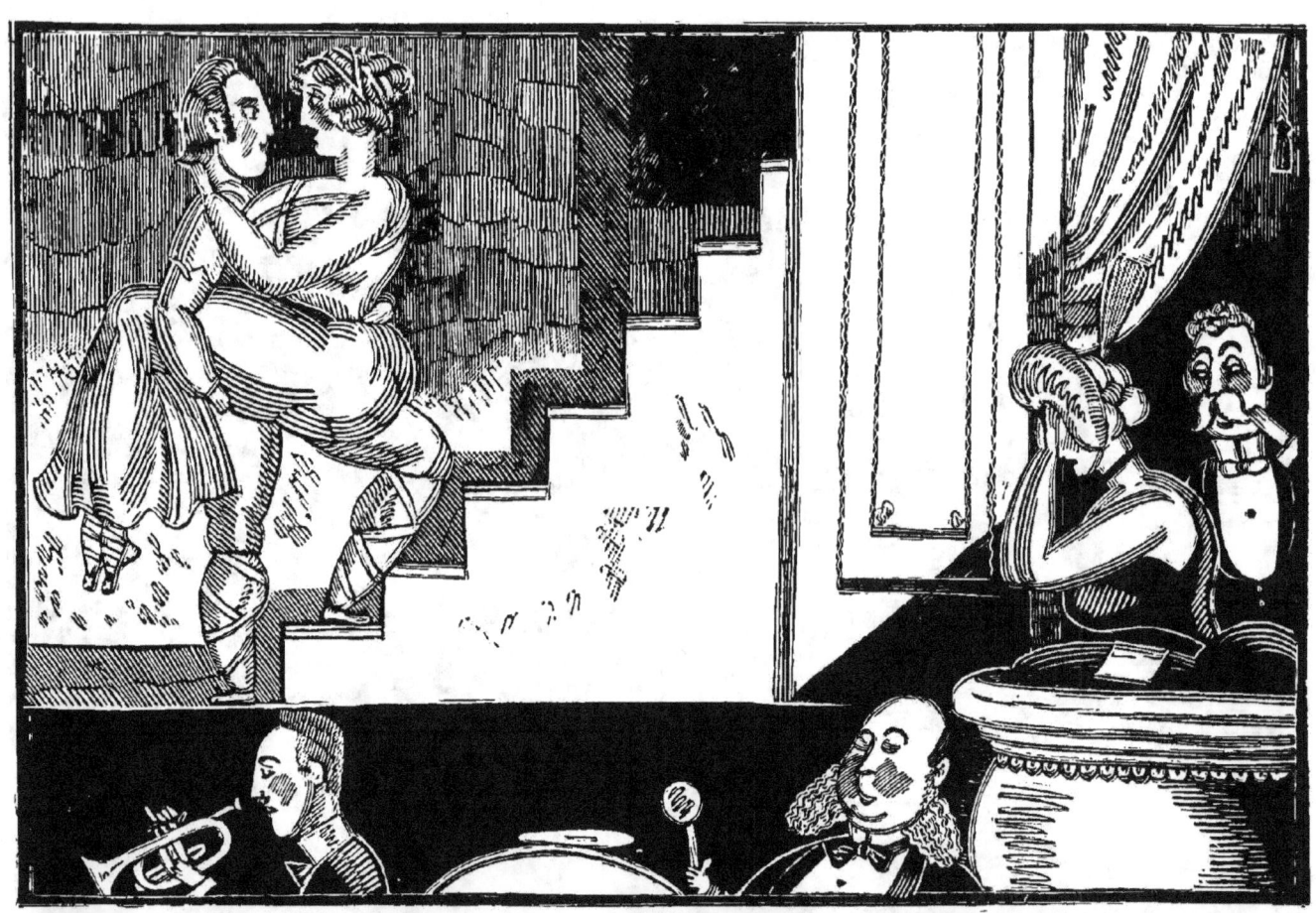

WHEN THE THEATRE WAS FRAUGHT WITH ROMANCE
OLGA NETHERSOLE PLAYS THE STAIRWAY SCENE from "SAPPHO"
ENGRAVED BY JOHN HELD JR WEIGHT 167 lbs STRIPPED

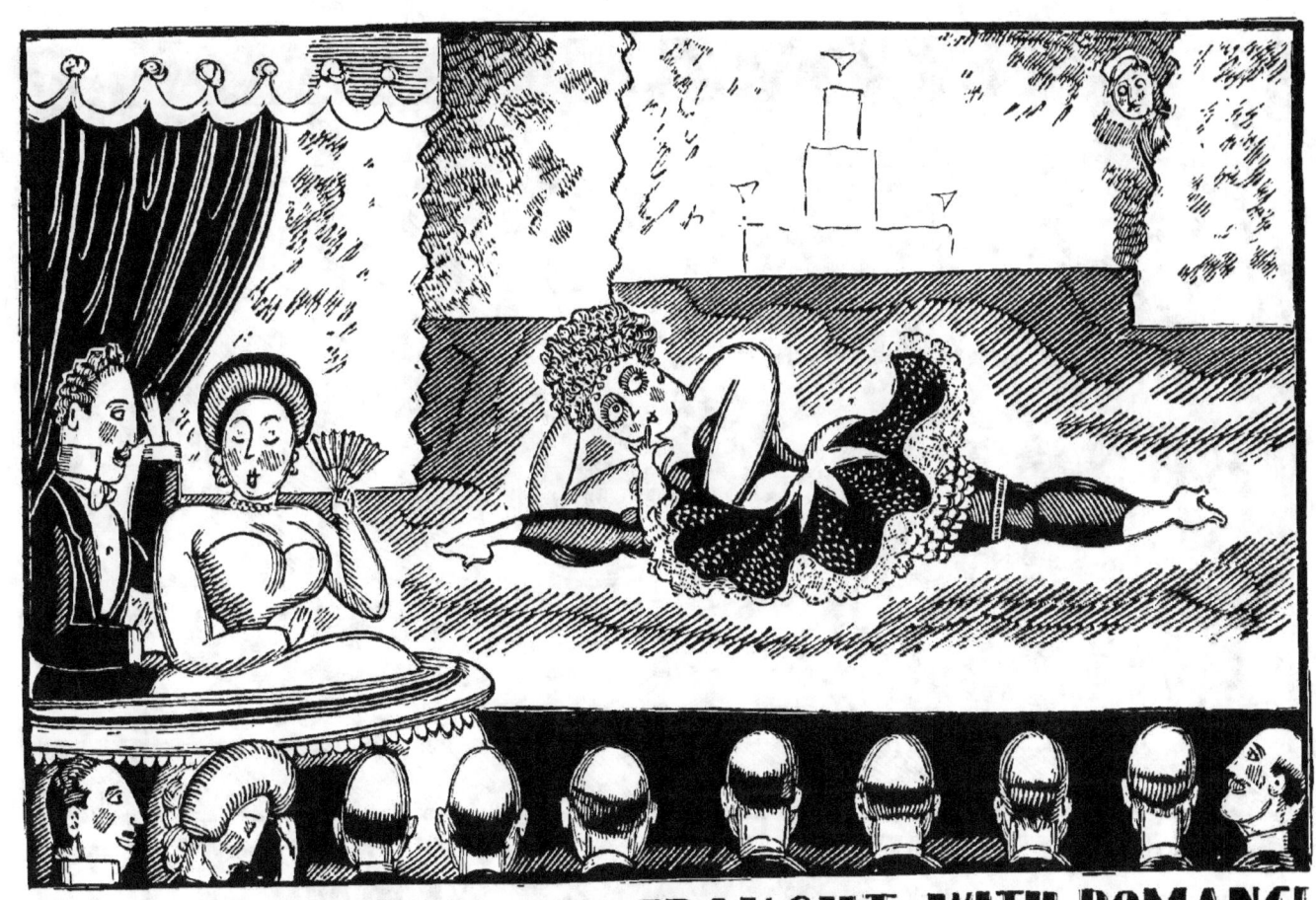

WHEN THE THEATRE WAS FRAUGHT WITH ROMANCE
DOING THE SPLIT
ENGRAVED BY JOHN HELD JR   MAN AND BOY

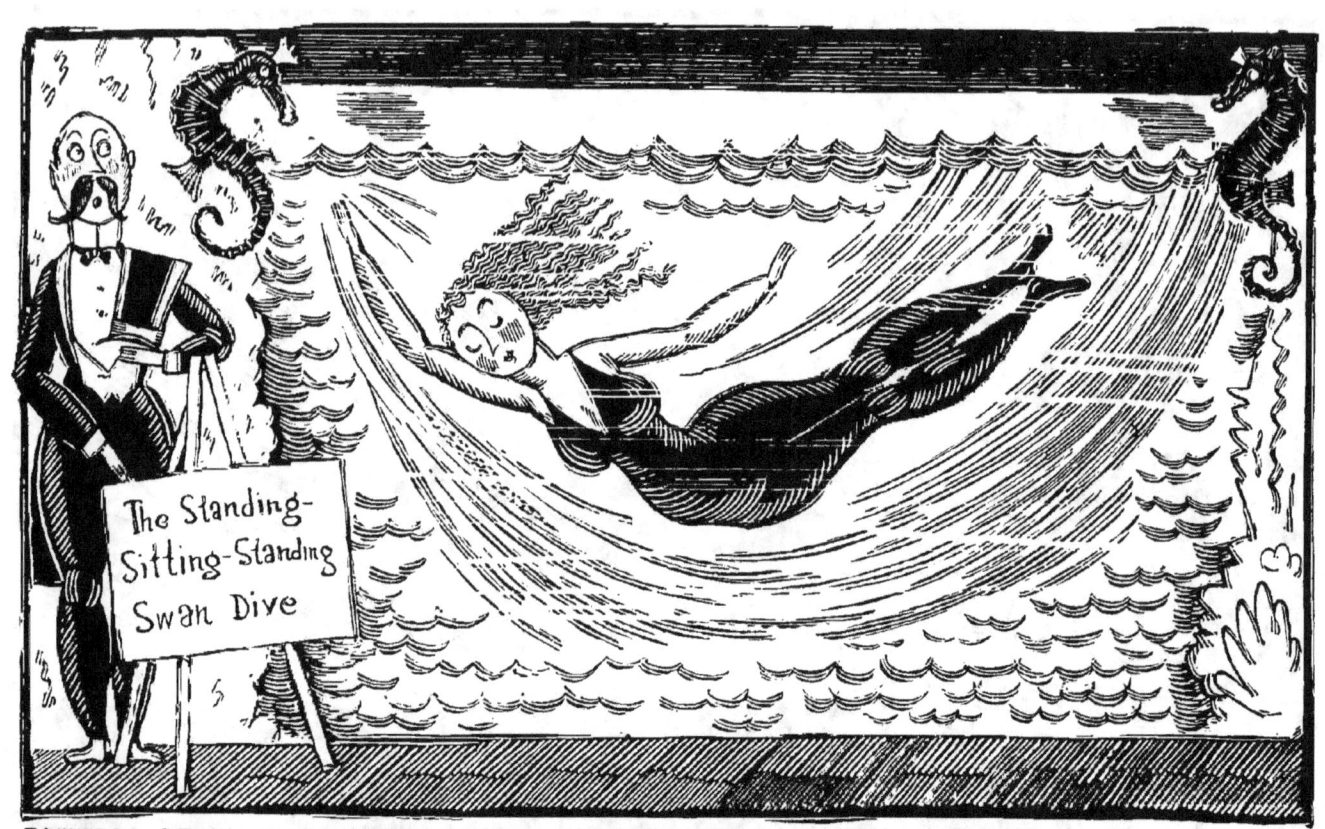

WHEN THE THEATRE WAS FRAUGHT WITH ROMANCE
The **DIVING VENUS**
DEFTLY ENGRAVED BY JOHN HELD JR - HISTORIAN

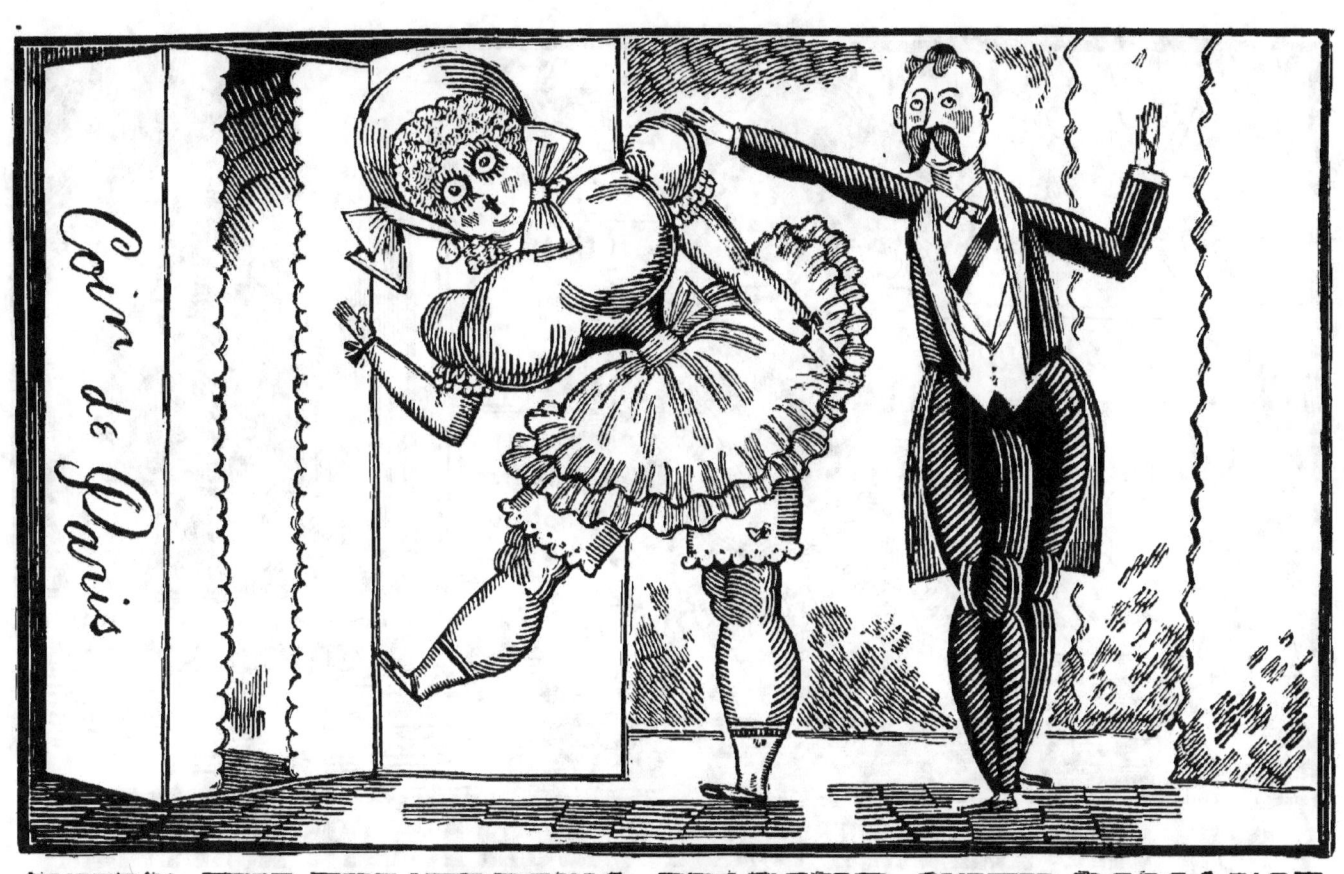

WHEN THE THEATRE WAS FRAUGHT WITH ROMANCE
"The MECHANICAL DOLL"
Engraved by JOHN HELD JR who TOOTS HIS OWN HORN

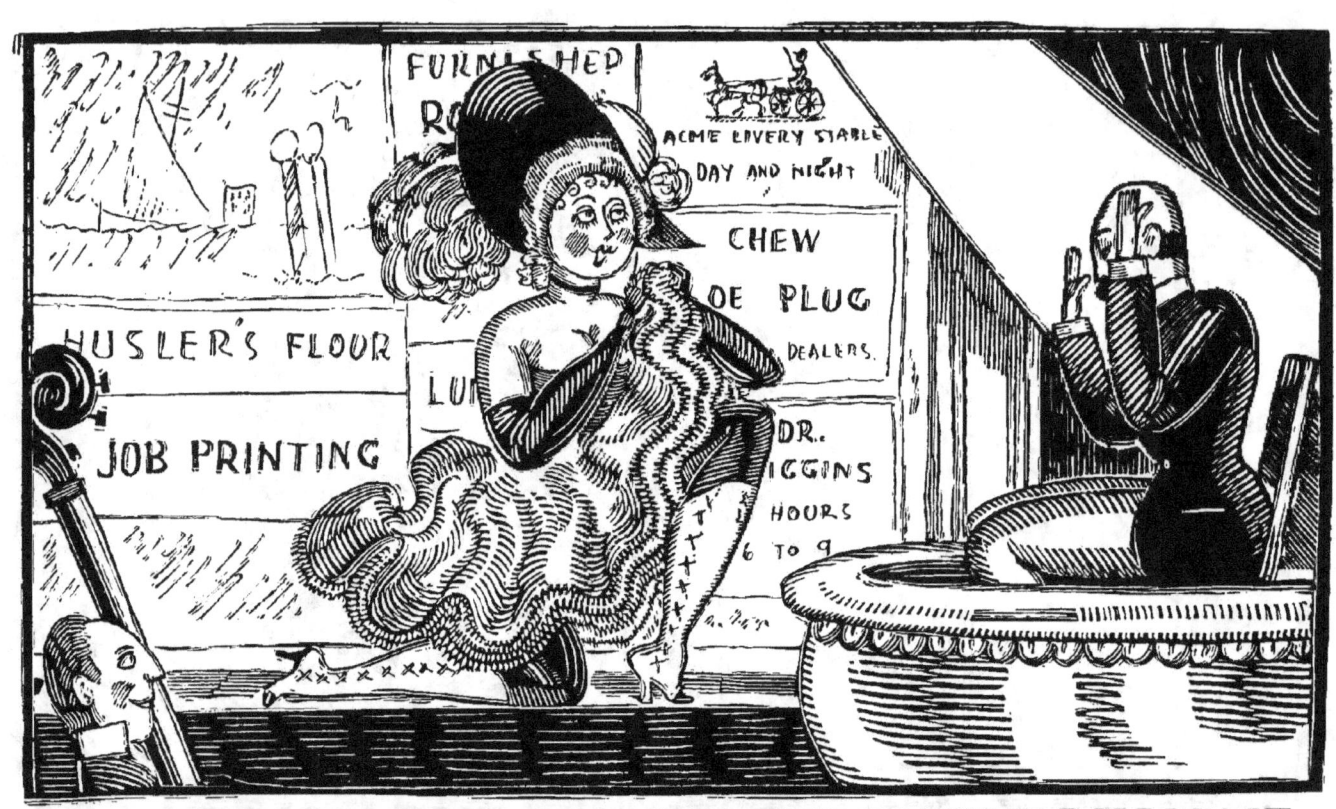

WHEN THE THEATRE WAS FRAUGHT WITH ROMANCE
THE SOUBRETTE SINGS A RACY SONG TO THE MAN IN THE BOX
ENg BY JOHN HELD JR WHO DEAR TO HIS HEART ARE THE SCENES OF HIS CHILDHOOD

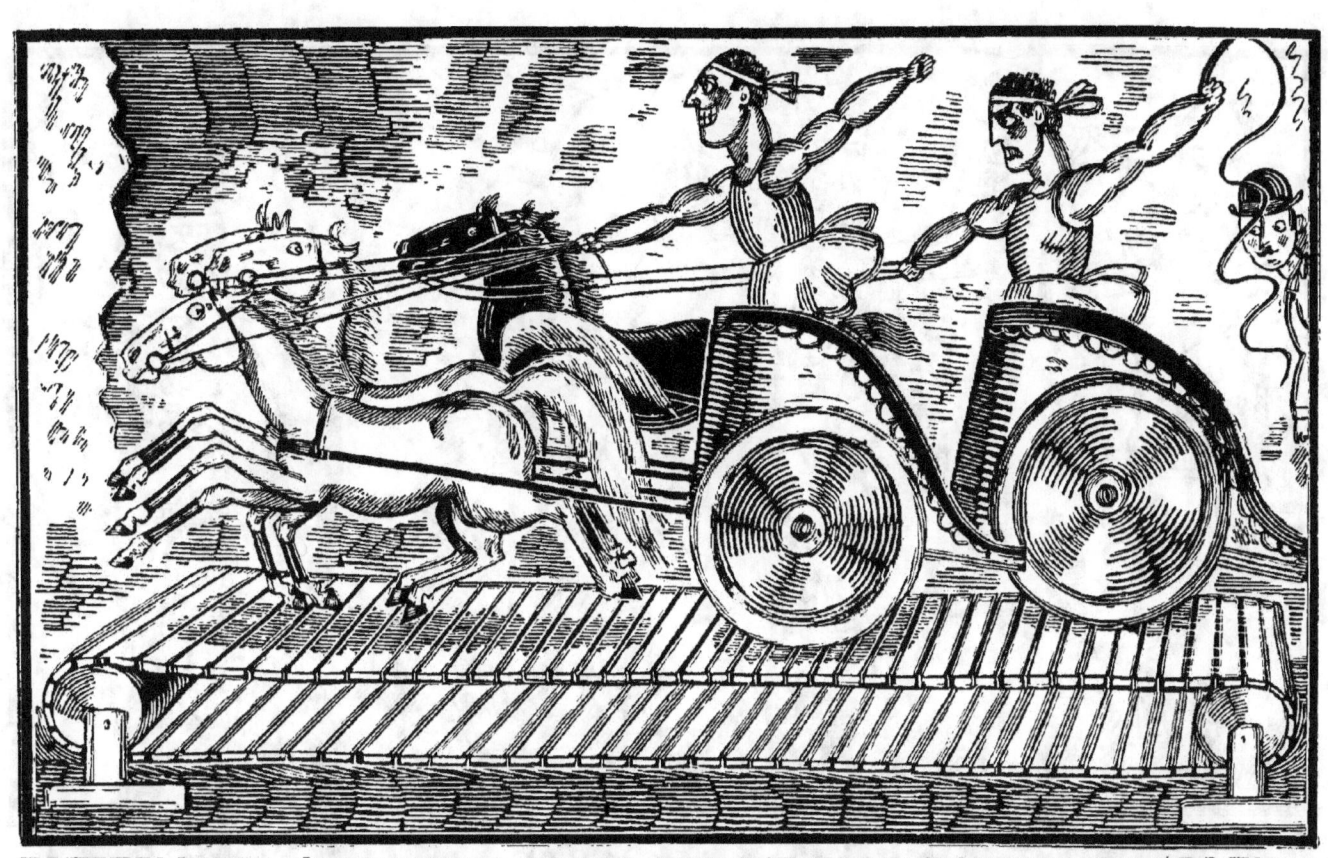

WHEN THE THEATRE WAS FRAUGHT WITH ROMANCE
BEN-HUR AND THE WHITE HORSES ALWAYS **WIN**
ENGRAVED BY **JOHN HELD JR** WHO SOMETIMES WONDERS WHAT ITS ALL ABOUT

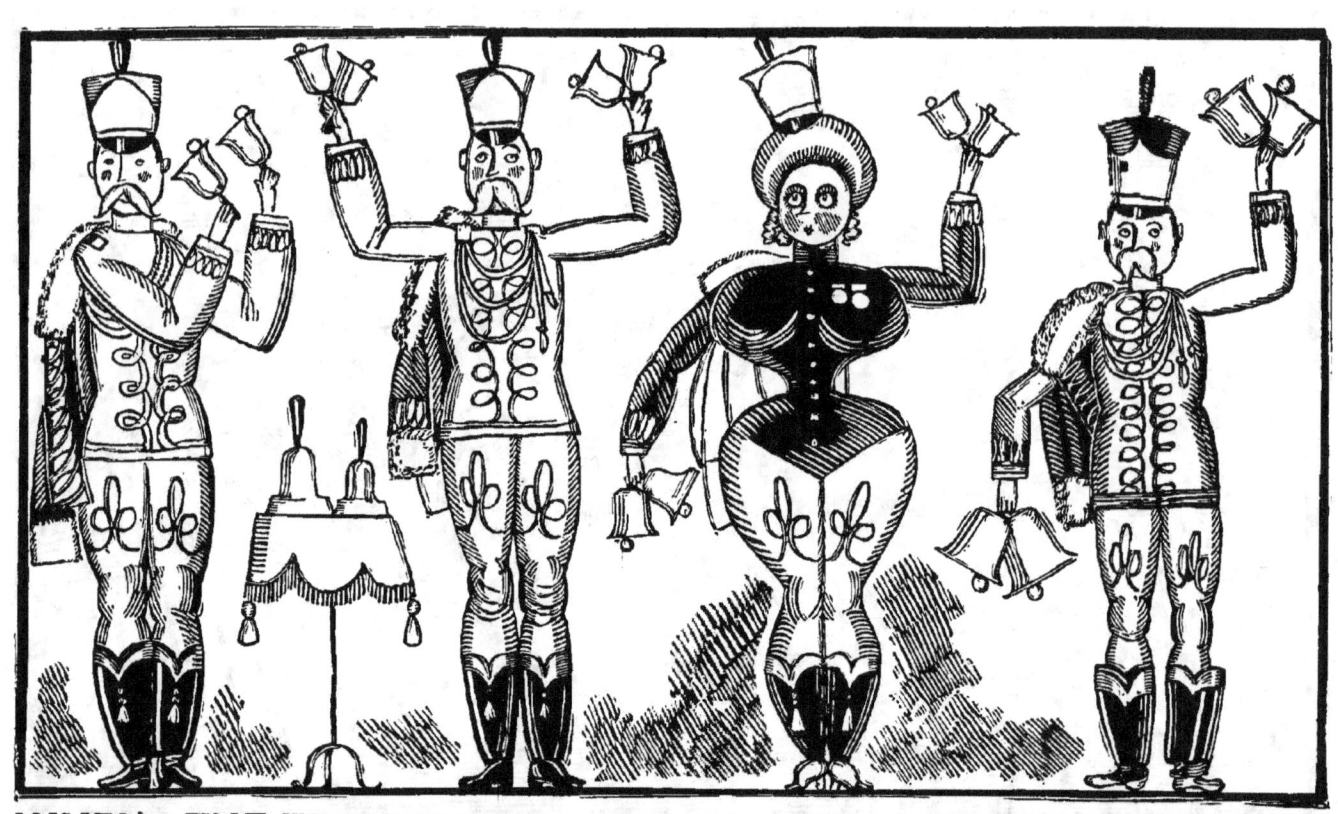

WHEN THE THEATRE WAS FRAUGHT WITH ROMANCE
THE ORIGINAL SWISS BELL RINGERS
ENGRAVED BY JOHN (BUDDY) HELD JR. AMERICA'S BOY FRIEND.

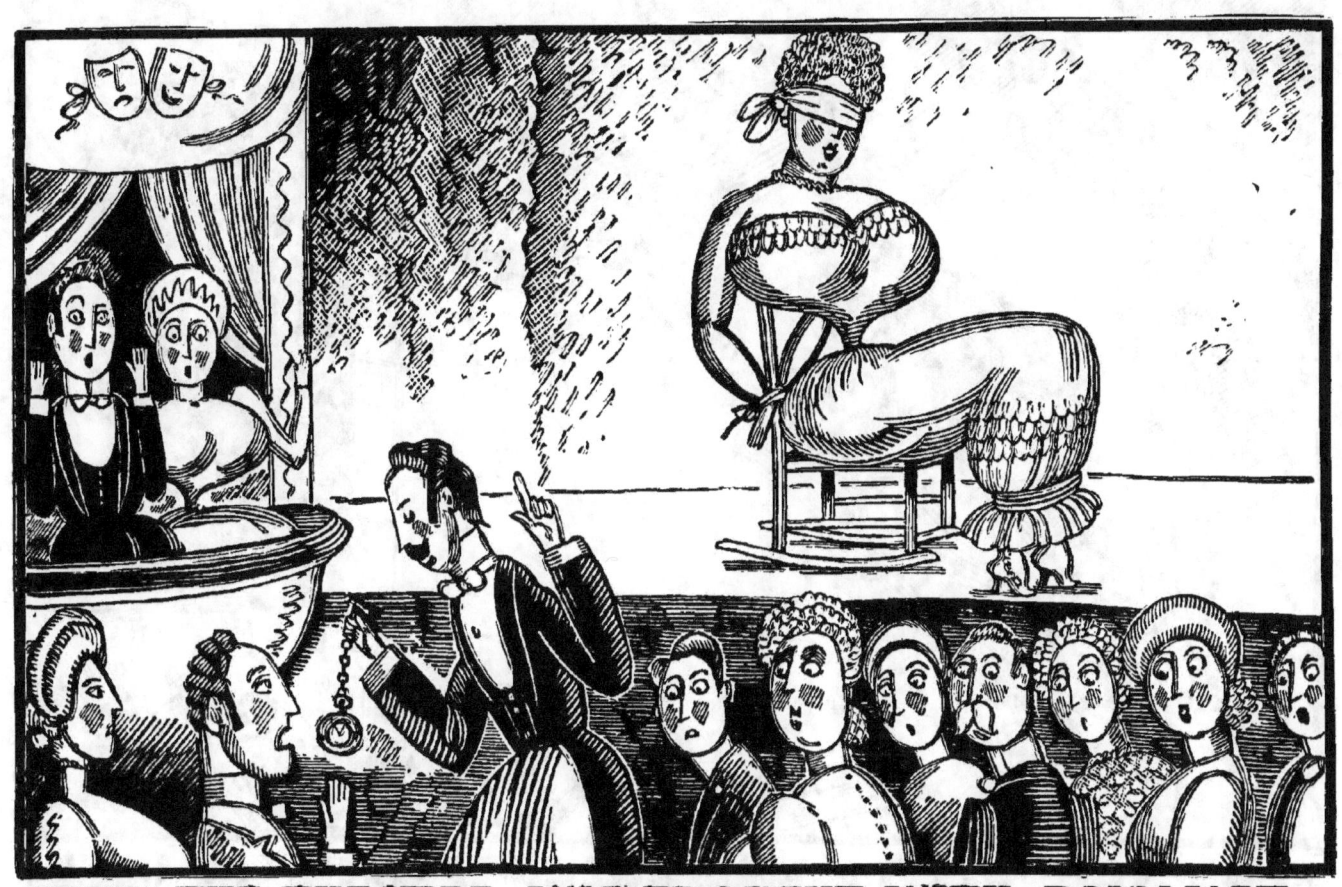

WHEN THE THEATRE WAS FRAUGHT WITH ROMANCE
ANNIE EVA FAY the MIND-READER TOLD YOU PAST, PRESENT AND FUTURE ALSO
THE NUMBER IN YOUR WATCH! ~ ENGRAVED by JOHN HELD JR
WHO IS A CHARMING COMPANION ~ SOUND OF WIND AND LIMB & GENEROUS TO A FAULT

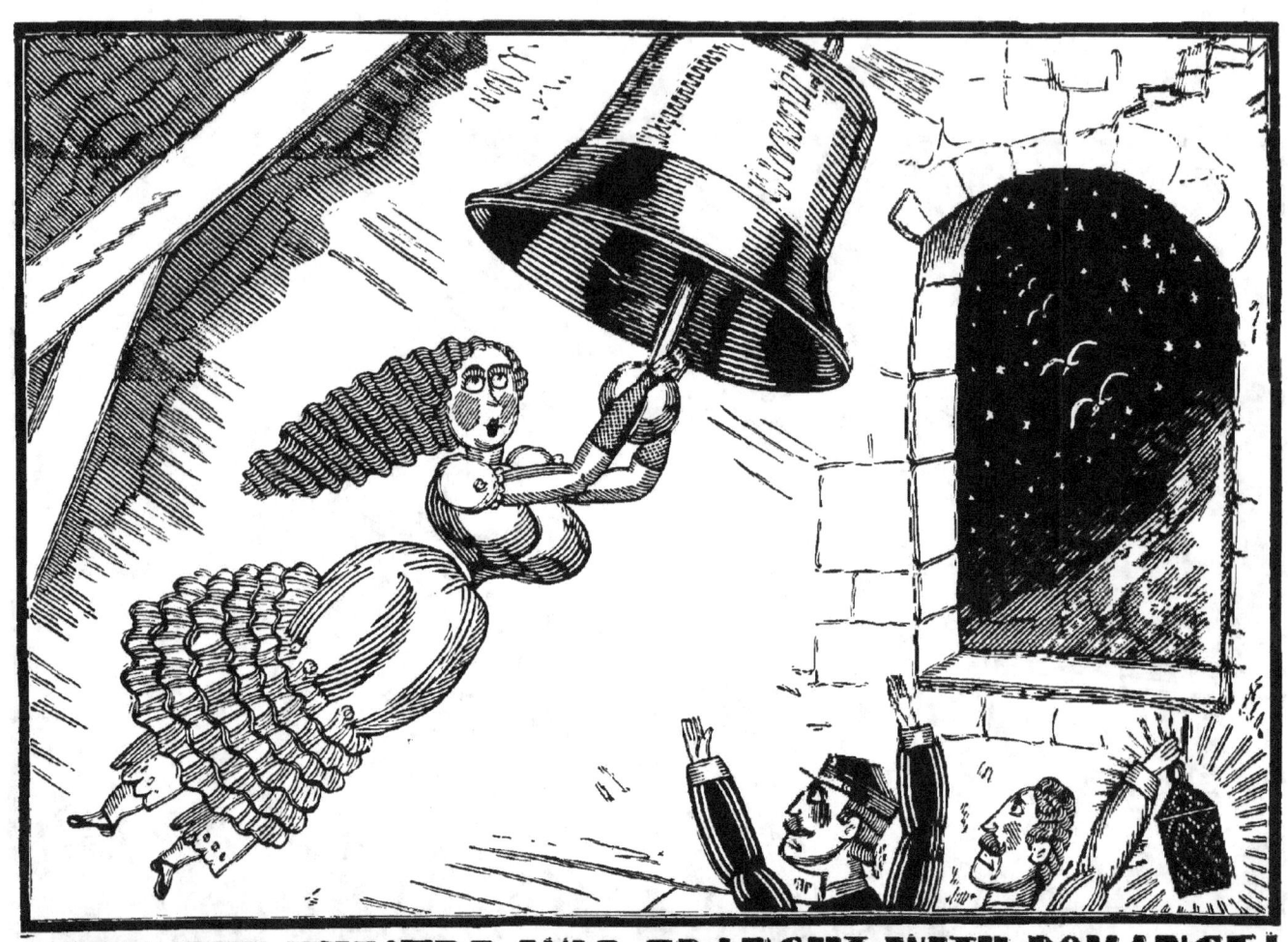

WHEN THE THEATRE WAS FRAUGHT WITH ROMANCE!
· MRS. LESLIE CARTER IN " THE HEART OF MARYLAND "
ENGRAVED BY JOHN HELD JR WHO DOESN'T REMEMBER VERY WELL.

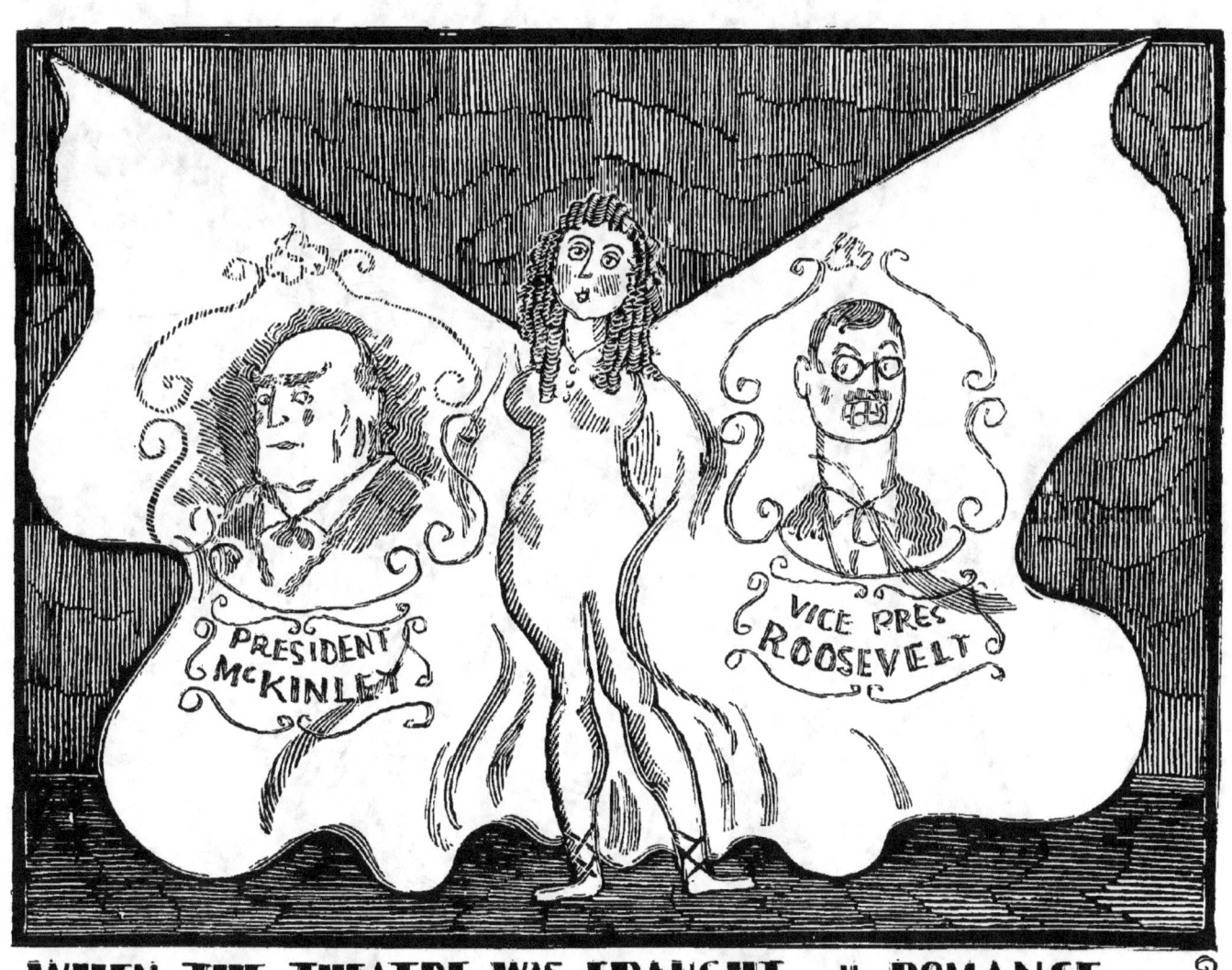

WHEN THE THEATRE WAS FRAUGHT with ROMANCE
THE STARTLING INNOVATION OF THE MAGIC-LANTERN SLIDE
IN CONJUNCTION WITH THE SERPENTINE DANCE
ENGRAVED BY JOHN HELD JR WHO IS GAME TO THE CORE

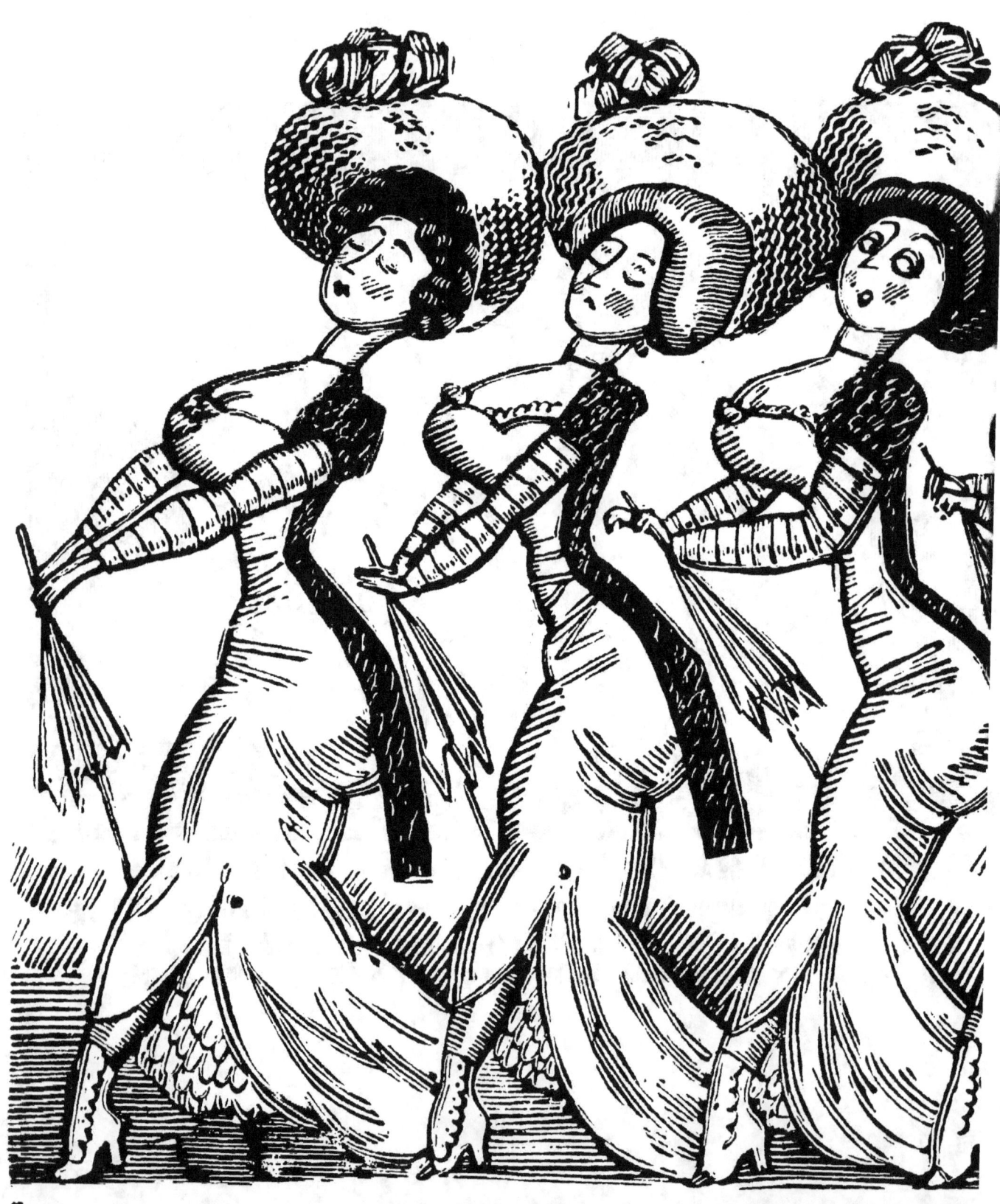

"TELL ME PRETTY MAIDEN ARE THERE ANY MORE AT HOME LIKE Y

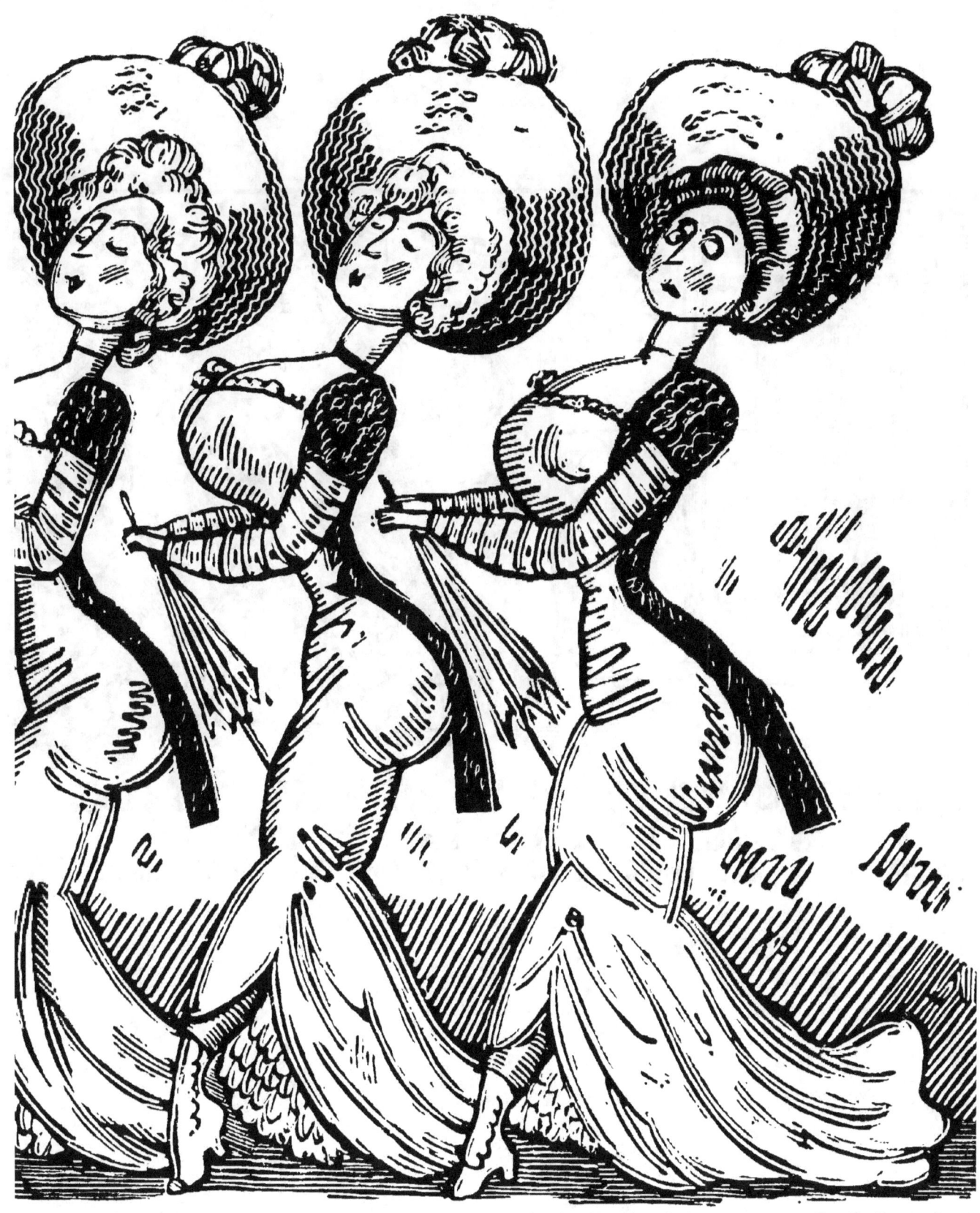

Eng by JOHN HELD JR   OH DEARY ME, HOW TIME DOES FLY

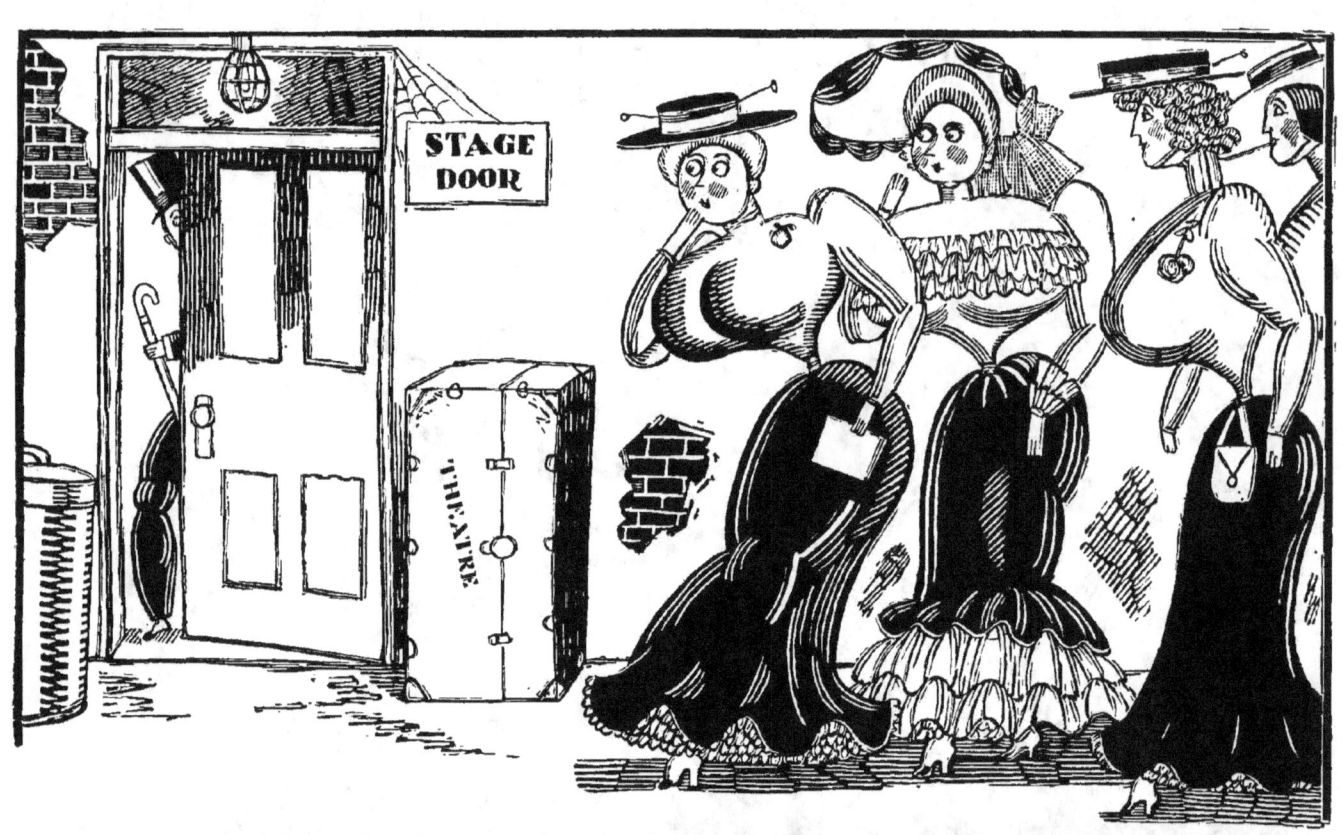

WHEN THE THEATRE WAS FRAUGHT WITH ROMANCE
WAITING FOR YOUNG "JACK" BARRYMORE
ENGRAVED BY JOHN HELD JR THE WELL KNOWN OUT-OF-TOWN MAN ABOUT TOWN

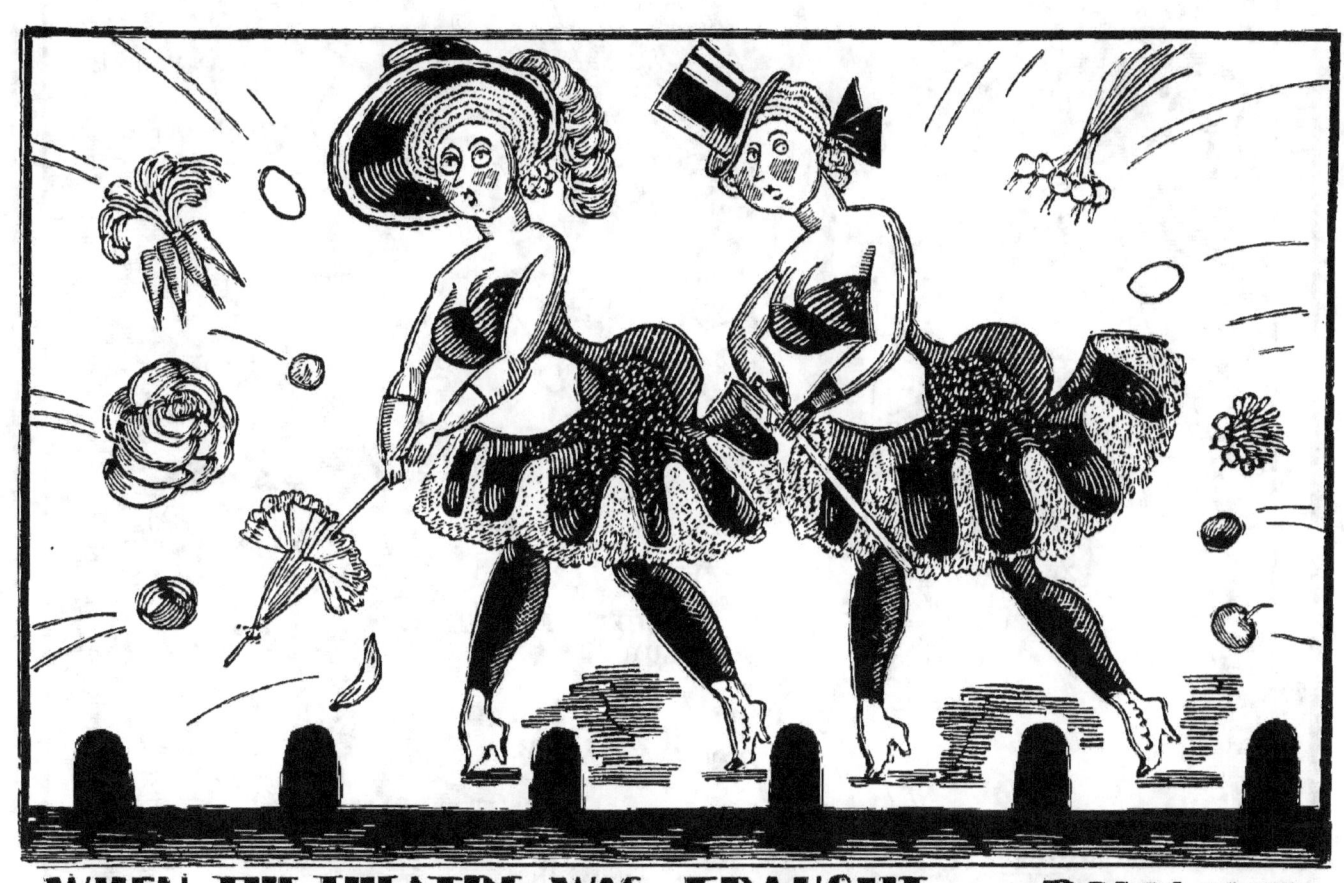

WHEN THE THEATRE WAS FRAUGHT with ROMANCE
THE CHERRY SISTERS
ENGRAVED BY **JOHN HELD JR** Who Is a SLY ELF

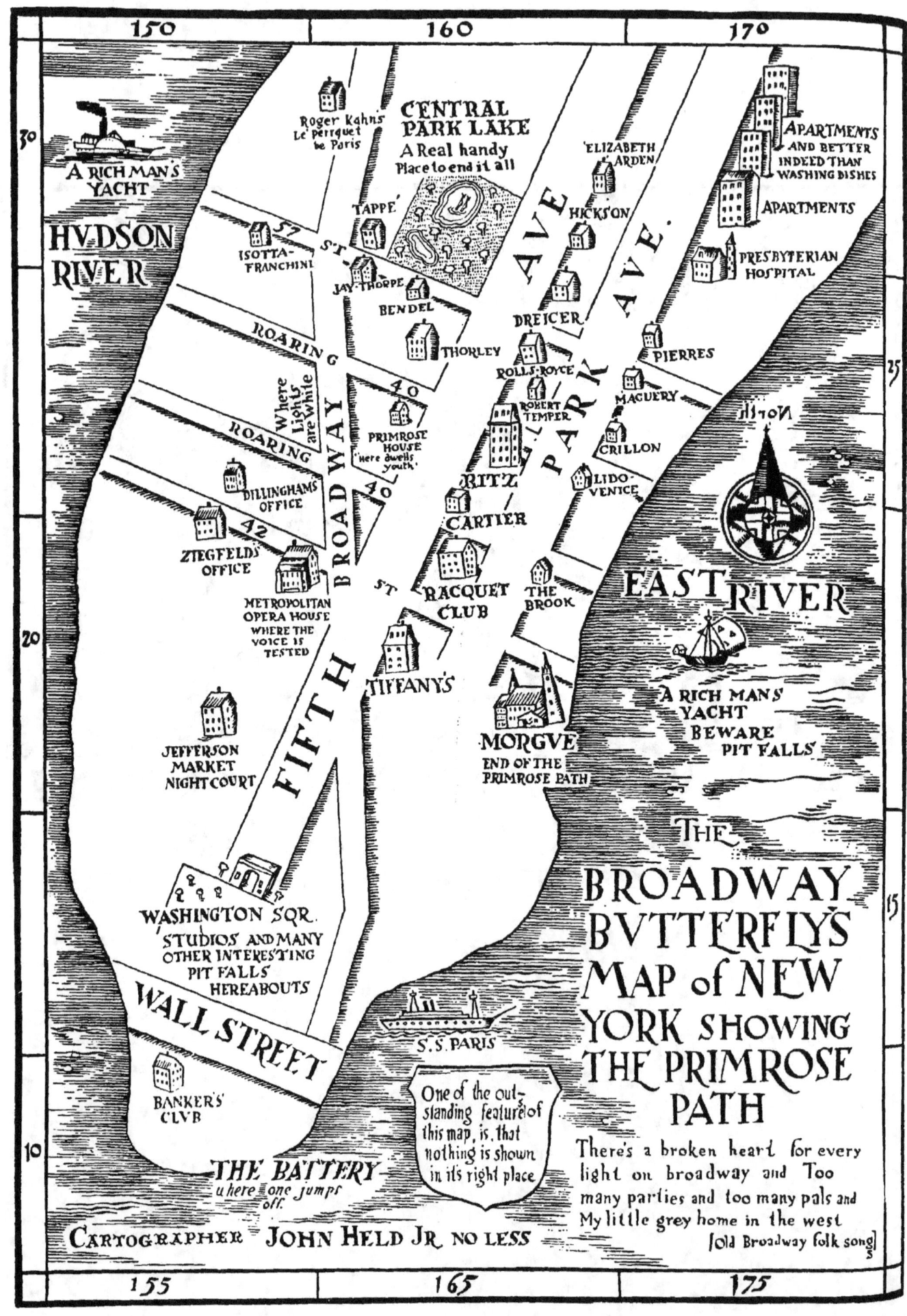

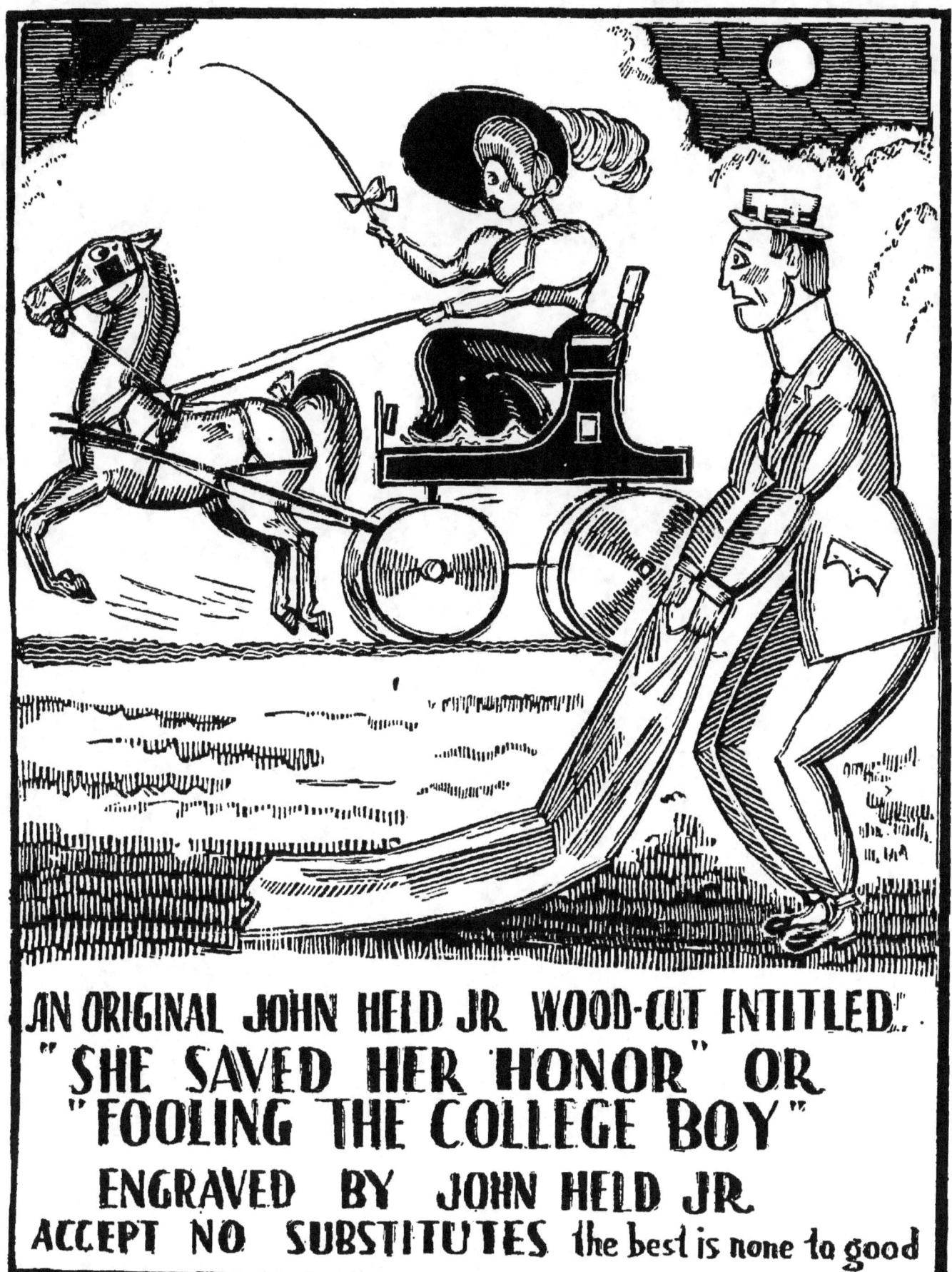

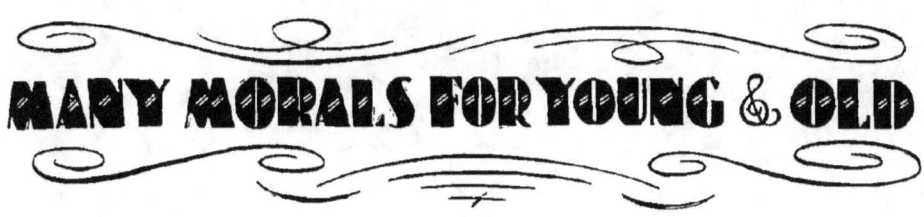

MANY MORALS FOR YOUNG & OLD

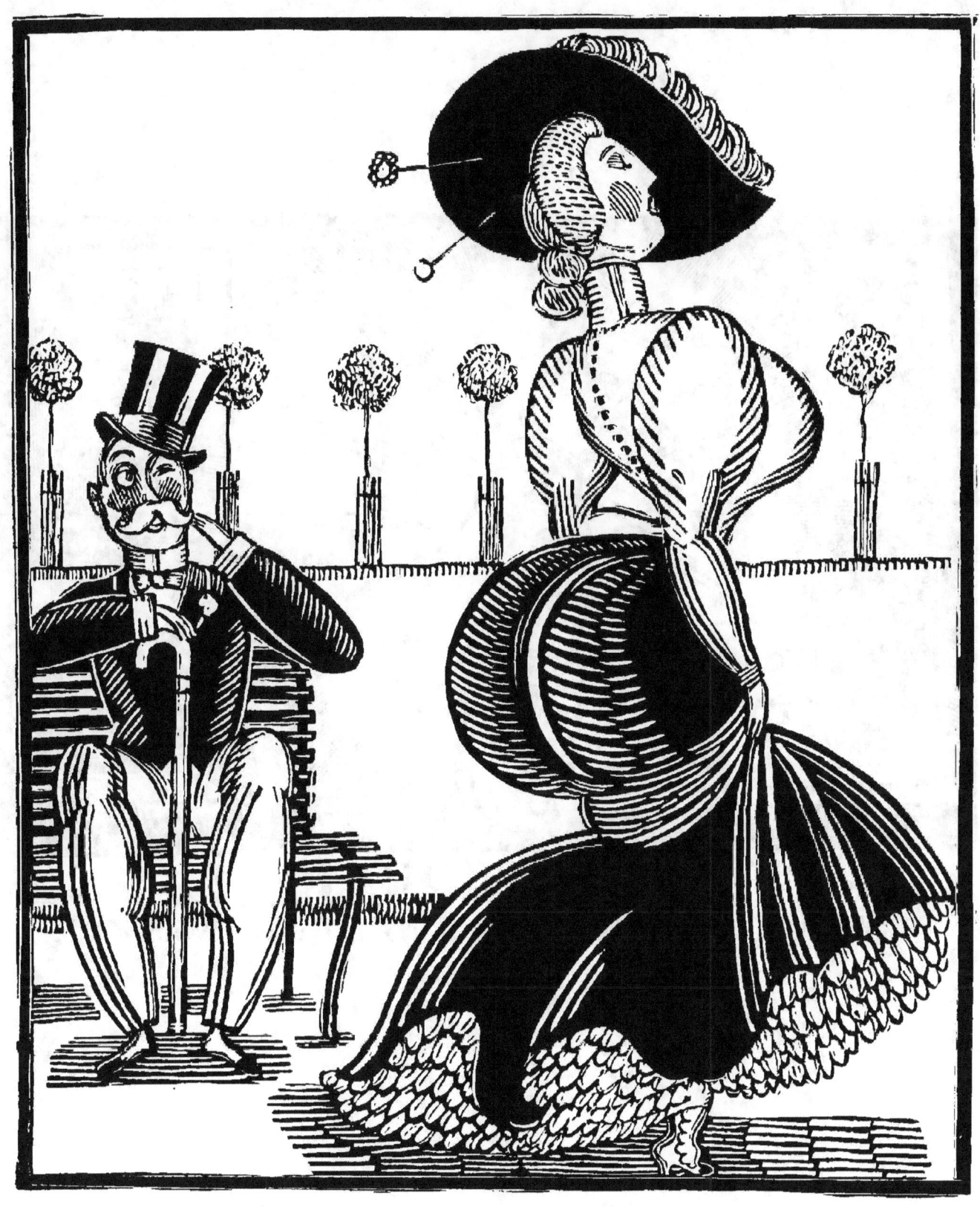

WHAT CHEEK!

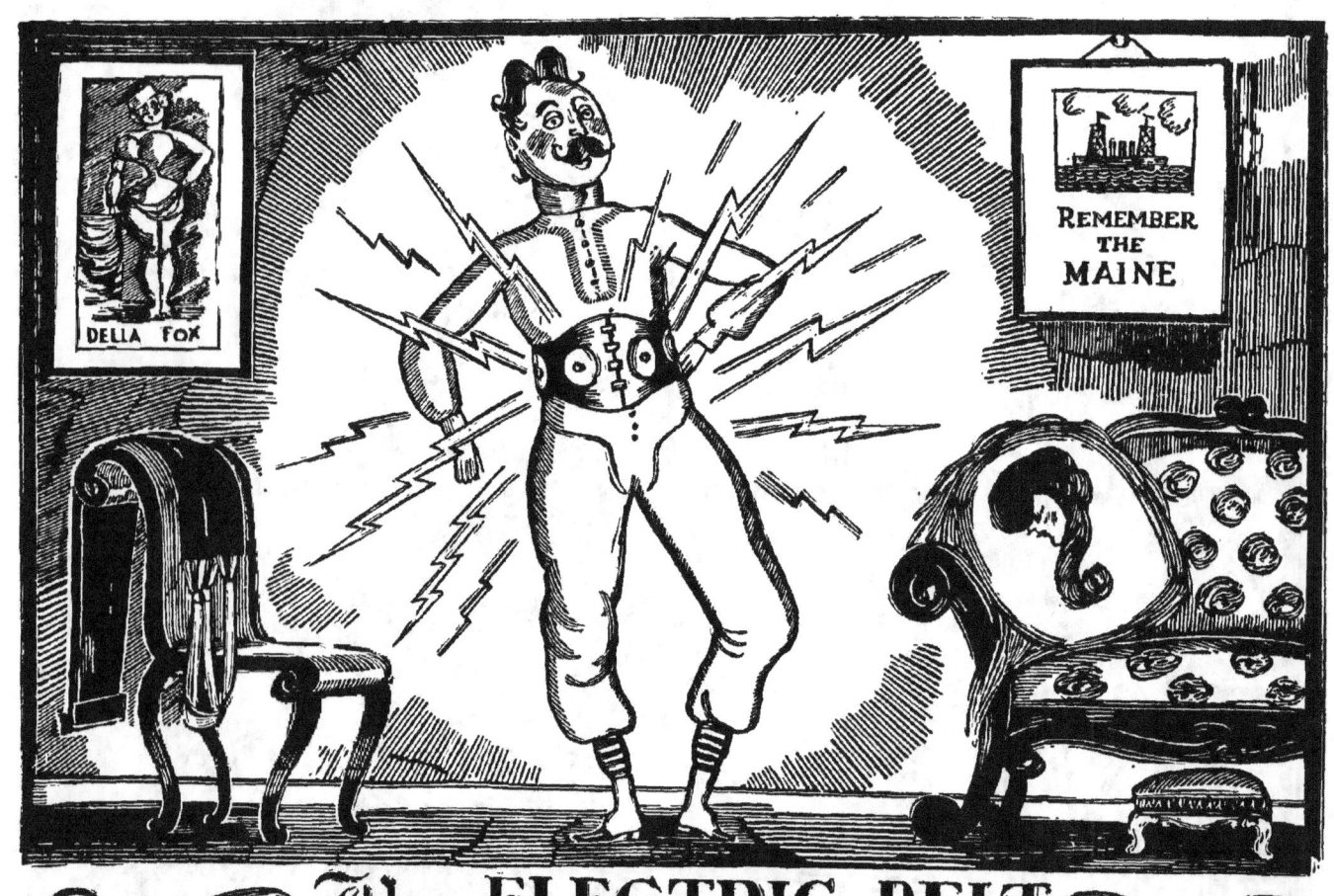

The ELECTRIC BELT

JOHN HELD JR REFLECTS the ROMANTIC PAST in WOOD-CUT. .

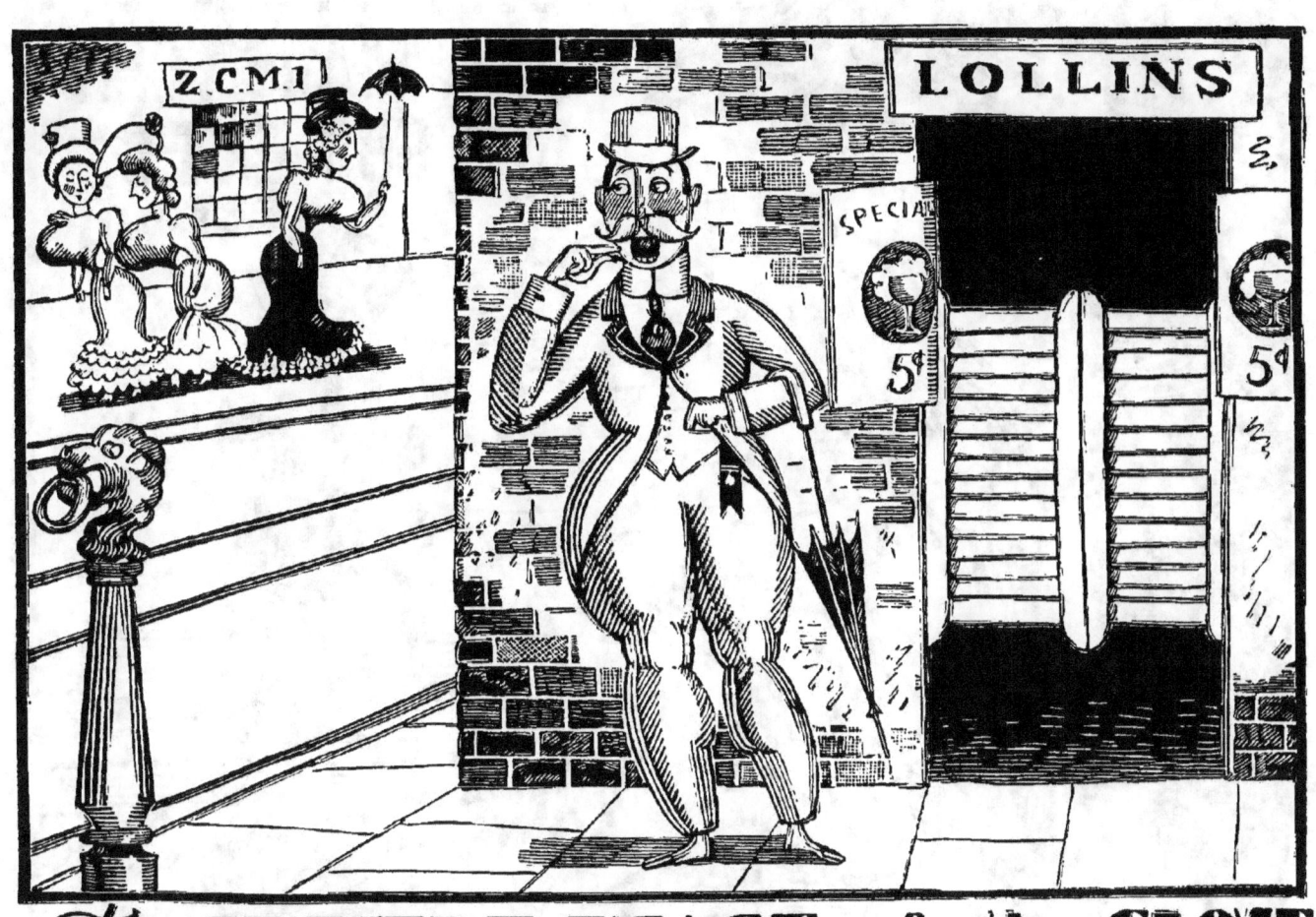

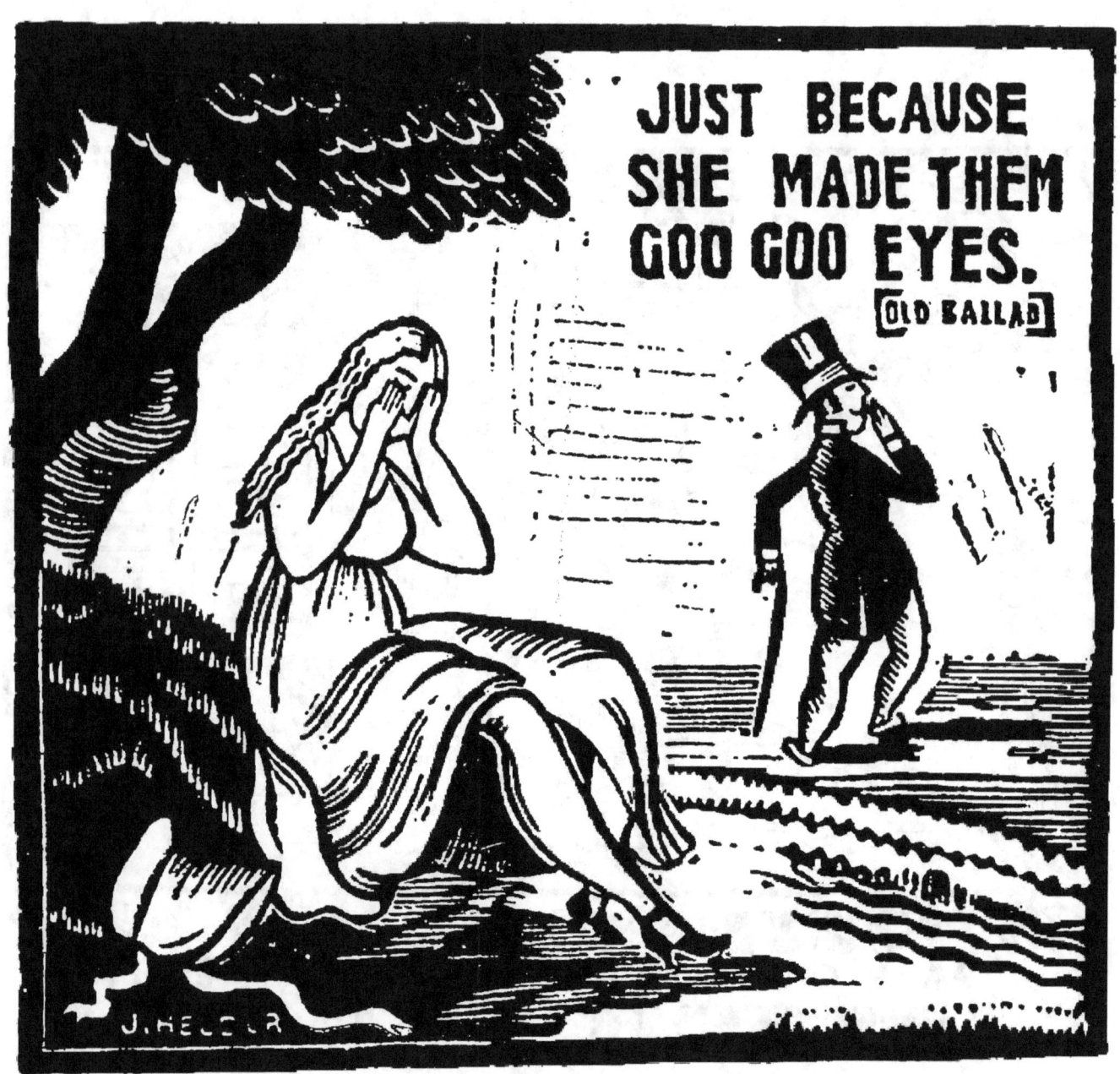

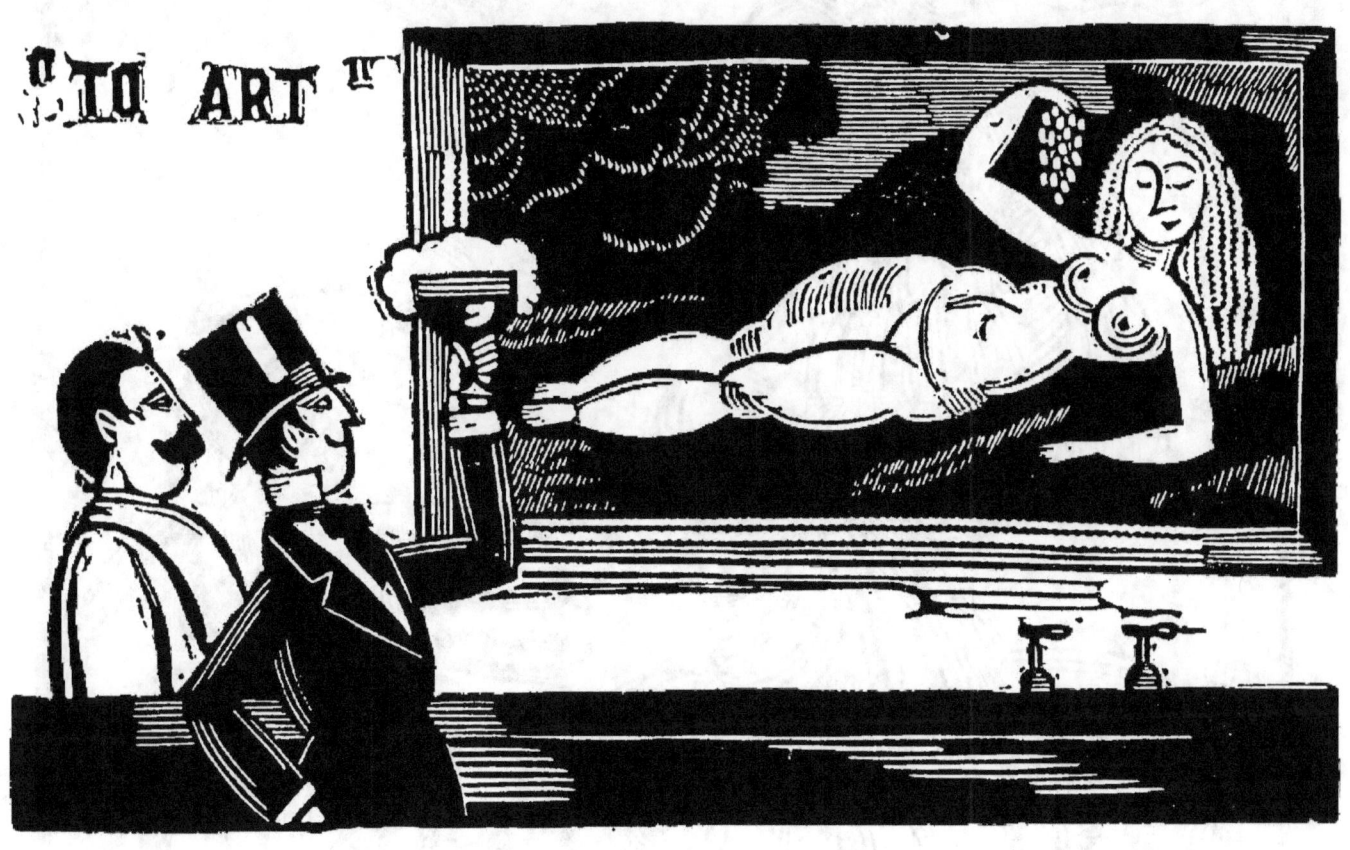

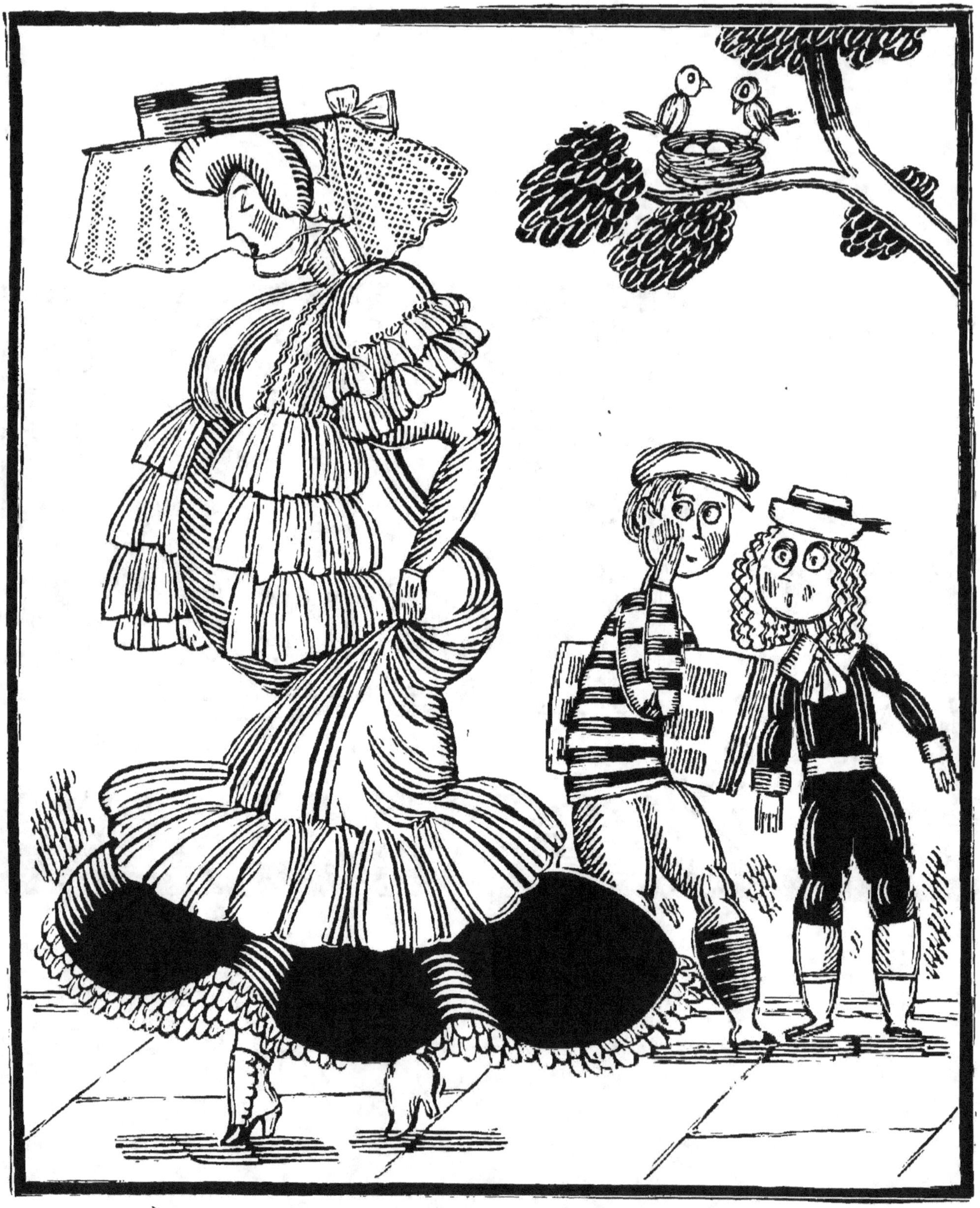

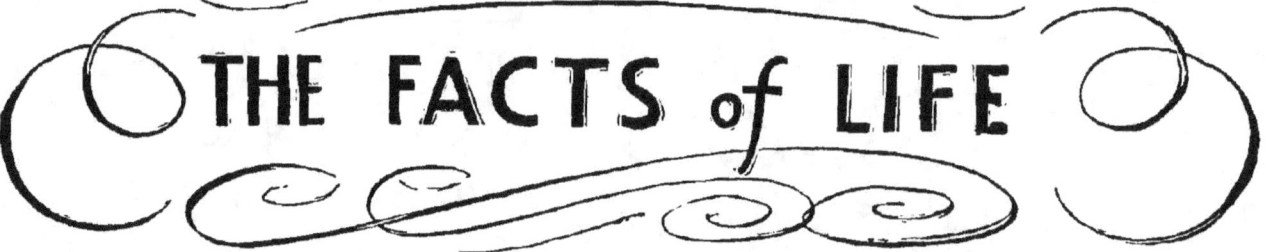

THE FACTS of LIFE

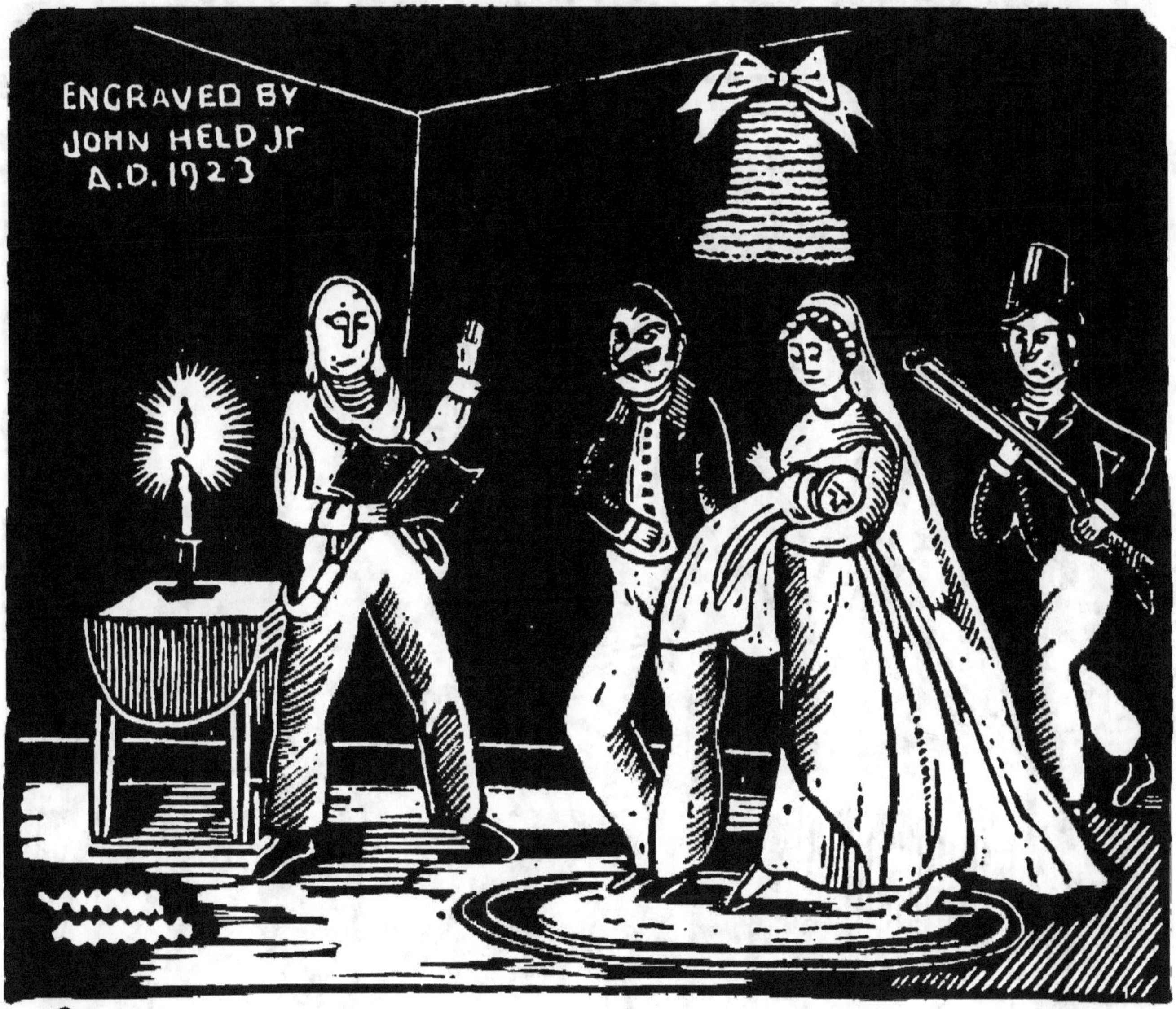

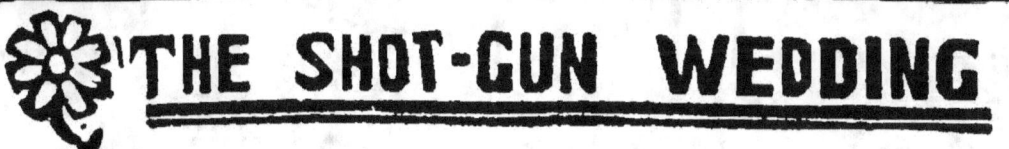

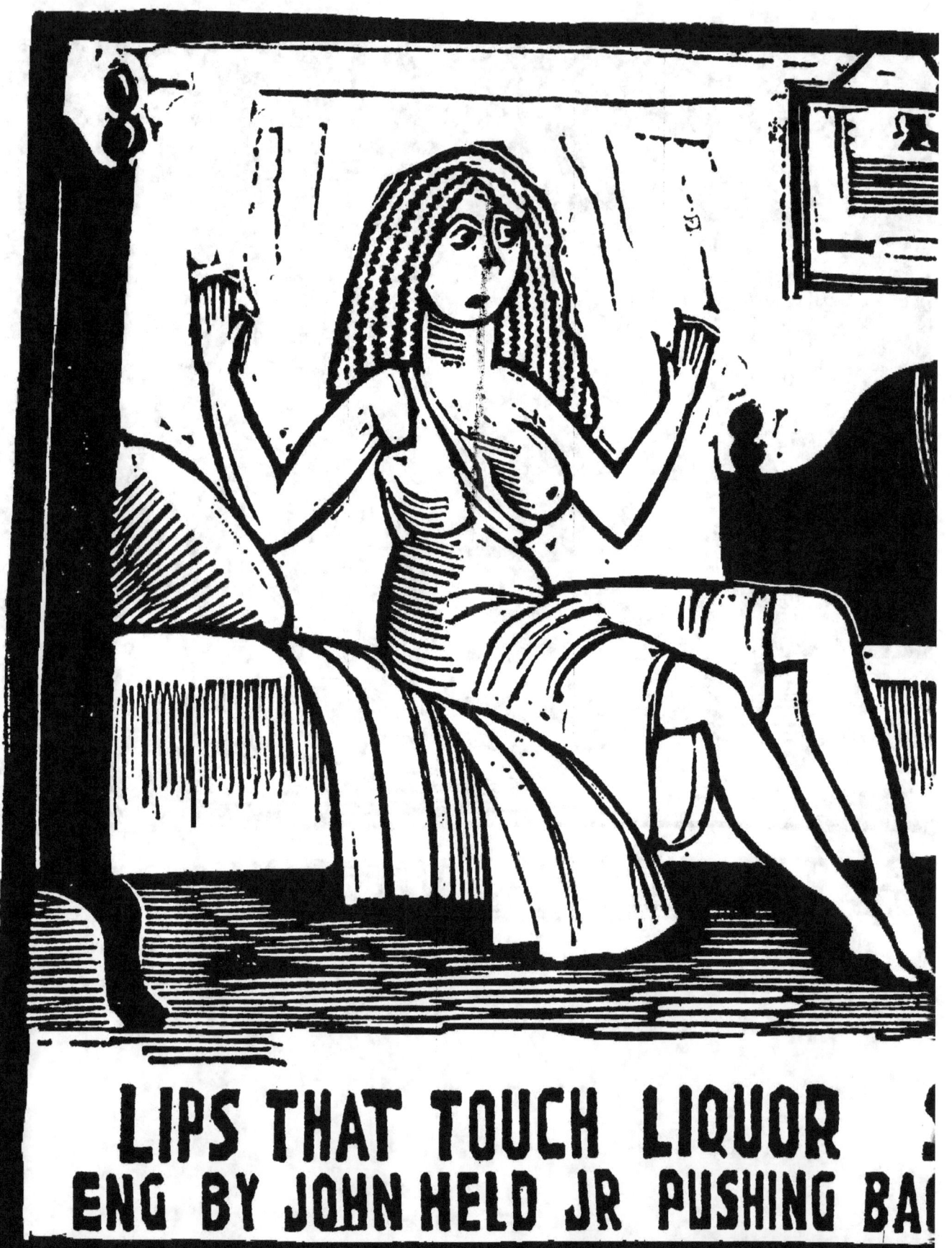

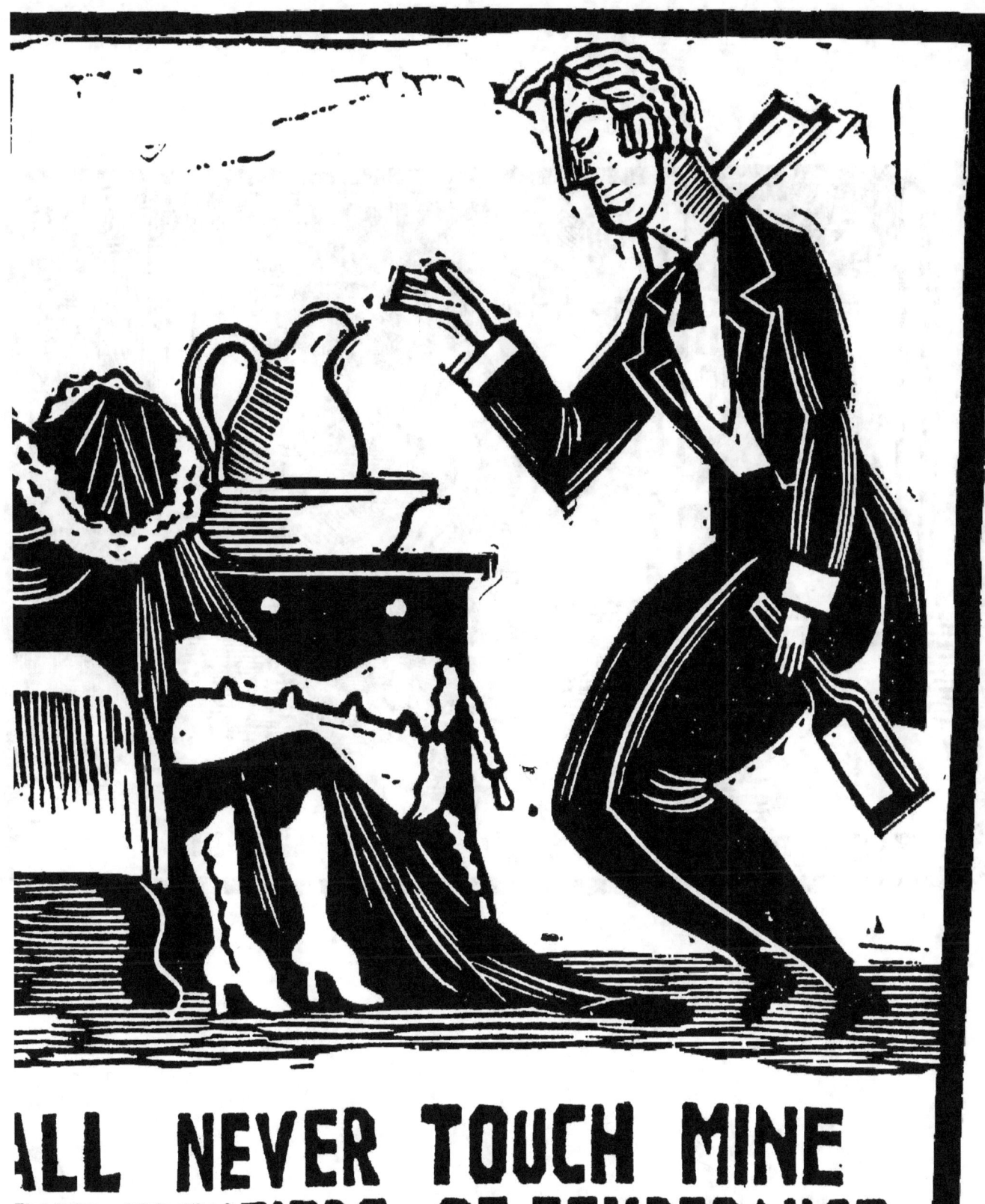

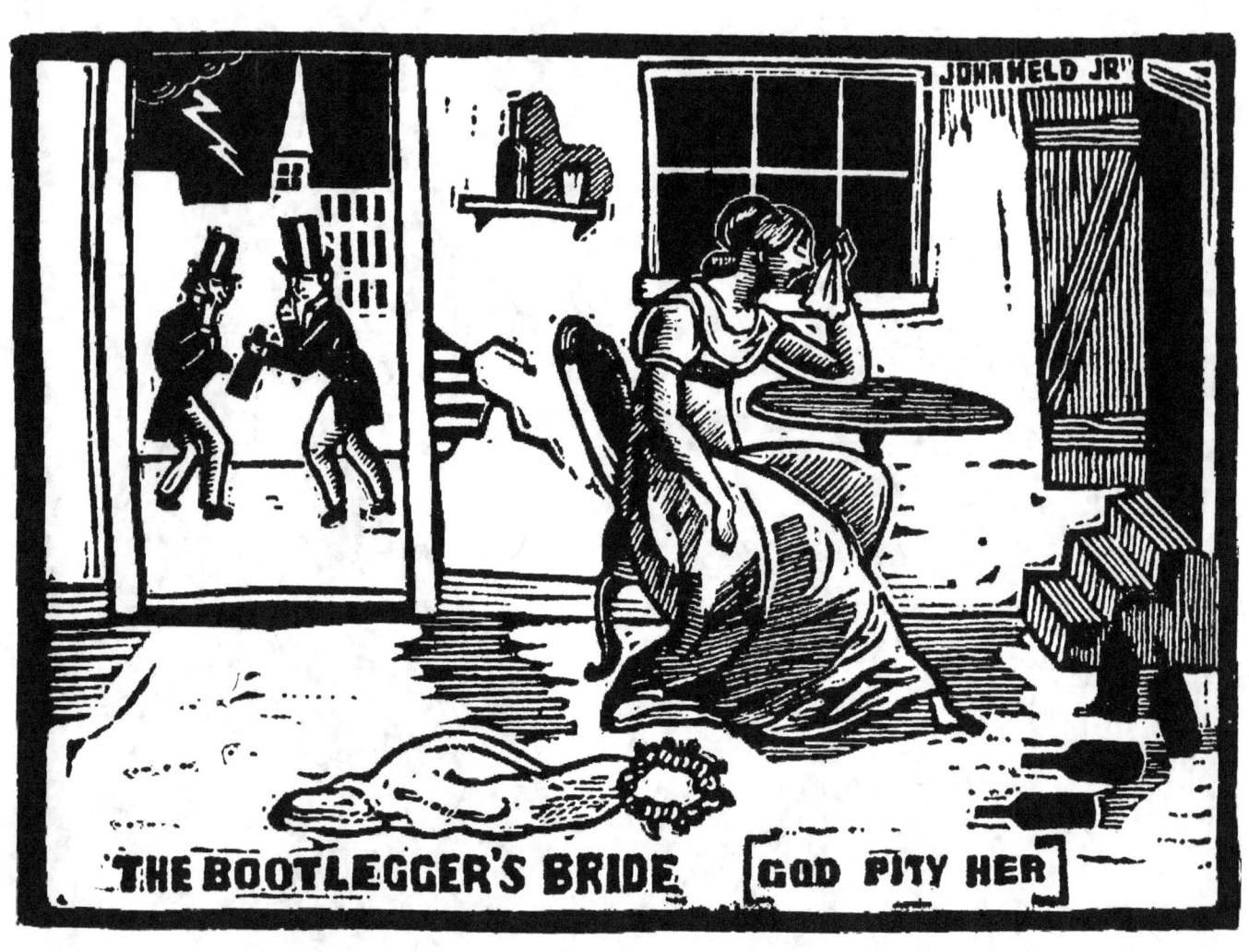

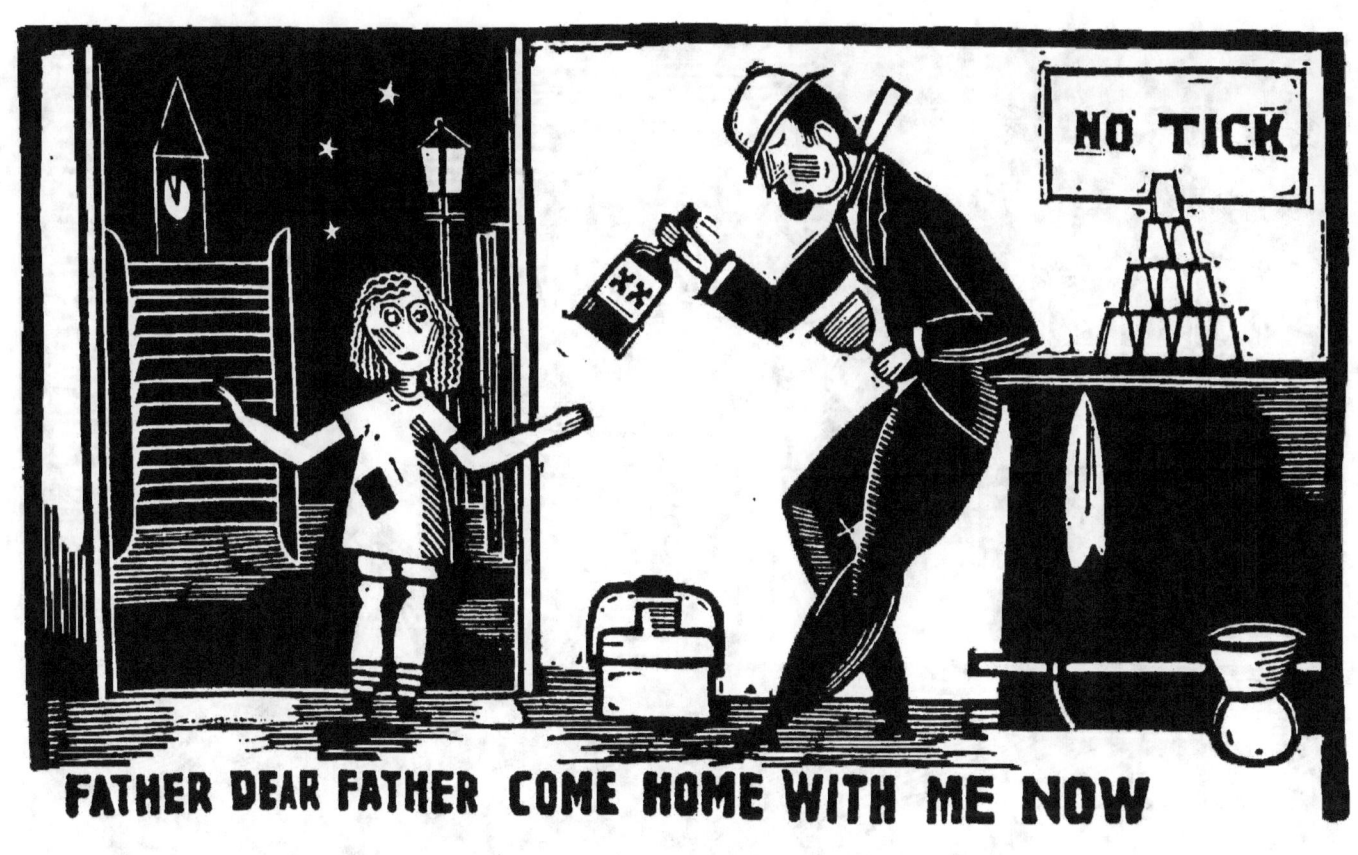

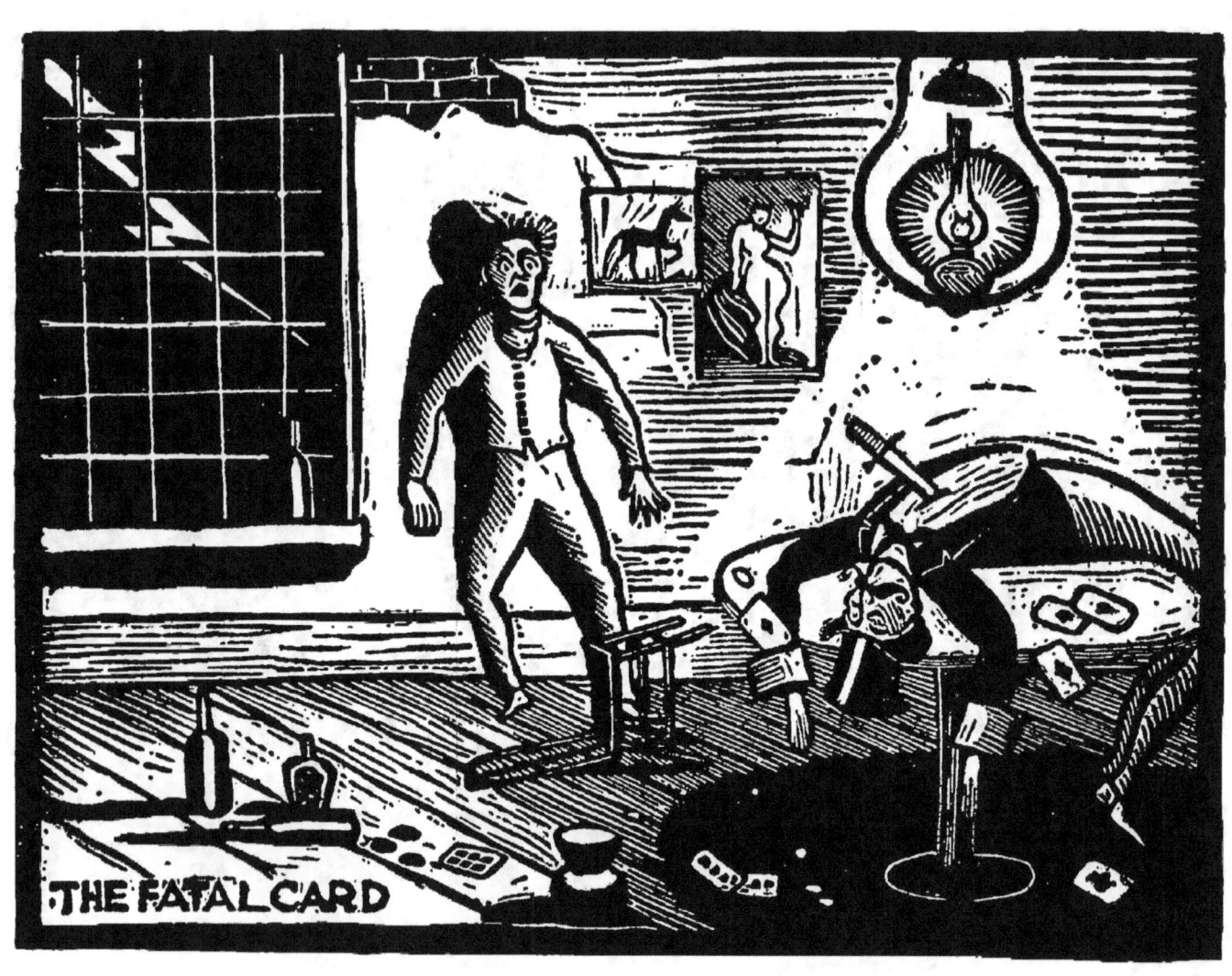

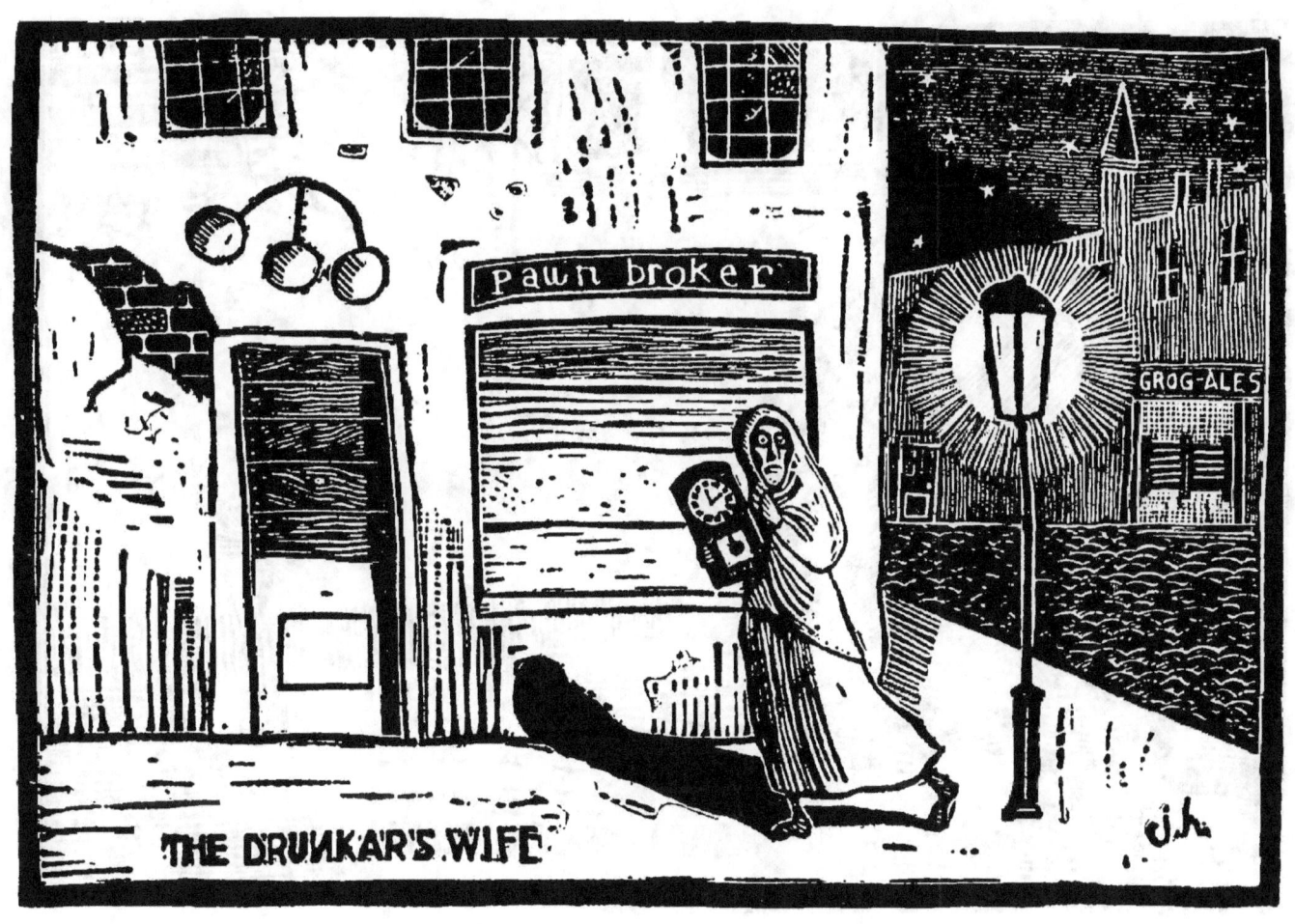

121

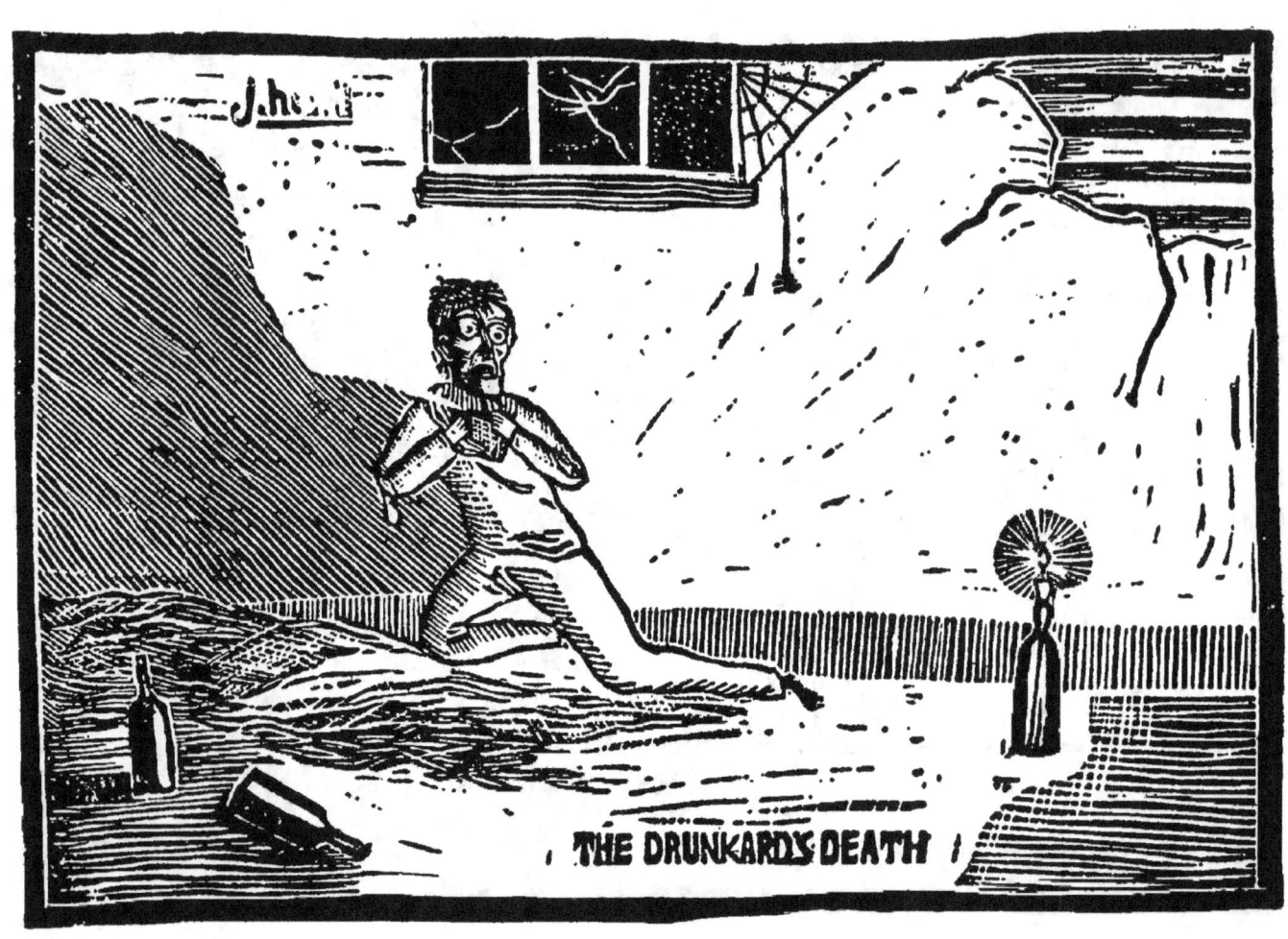

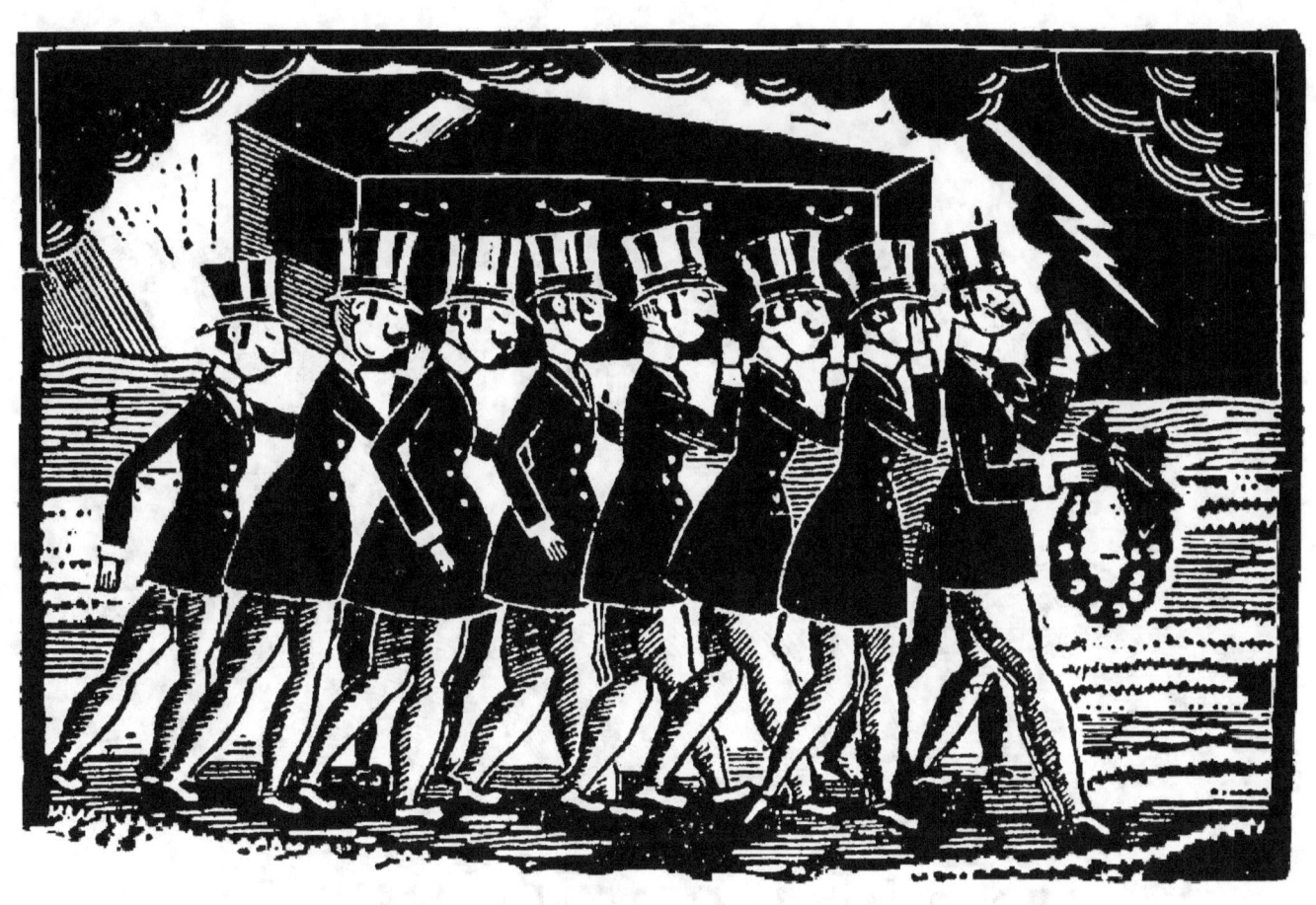

"LET 16 GAMBLERS COME CARRY MY COFFIN"

OLD REFRAIN   ENGRAVED   BY   JOHN HELD JR

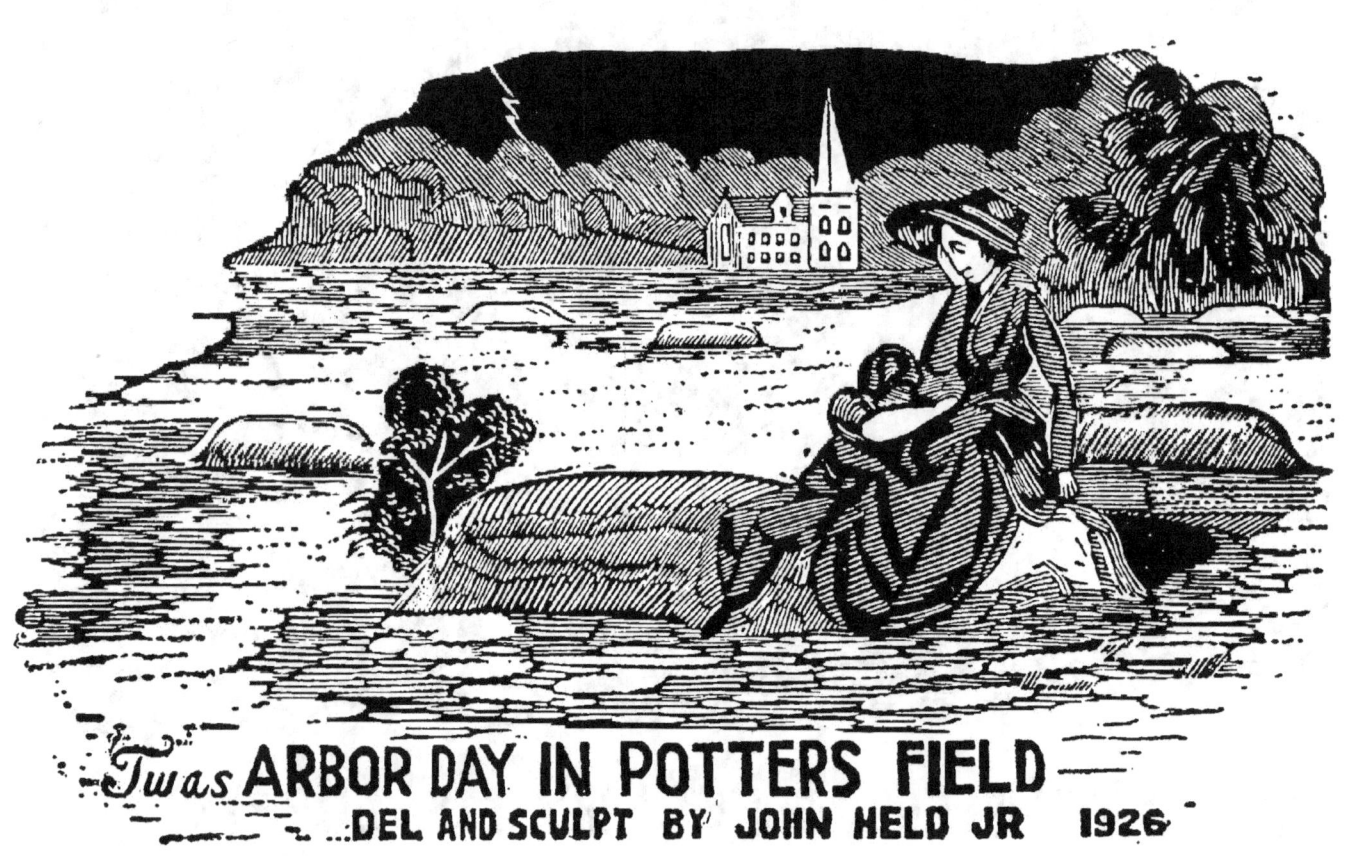

Twas ARBOR DAY IN POTTERS FIELD
...DEL AND SCULPT BY JOHN HELD JR 1926

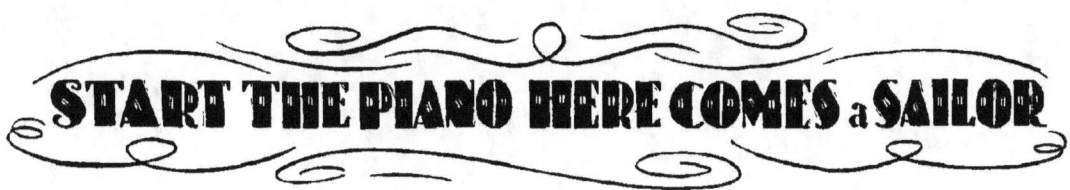

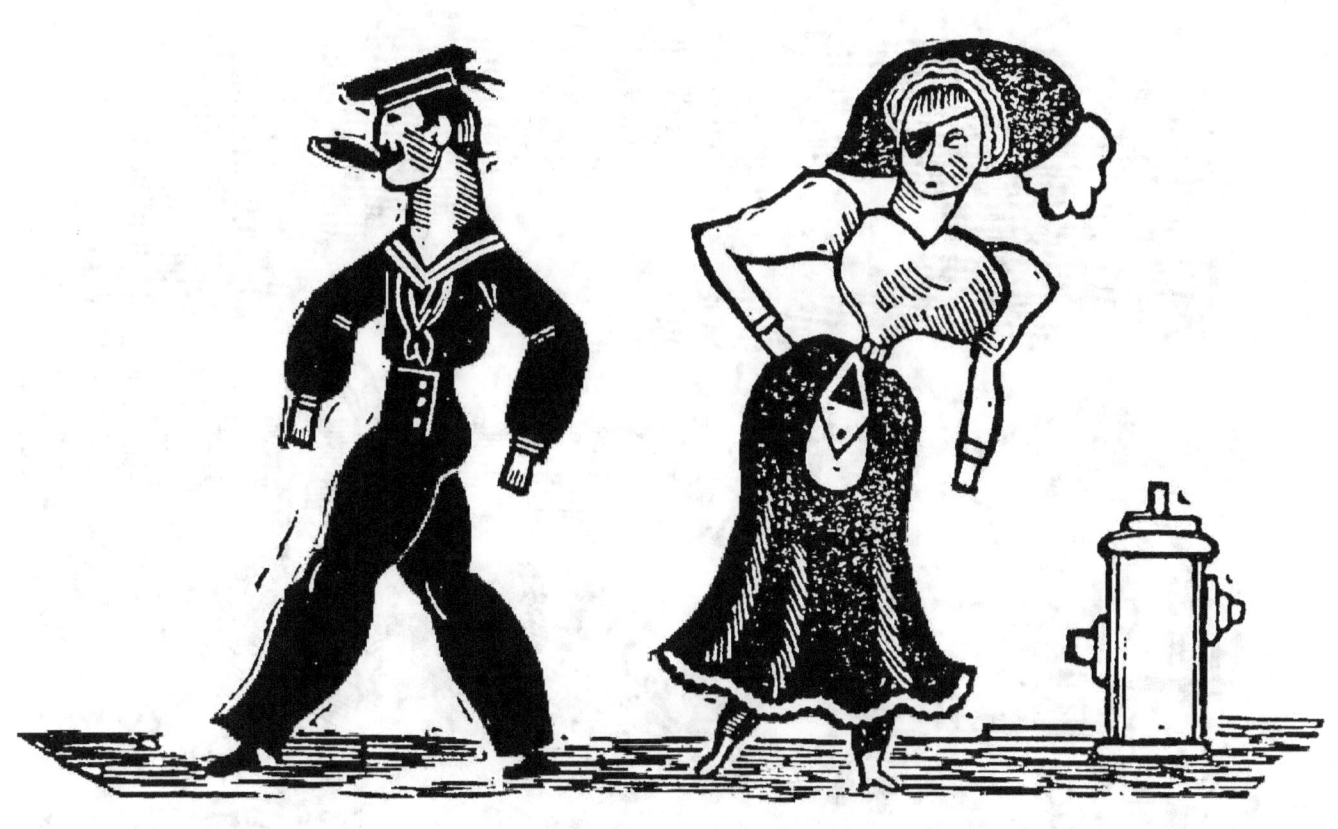

AN ENGRAVING BY JOHN HELD JR THAT BORDERS THE SUBLIME

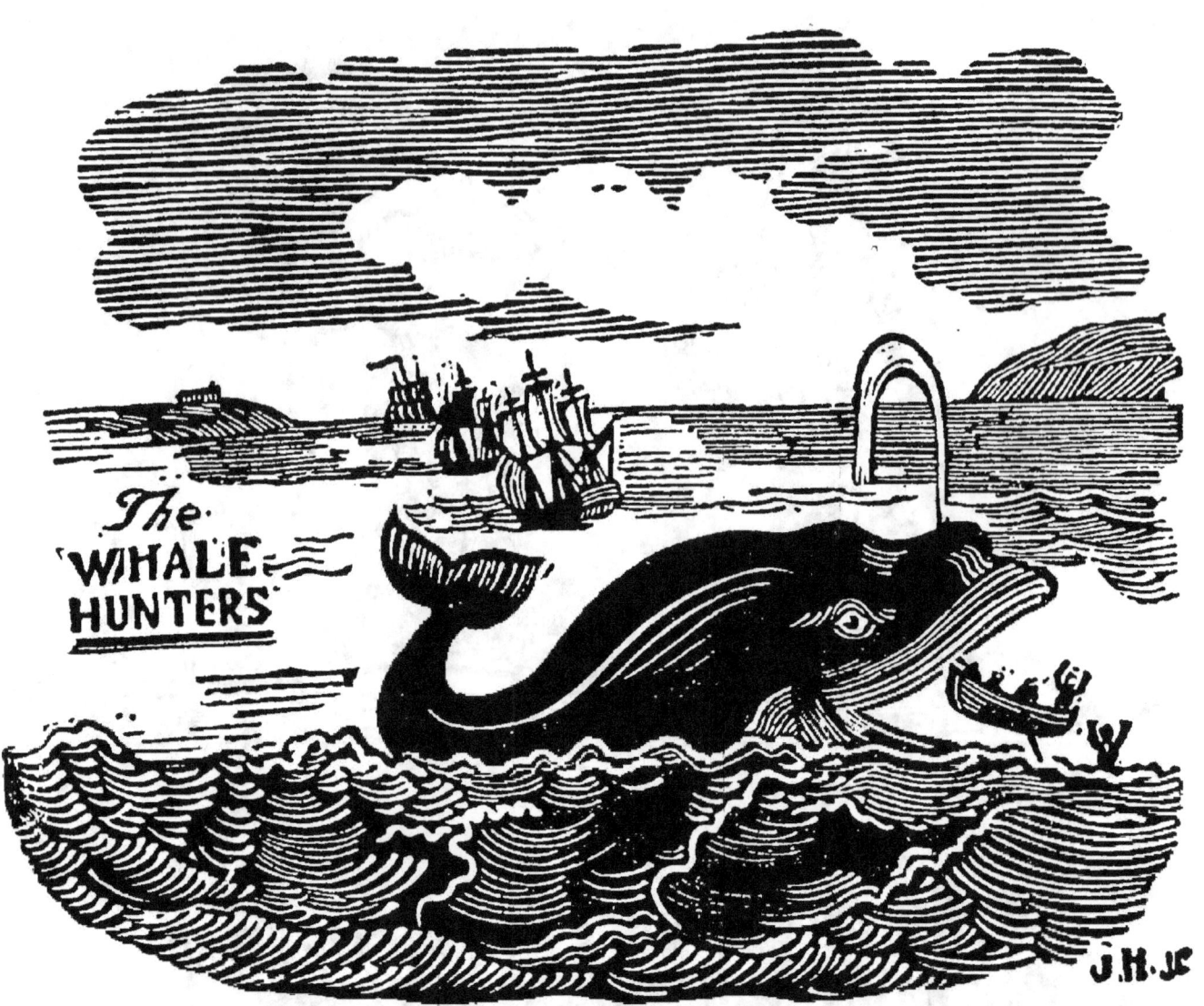

RISKING LIFE AND LIMB TO SECURE OIL FOR ACTORS HAIR
AN ENGRAVING WITH A MESSAGE BY JOHN HELD JR

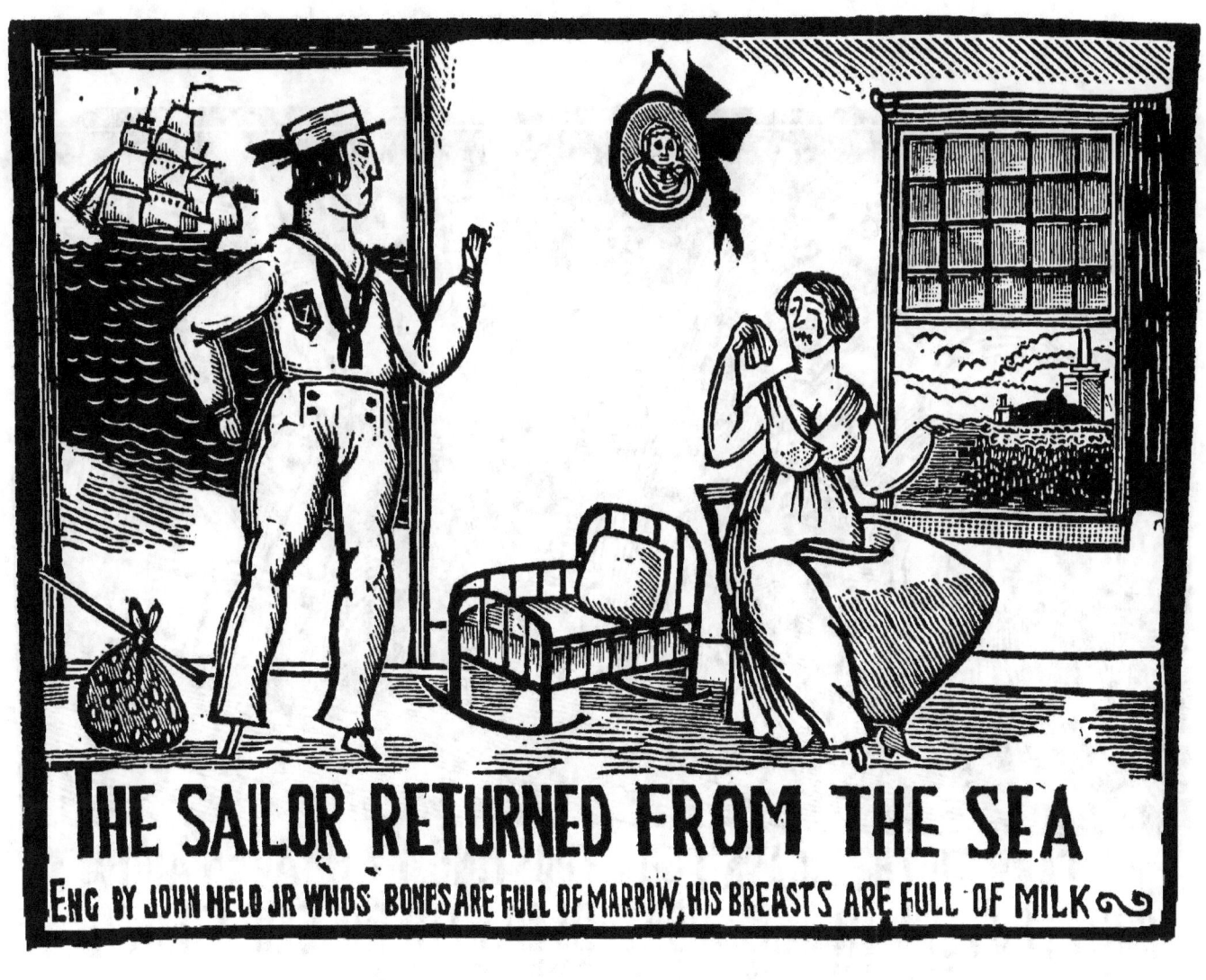

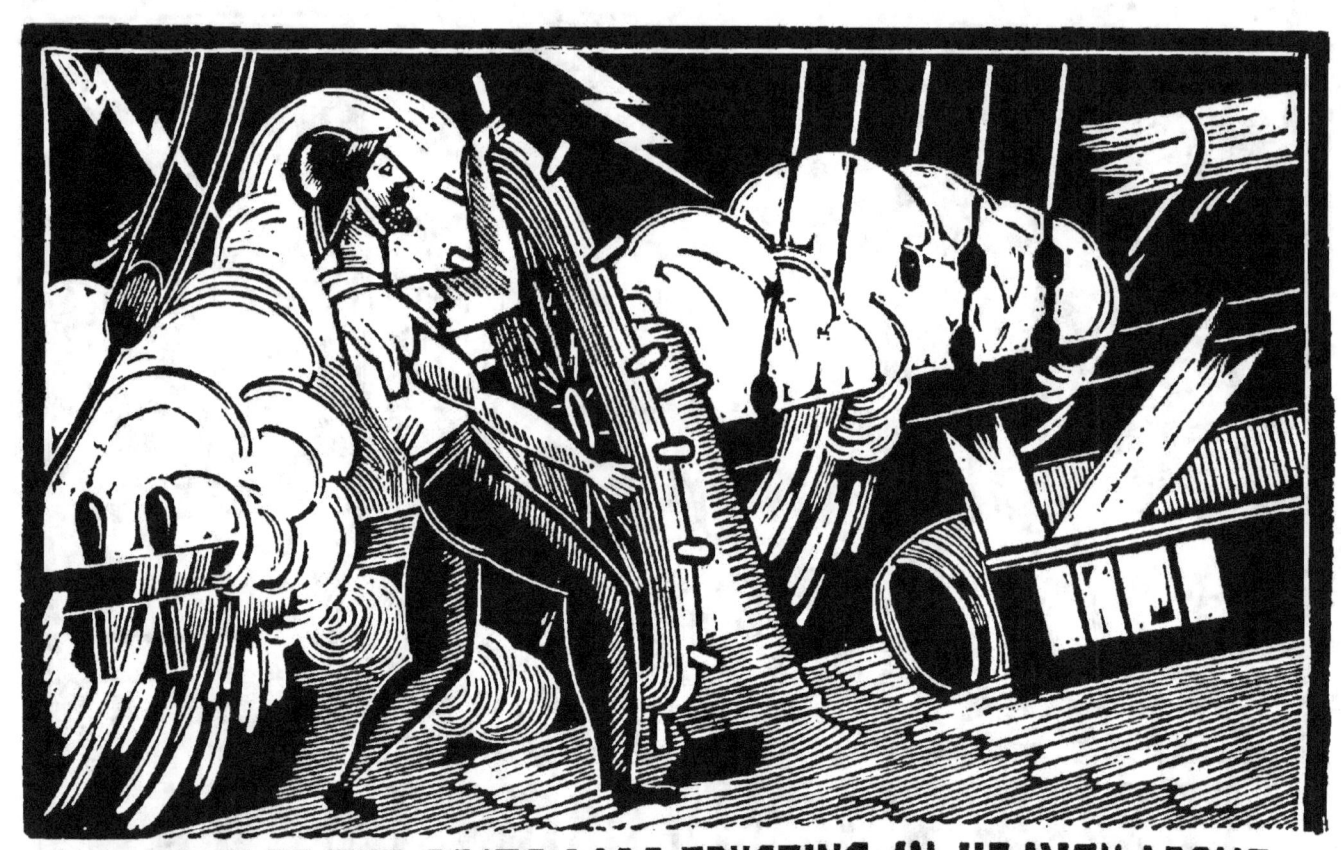

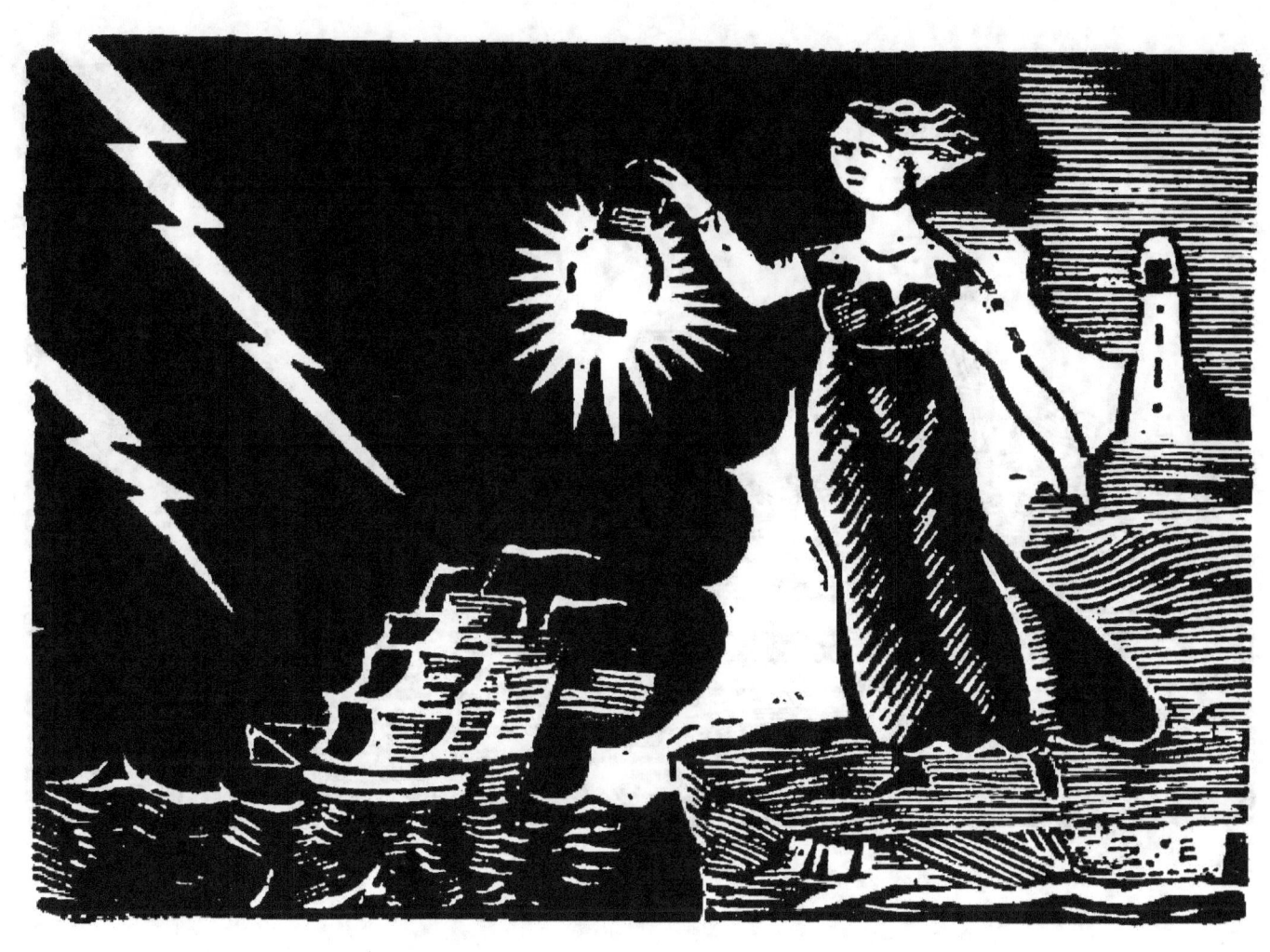

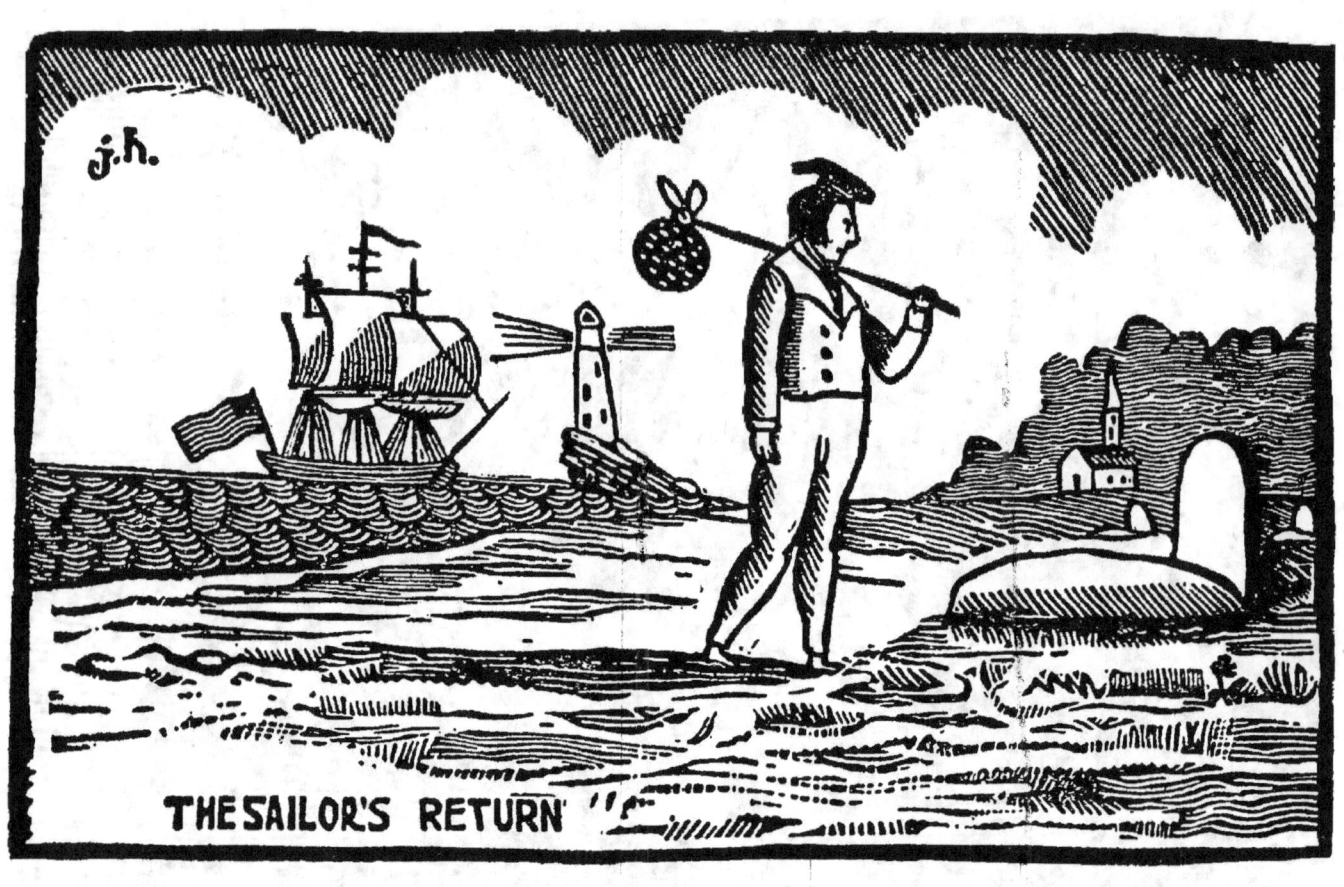

THE SAILOR'S RETURN

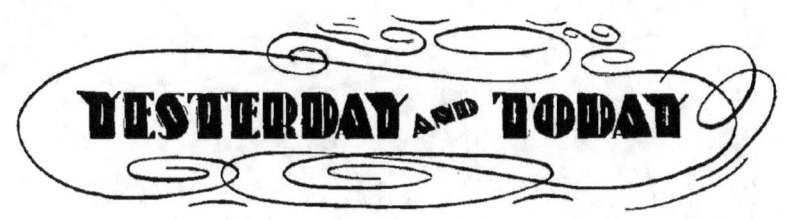

YESTERDAY AND TODAY

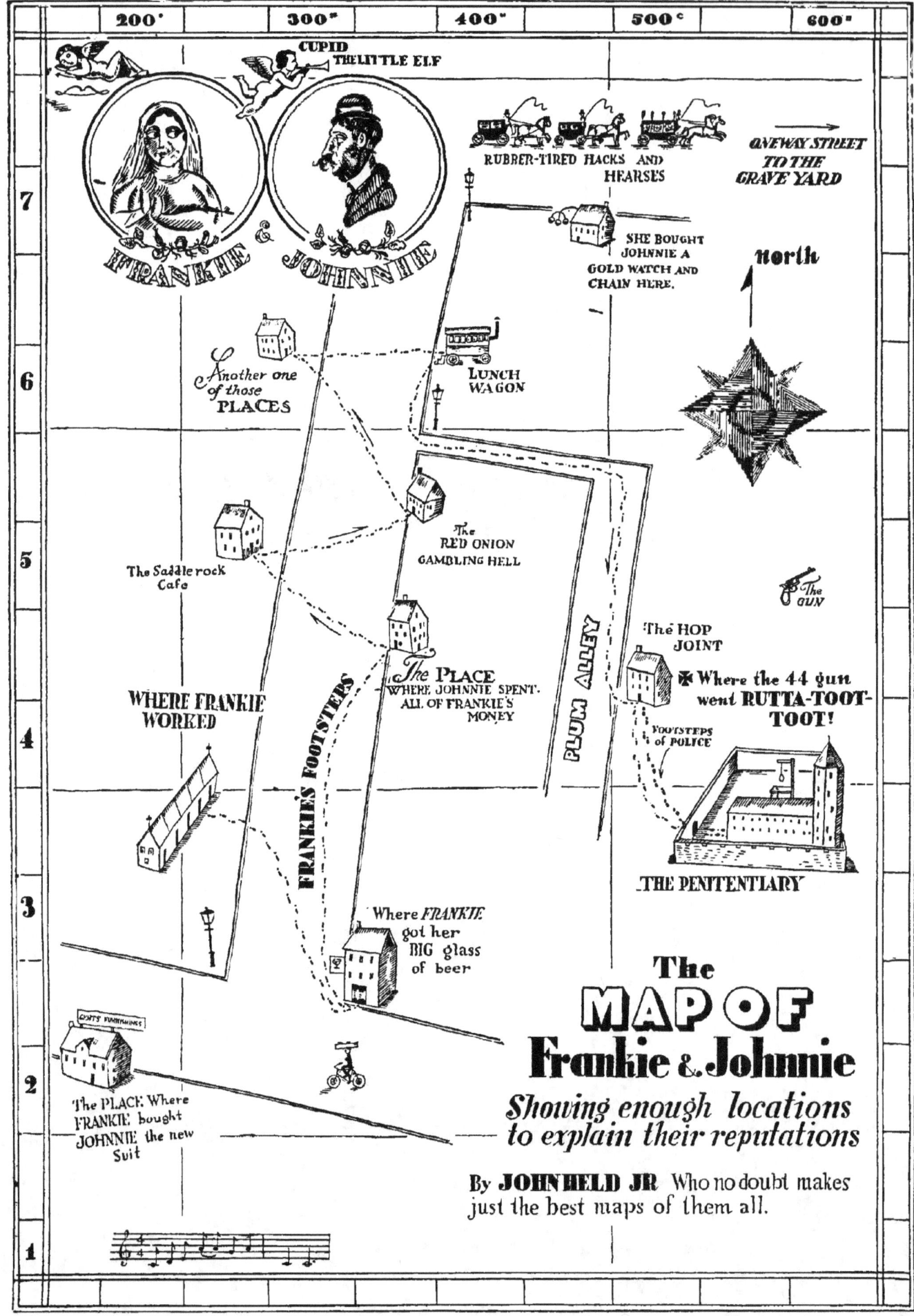

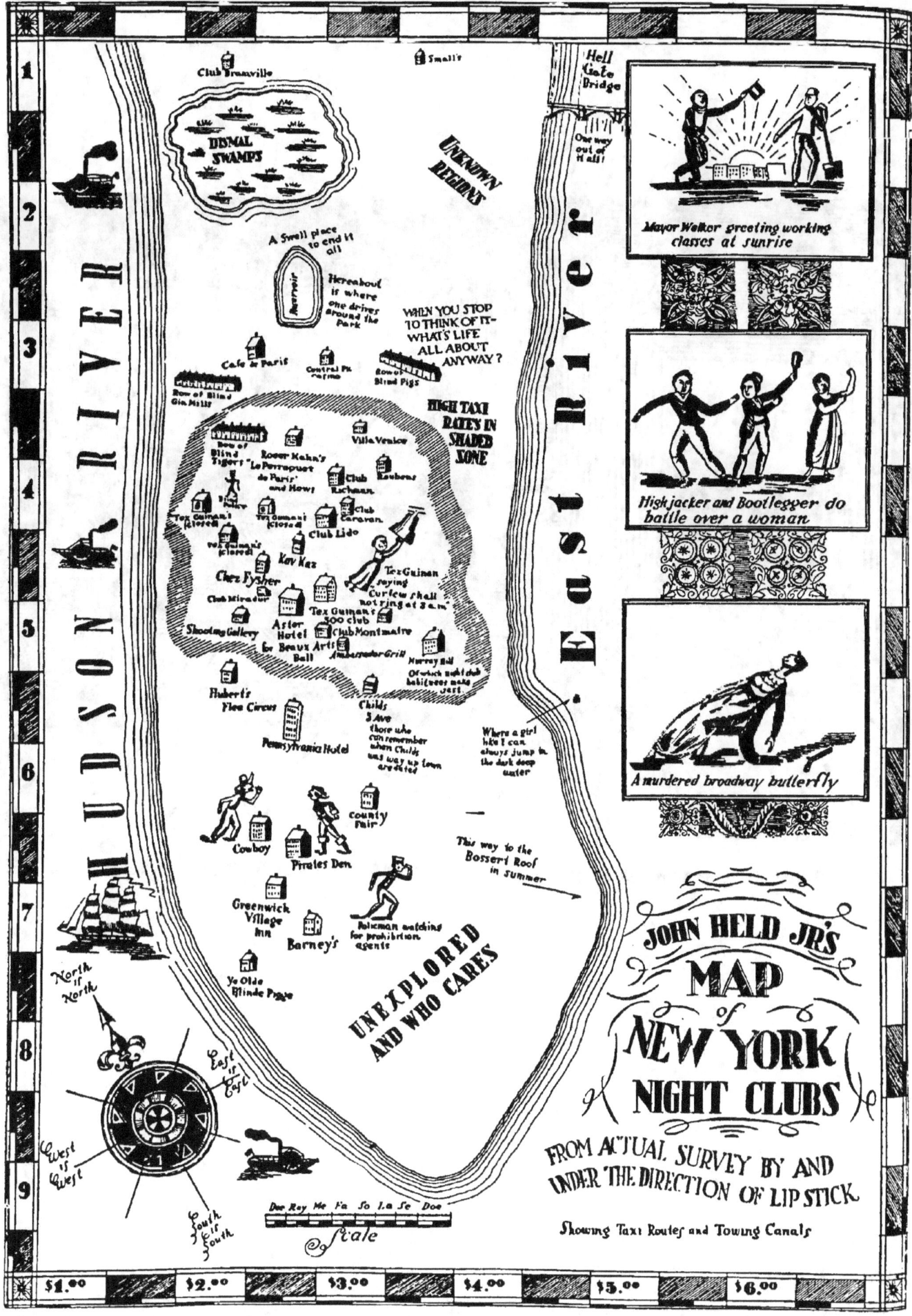

JOHN HELD JR'S
MAP
of
NEW YORK
NIGHT CLUBS

FROM ACTUAL SURVEY BY AND
UNDER THE DIRECTION OF LIP STICK

Showing Taxi Routes and Towing Canals

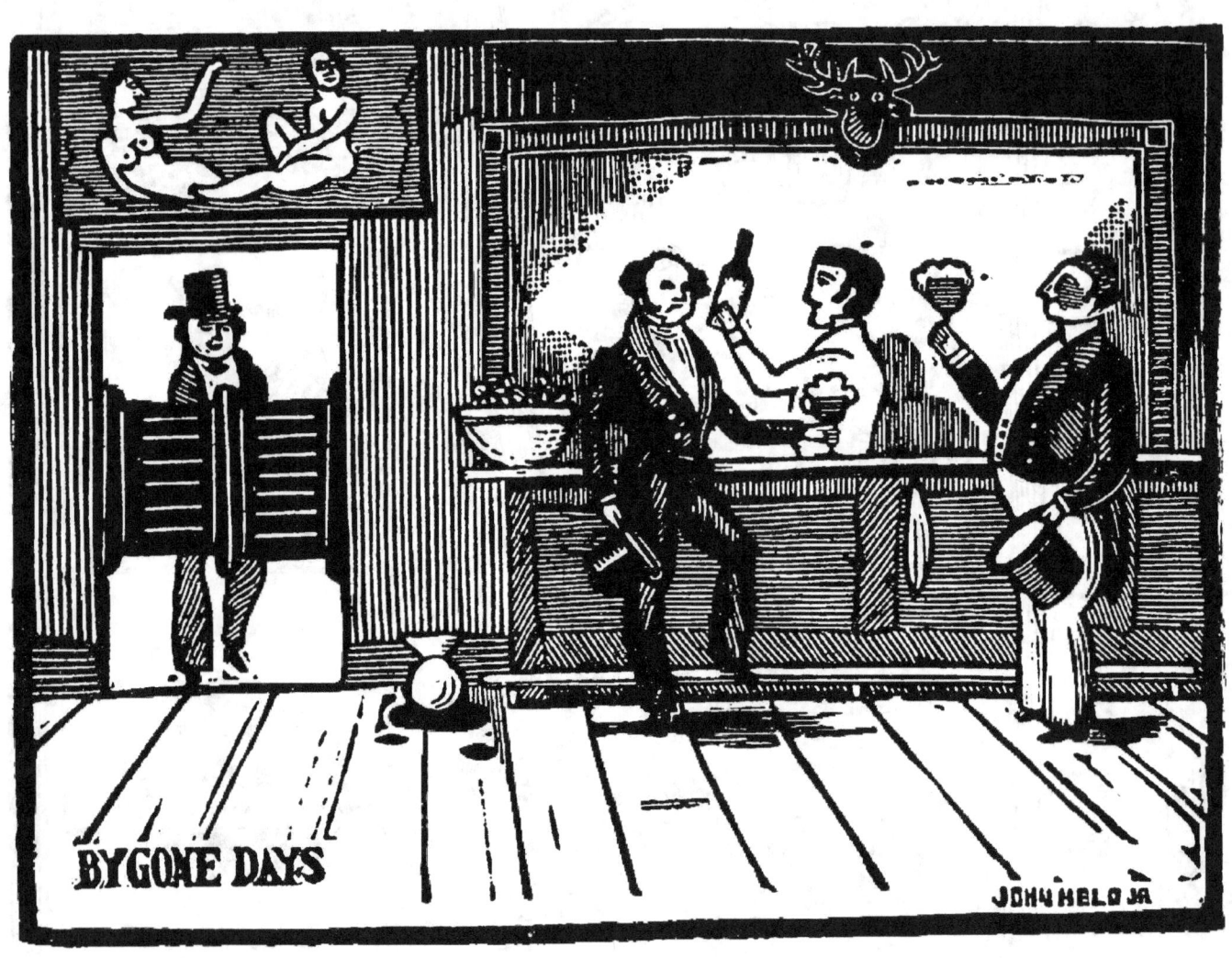

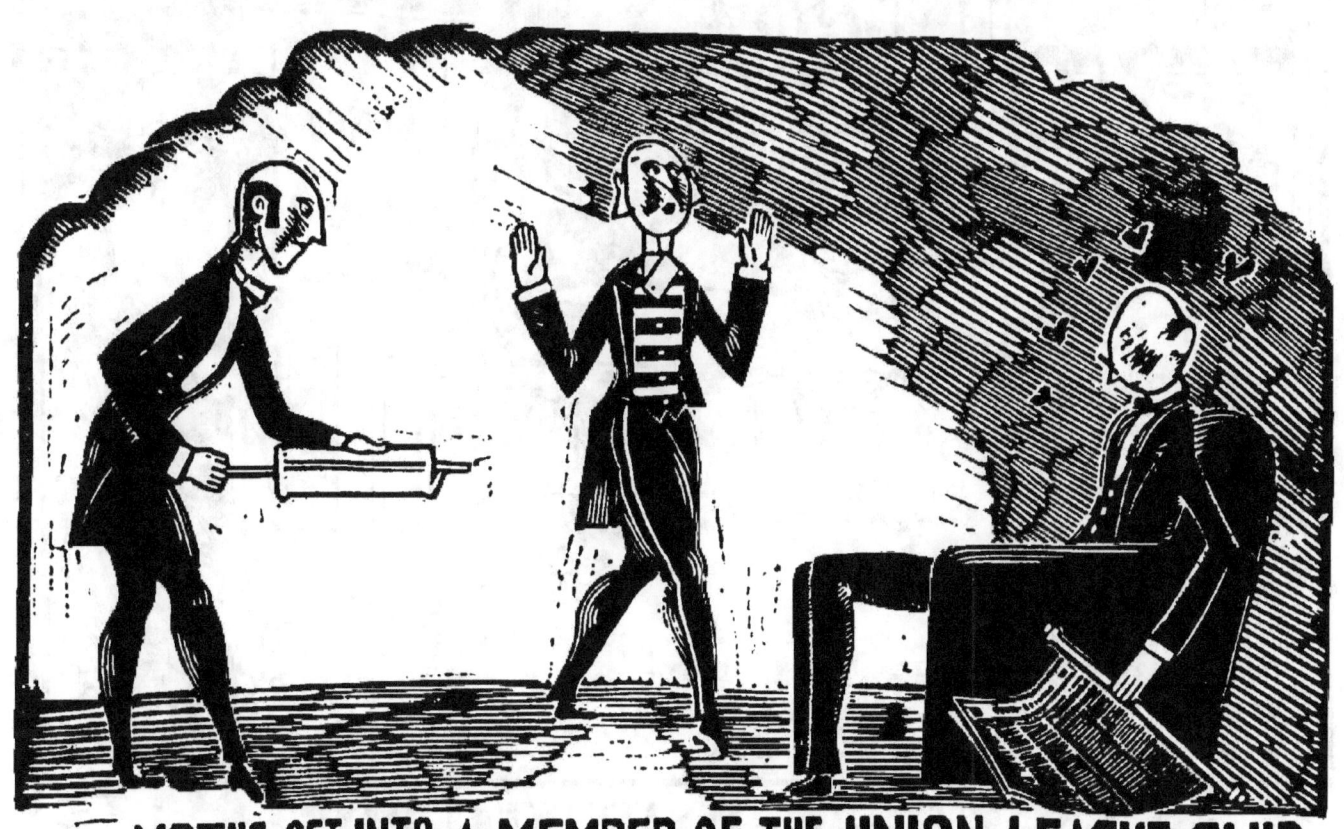

MOTHS GET INTO A MEMBER OF THE UNION LEAGUE CLUB
ENGRAVED BY NONE OTHER THAN JOHN HELD JR.

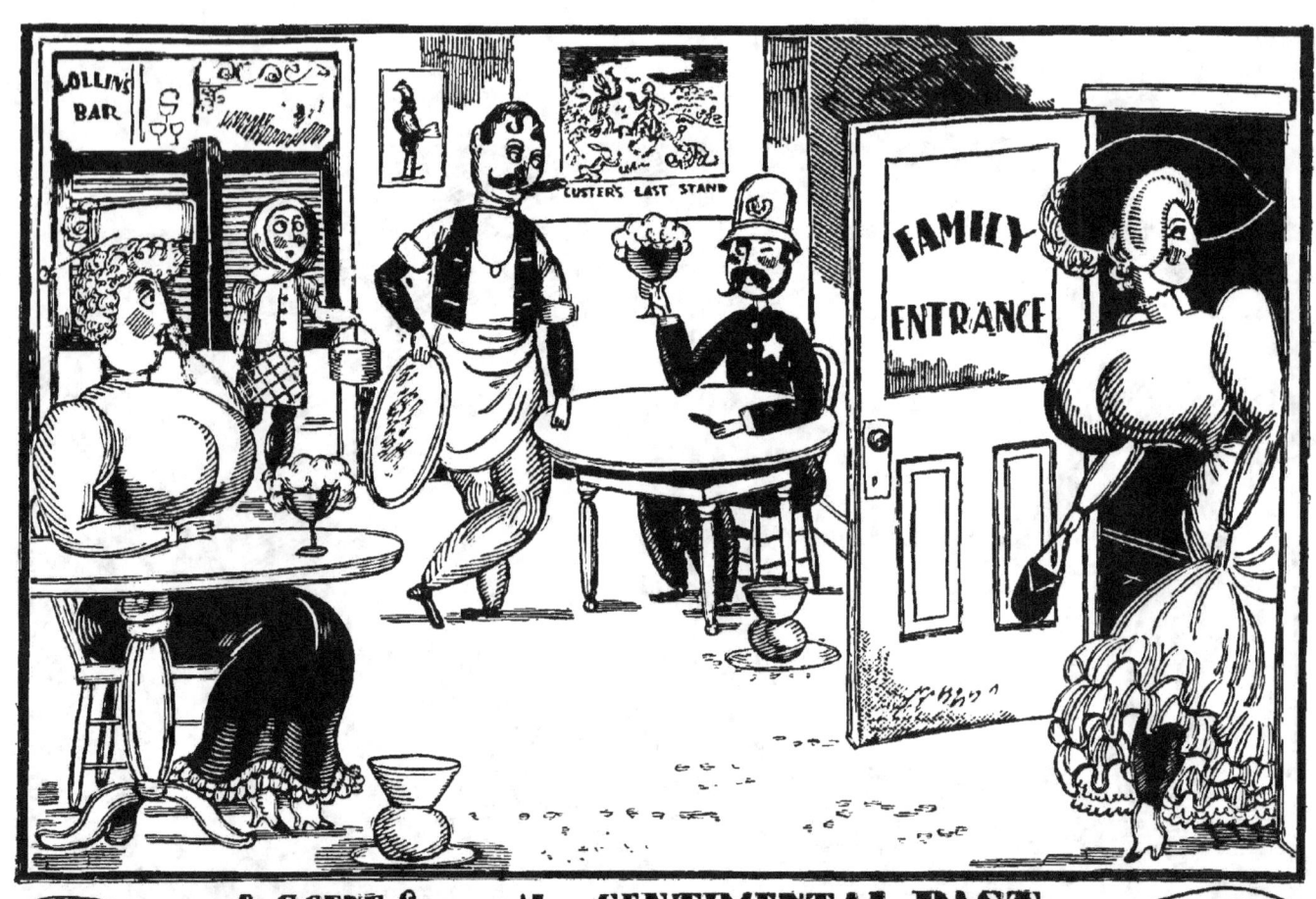

A SCENE from the SENTIMENTAL PAST
THAT ROMANTIC SPOT KNOWN AS THE "BACK ROOM" AH-ME!
ENGRAVED BY JOHN HELD JR WHO IS FAMED IN SONG AND STORY

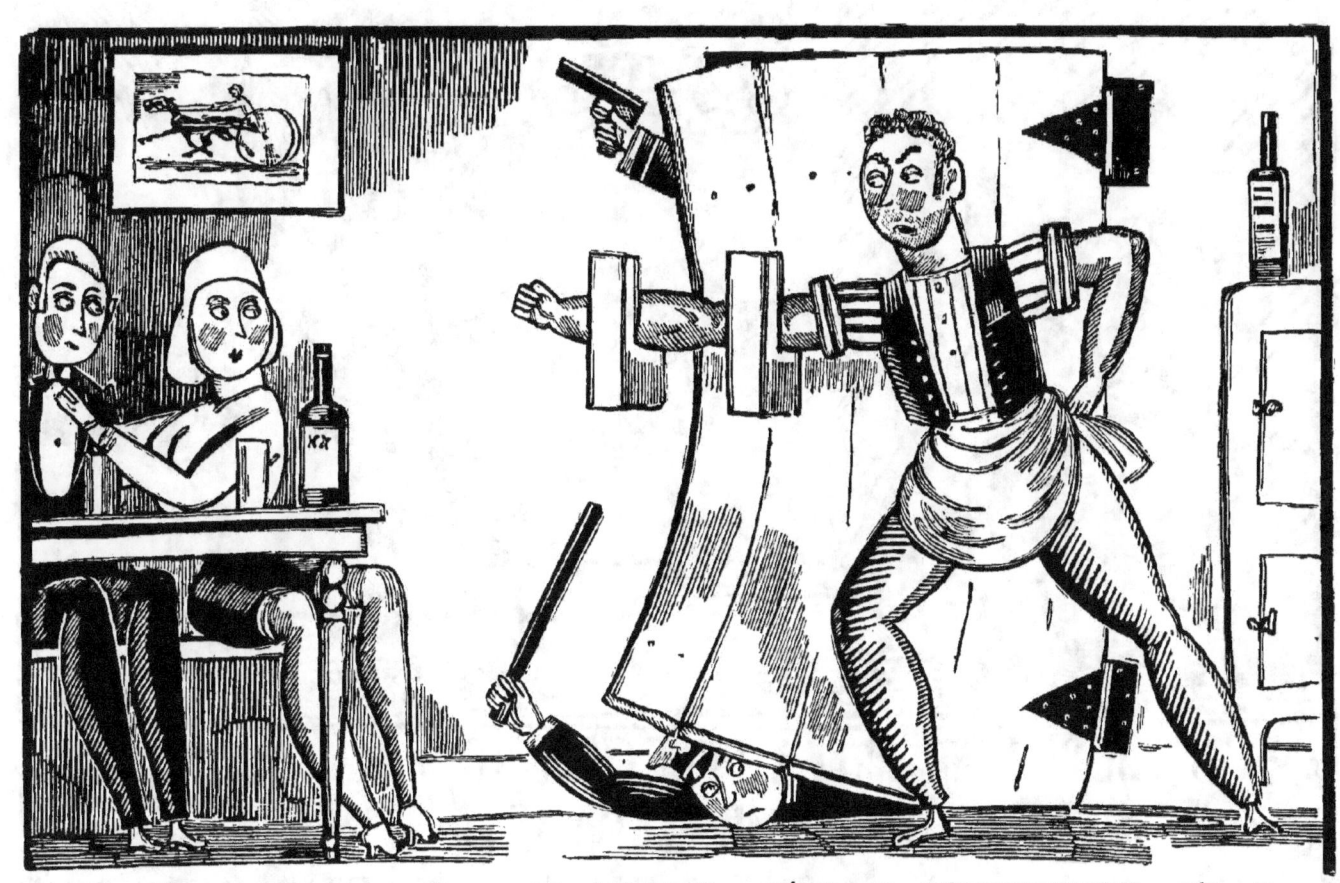

A Raid at the DAVY CROCKETT Club

an old Imitation Wood-cut by John Held jr [it's the old John.]

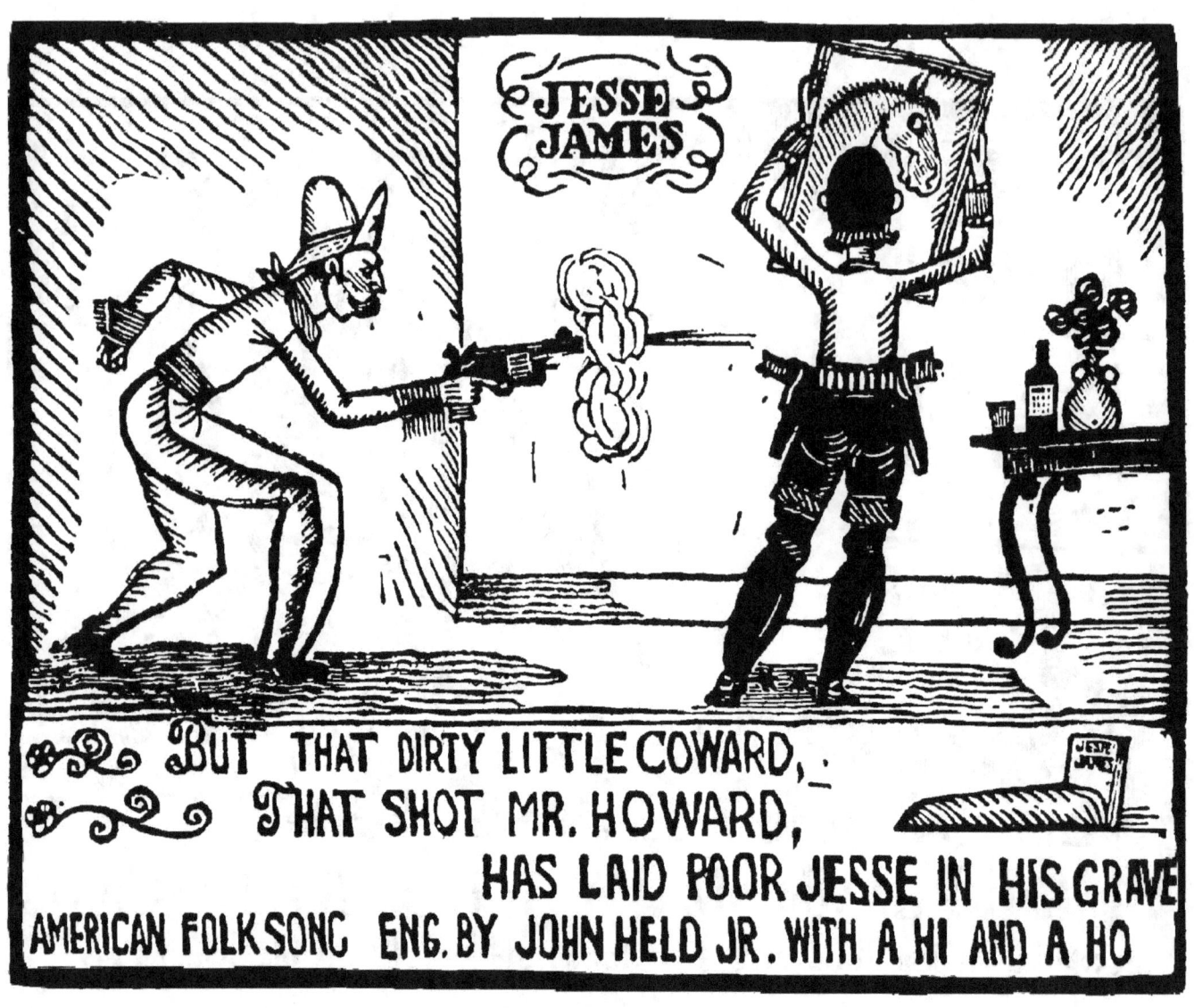

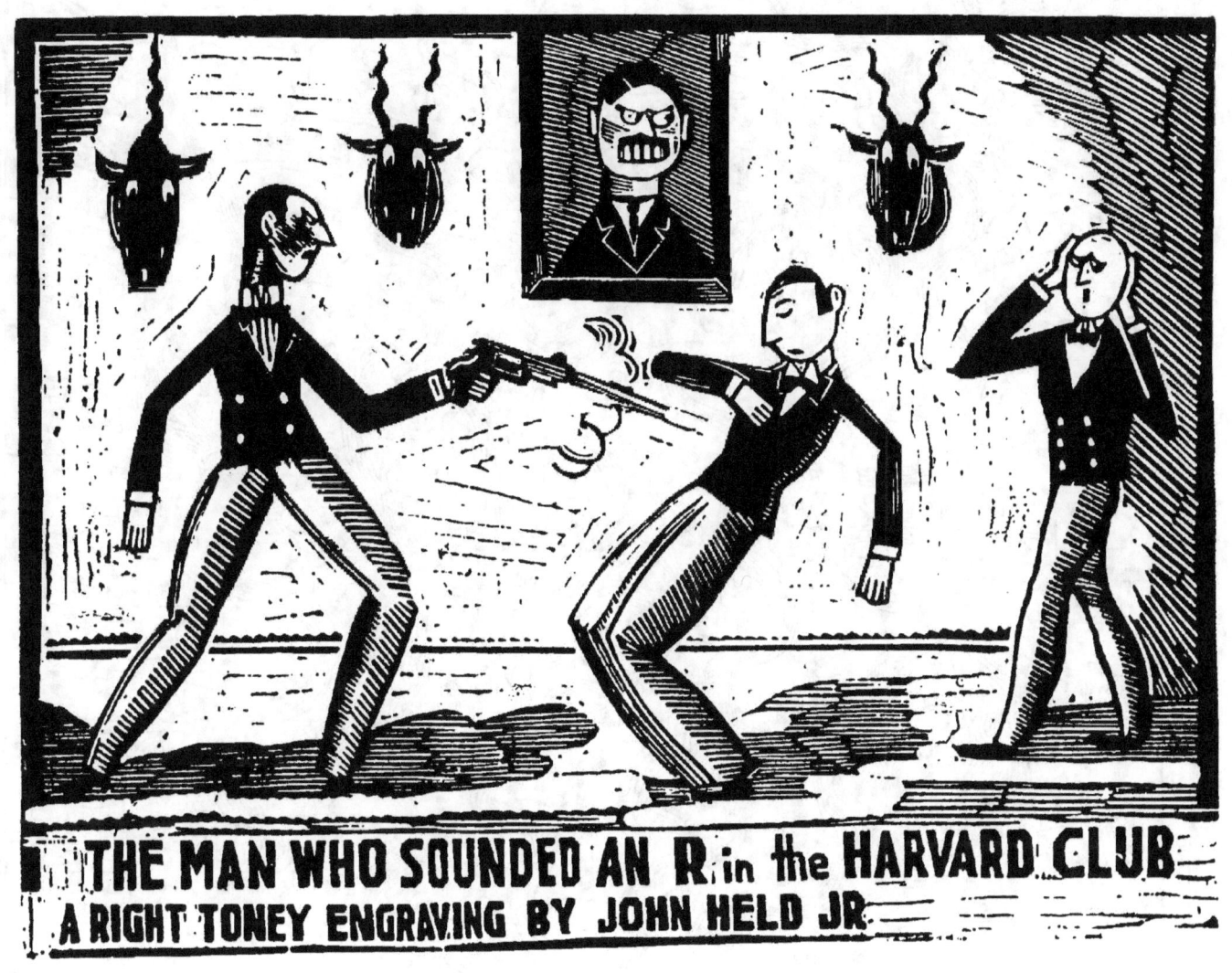

MAP OF AN IMAGINARY ESTATE FOR AN INVETERATE FLY-FISHERMAN CONCEIVED AND ENGROSSED BY JOHN HELD JR.

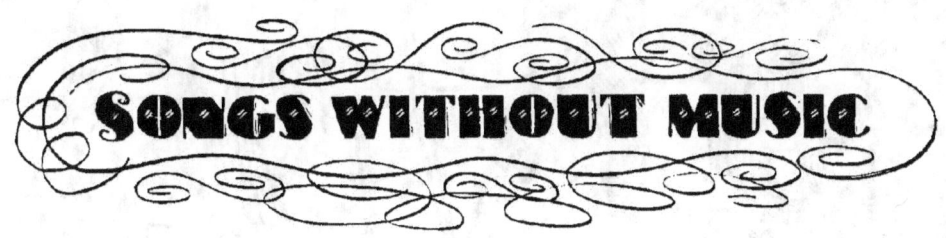

SONGS WITHOUT MUSIC

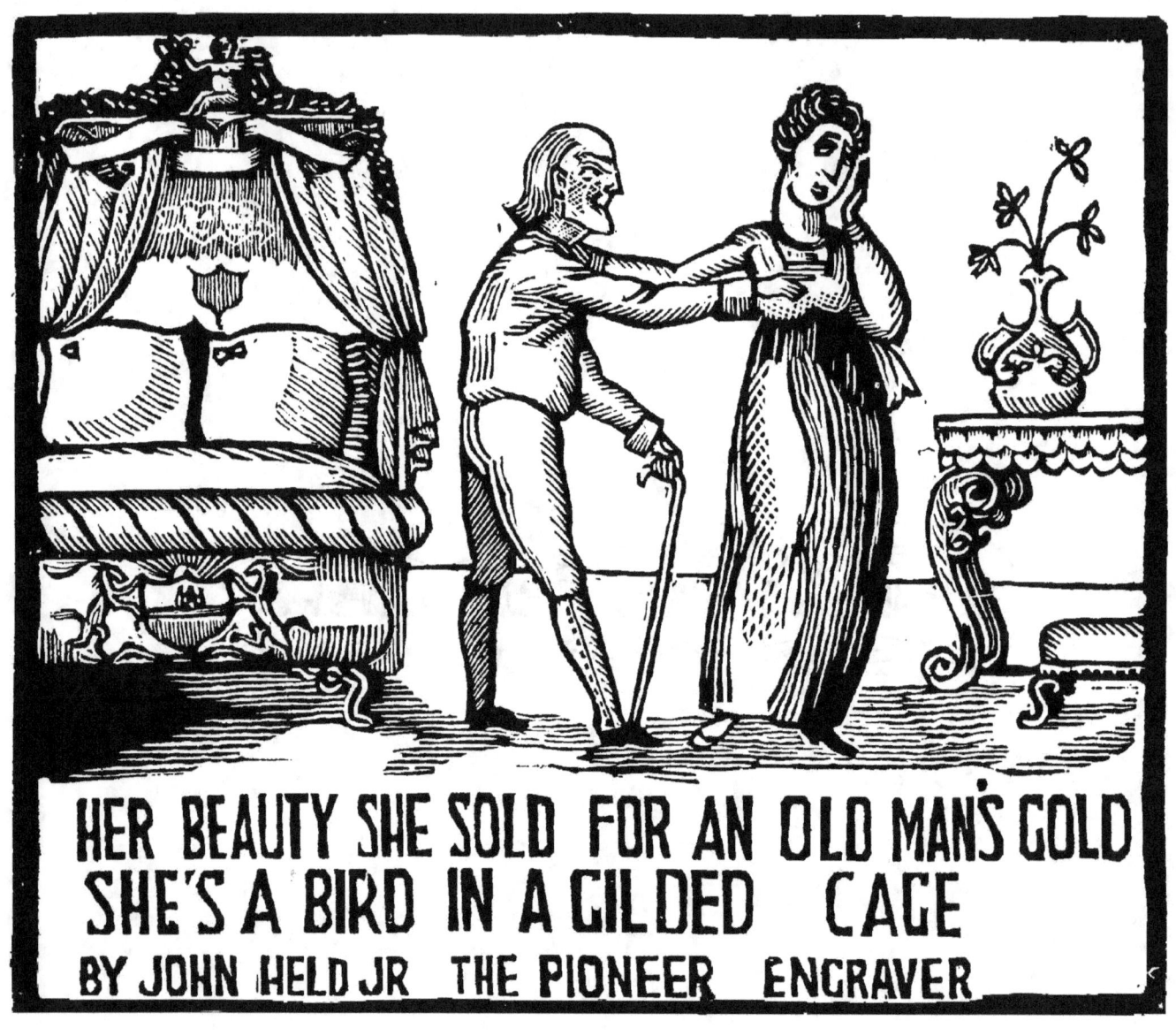

HER BEAUTY SHE SOLD FOR AN OLD MAN'S GOLD
SHE'S A BIRD IN A GILDED CAGE
BY JOHN HELD JR THE PIONEER ENGRAVER

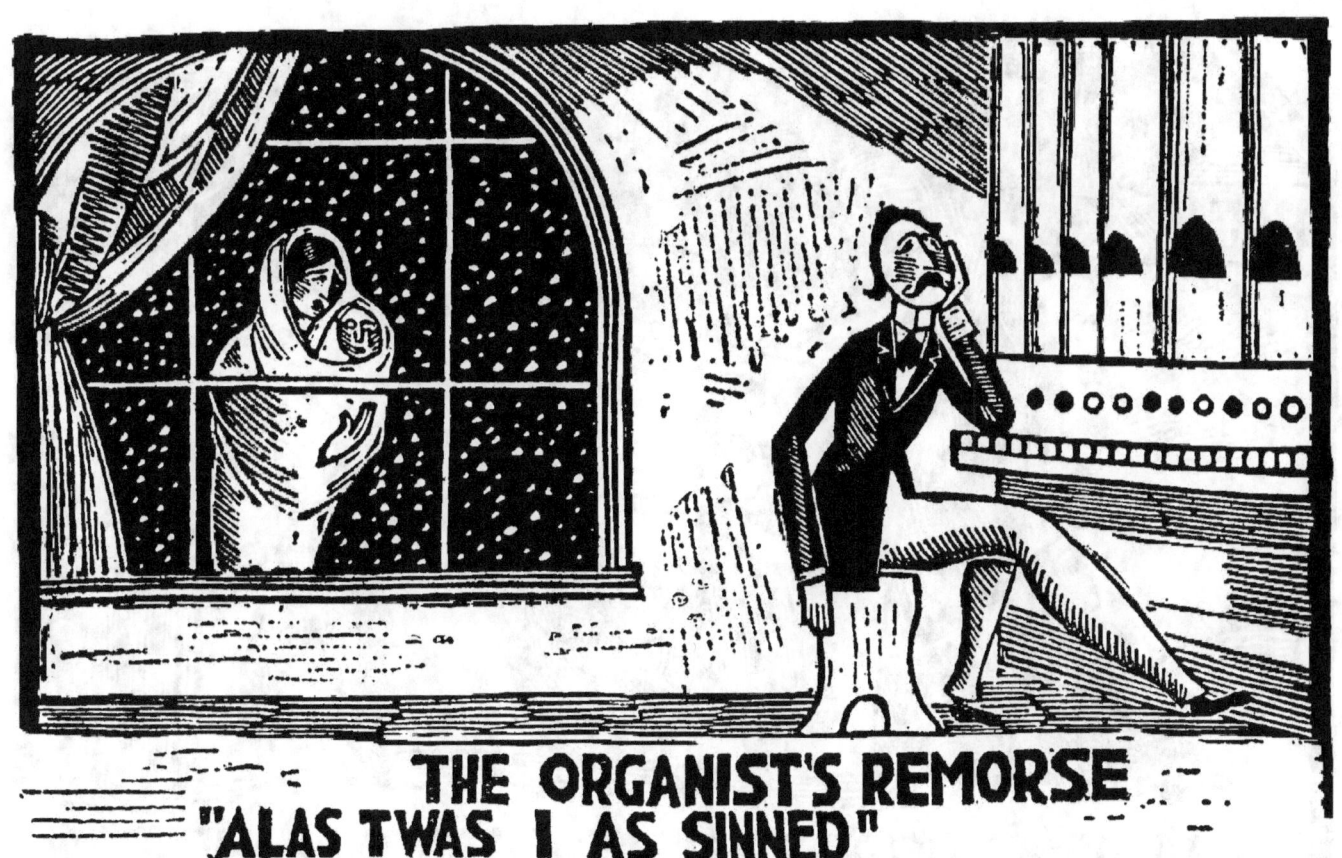

THE ORGANIST'S REMORSE
"ALAS TWAS I AS SINNED"
ENG BY JOHN HELD JR. NONE GENUINE WITHOUT THE SIGNATURE

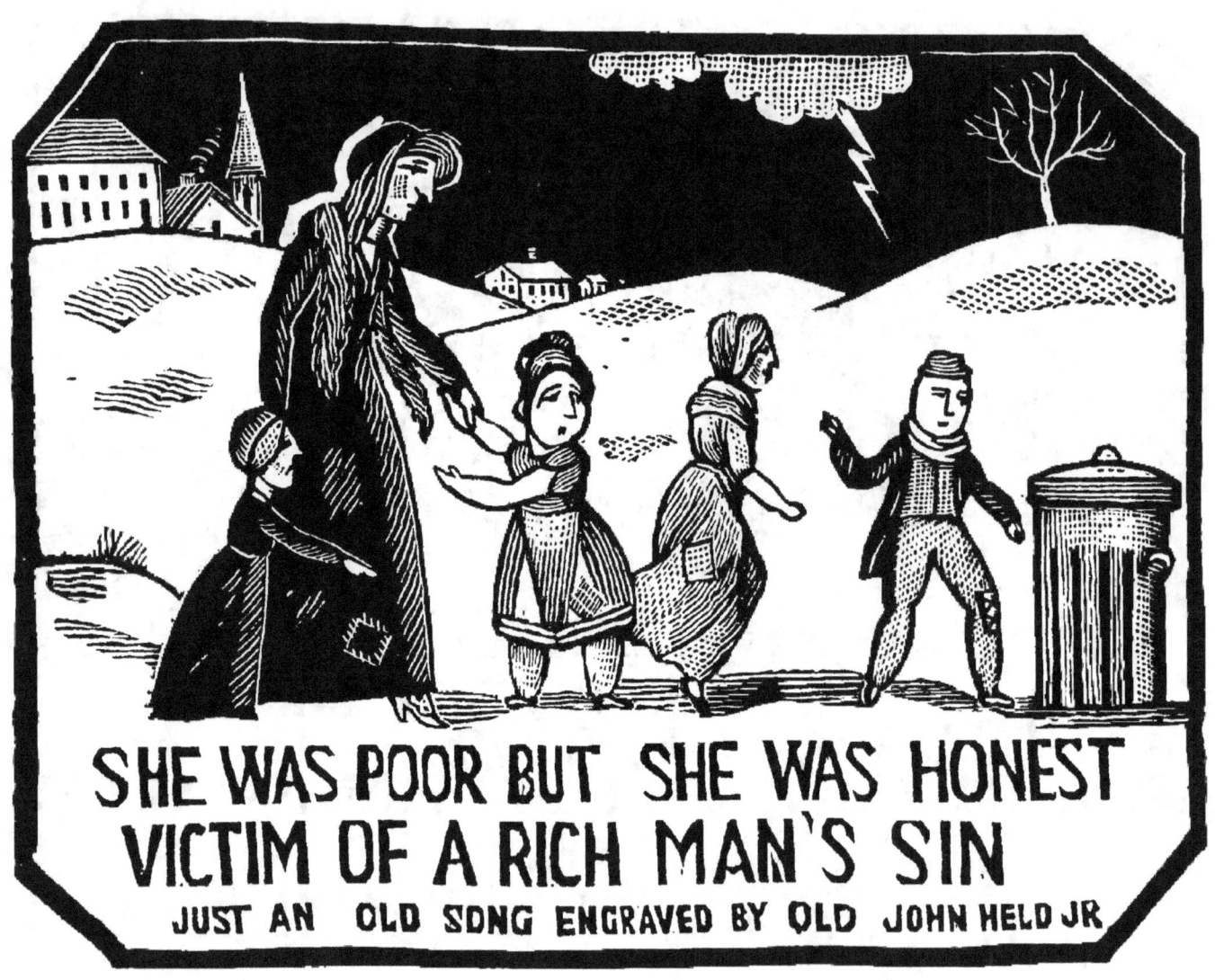

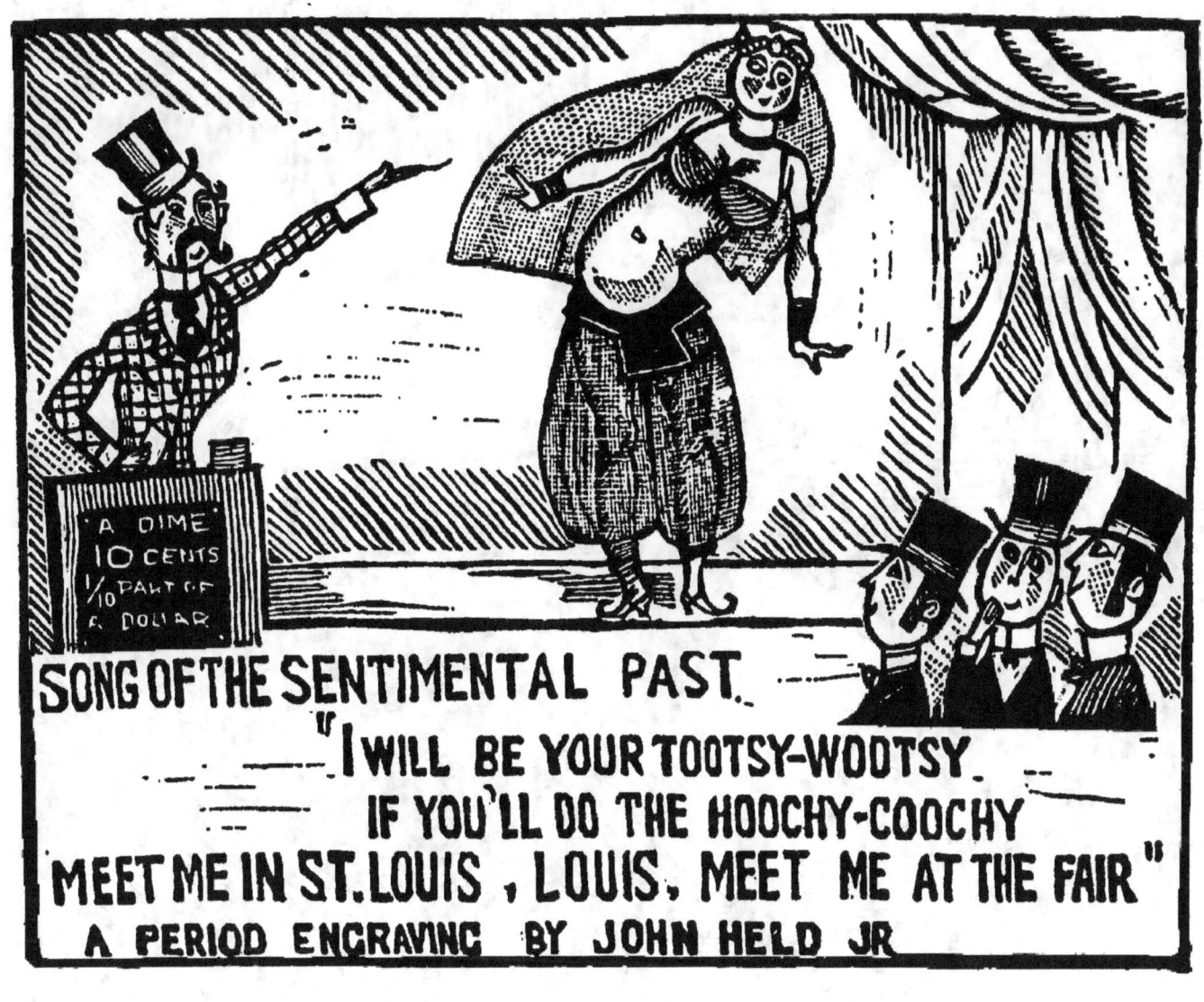

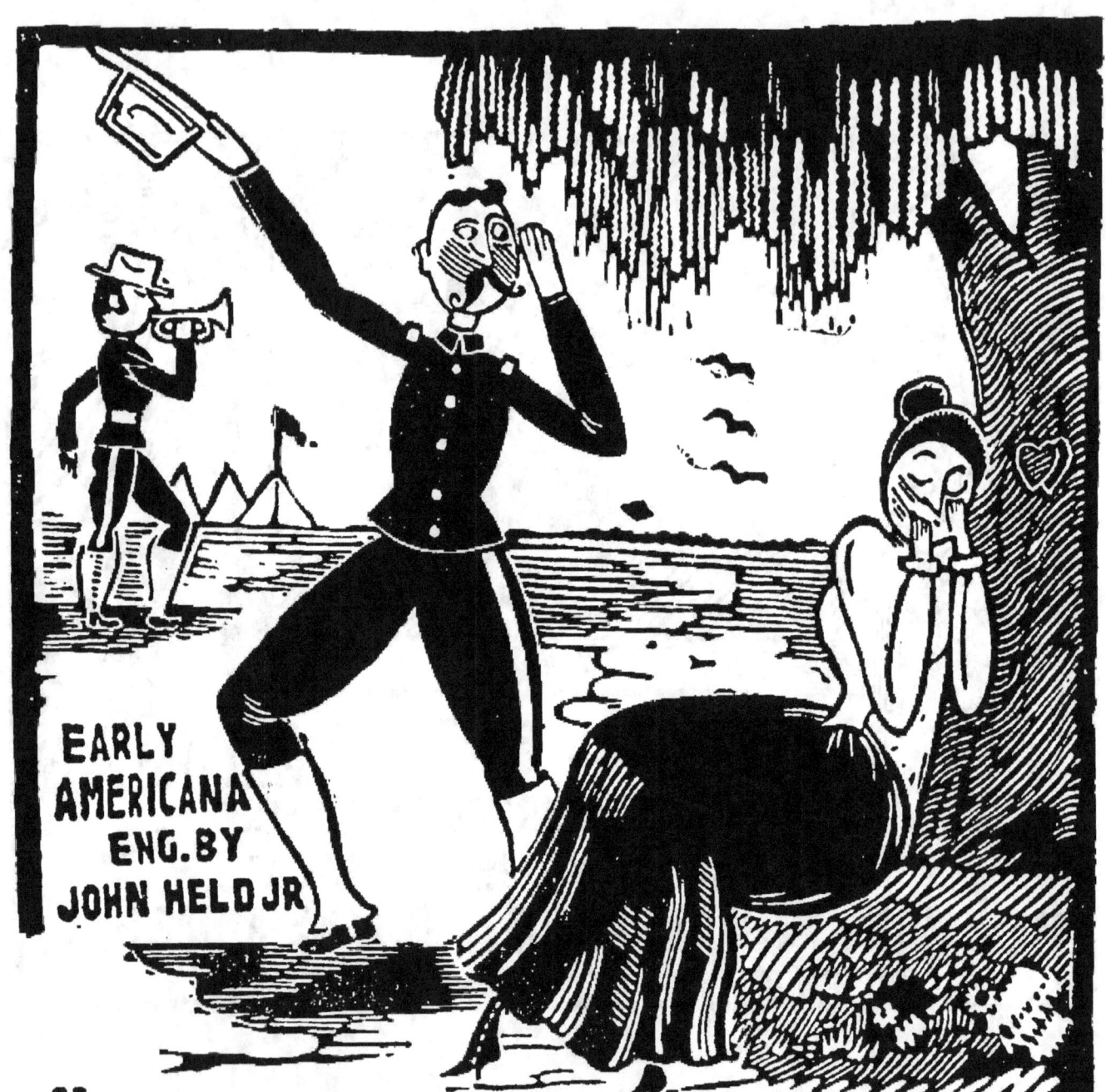

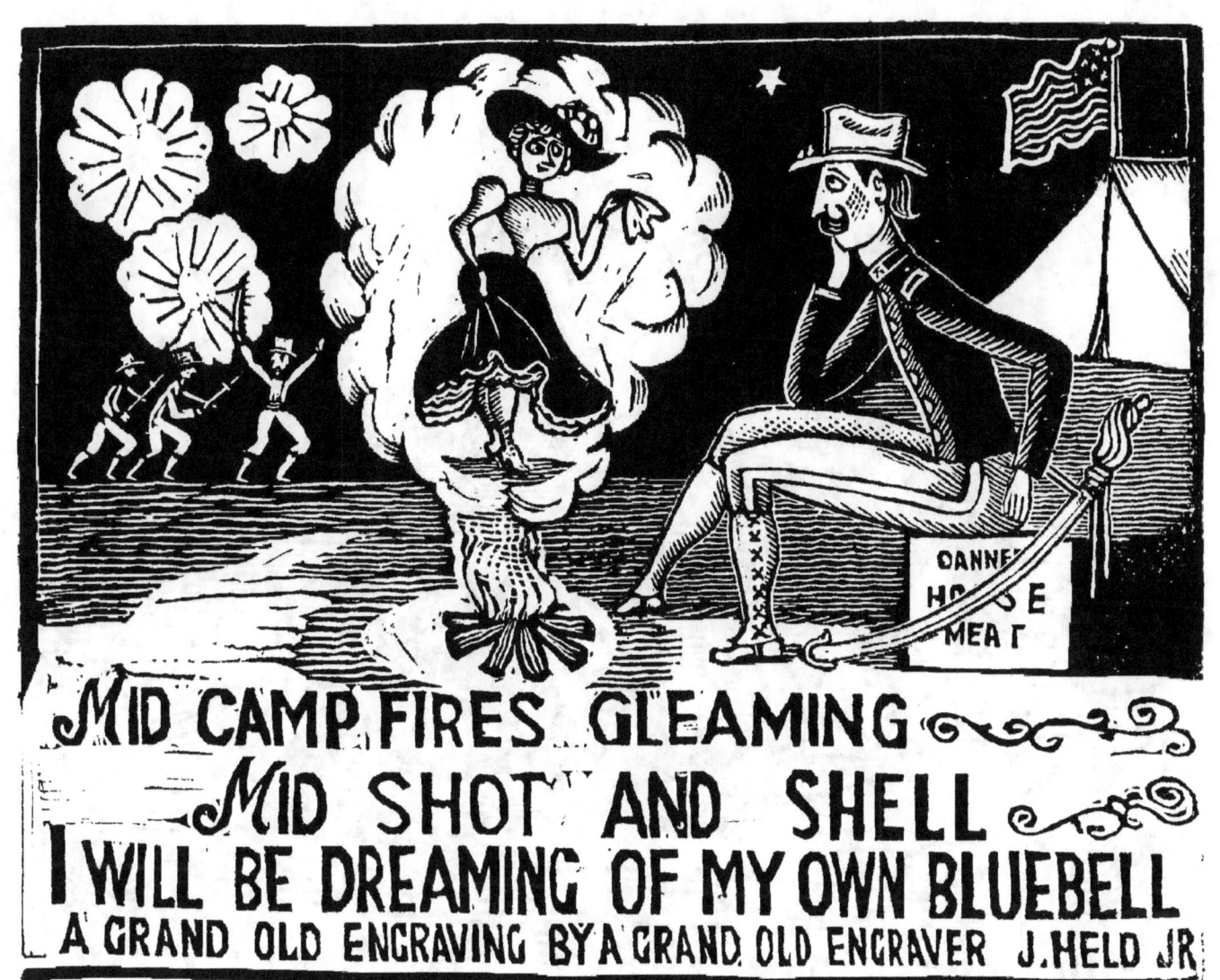

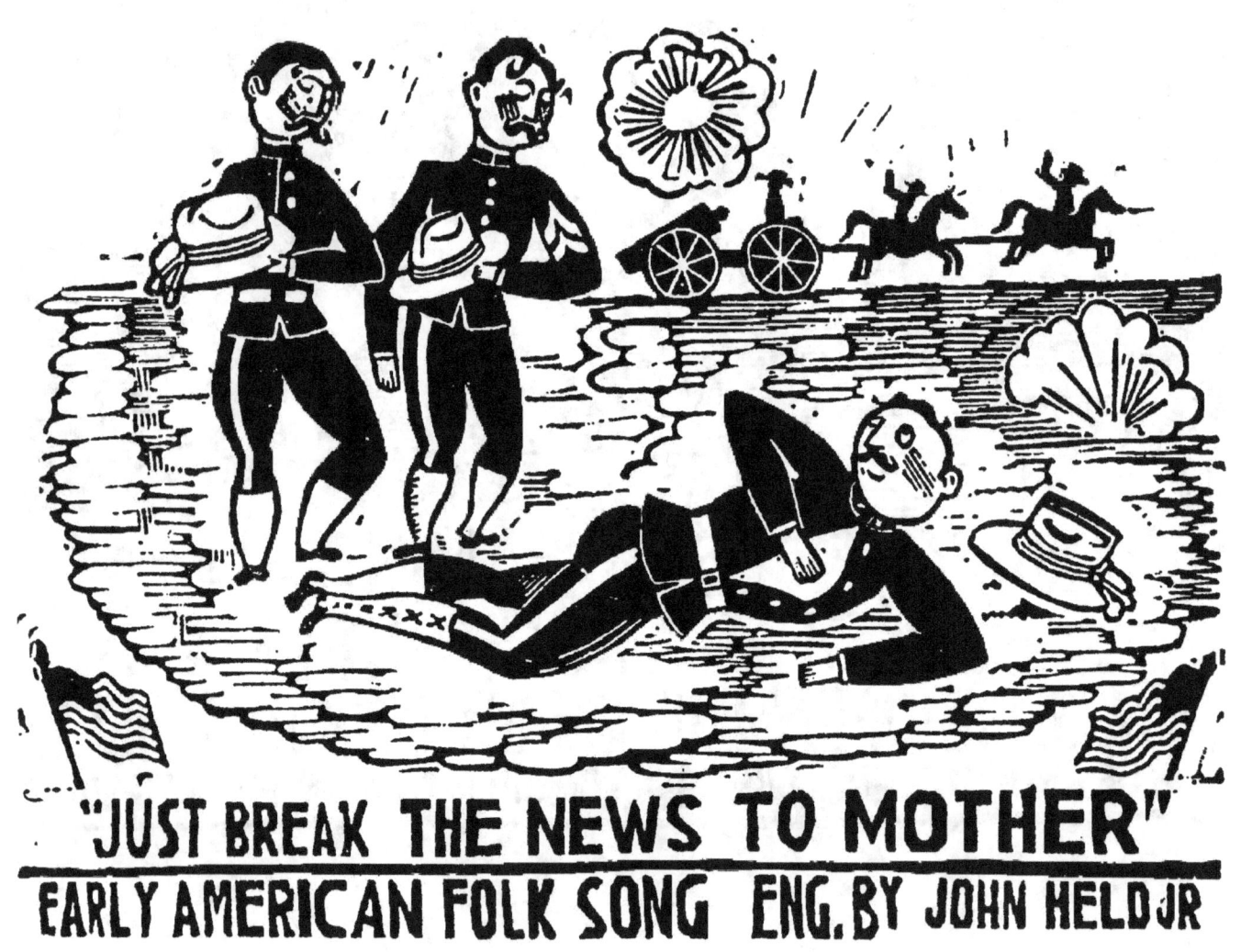

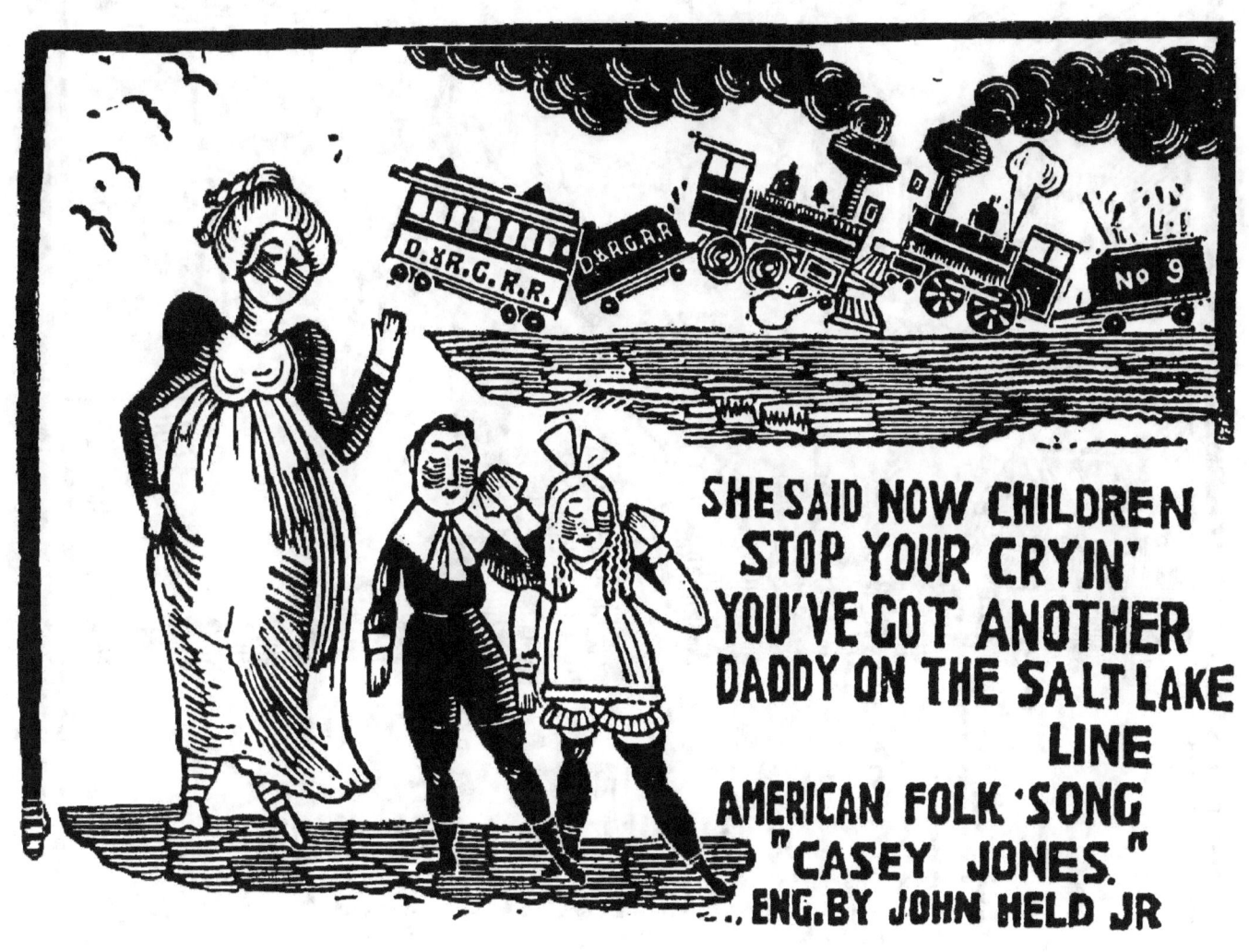

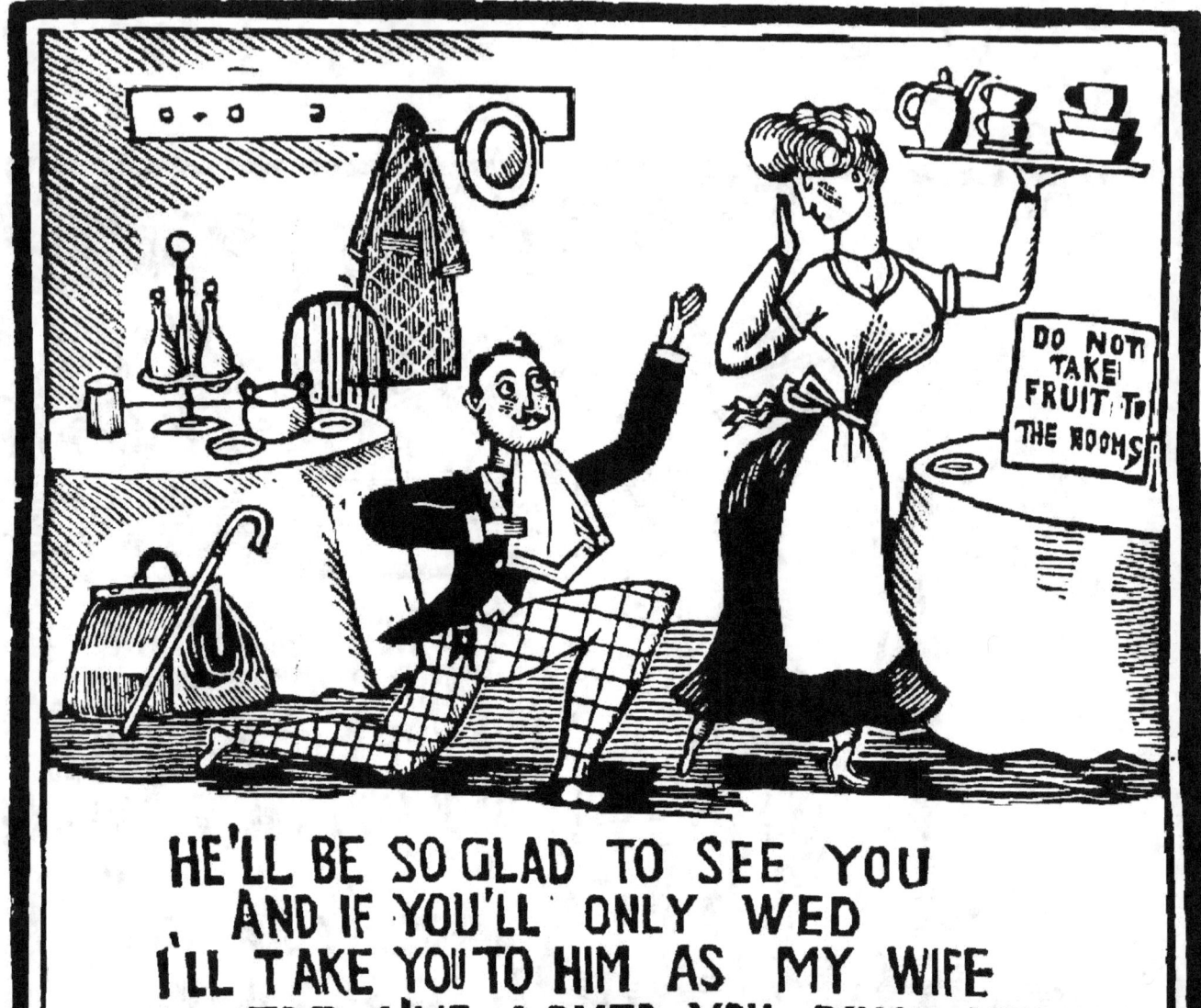

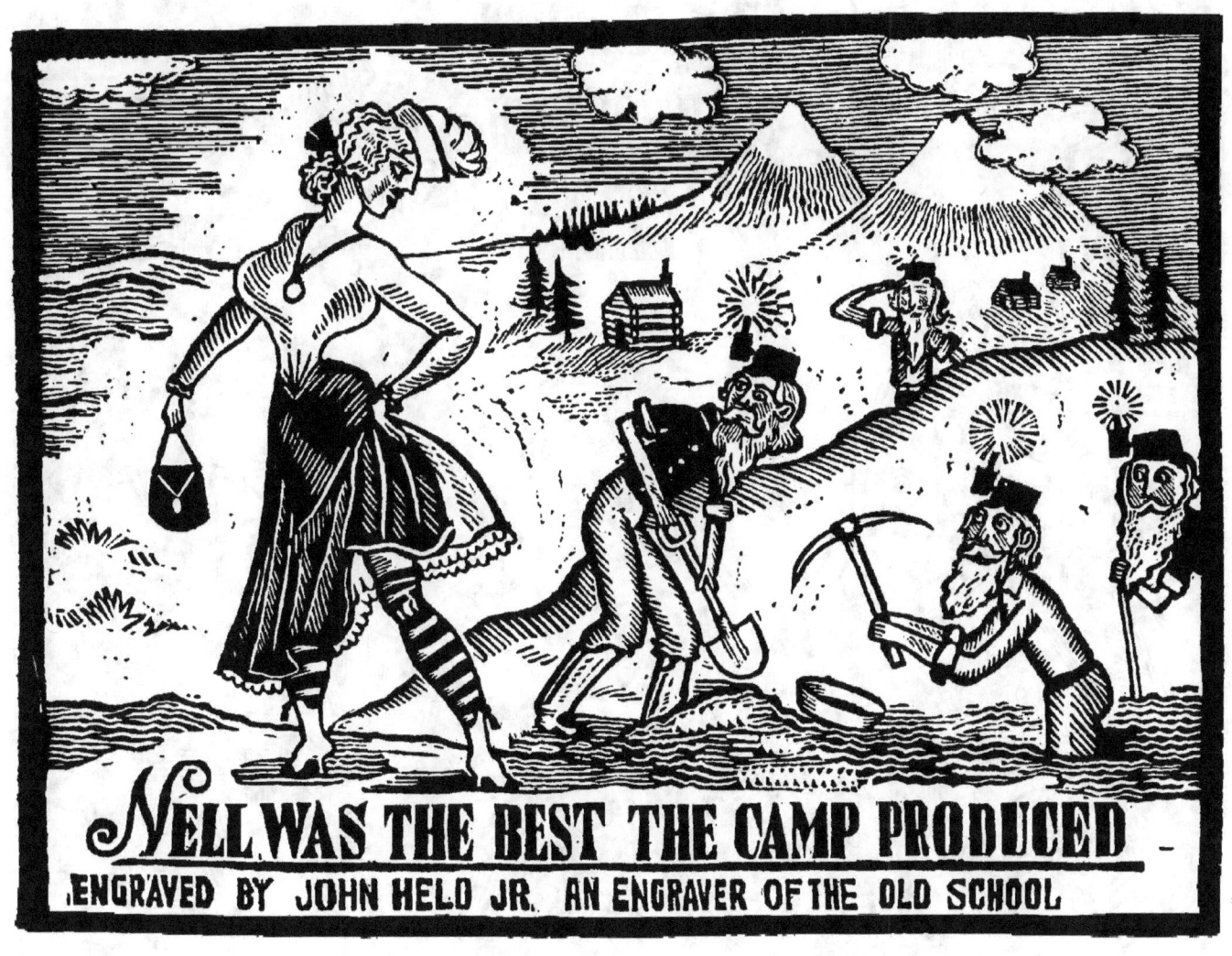

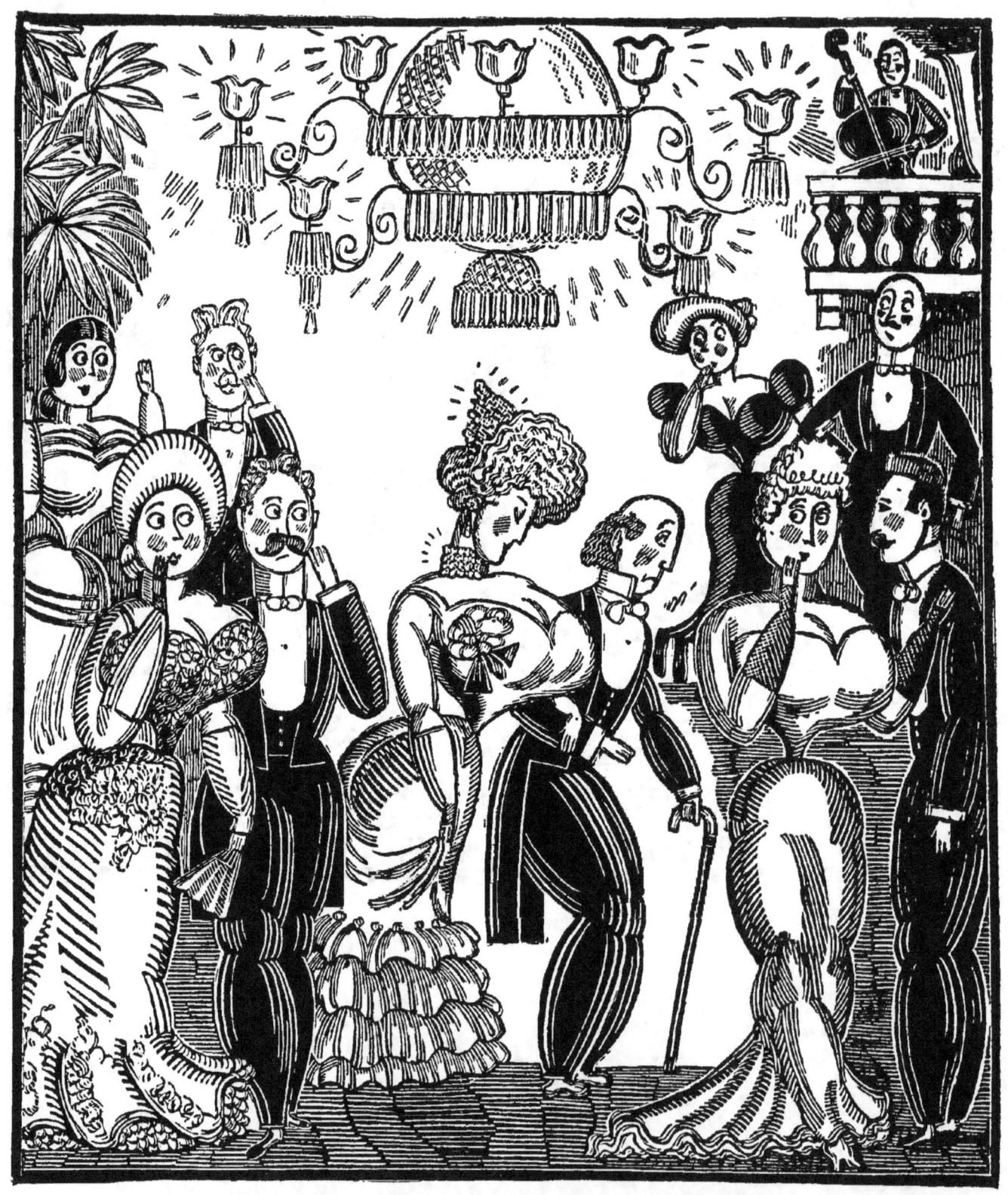

"THE BALL-ROOM WAS FILLED WITH FASHIONS THRONG. IT SHONE WITH A THOUSAND LIGHTS."

A ROMANTIC SITUATION IN THE BALLADE ENG. BY THAT FAMOUS OLD SENTIMENTALIST JOHN HELD JR WHO DANCES WITH TEARS IN HIS EYES

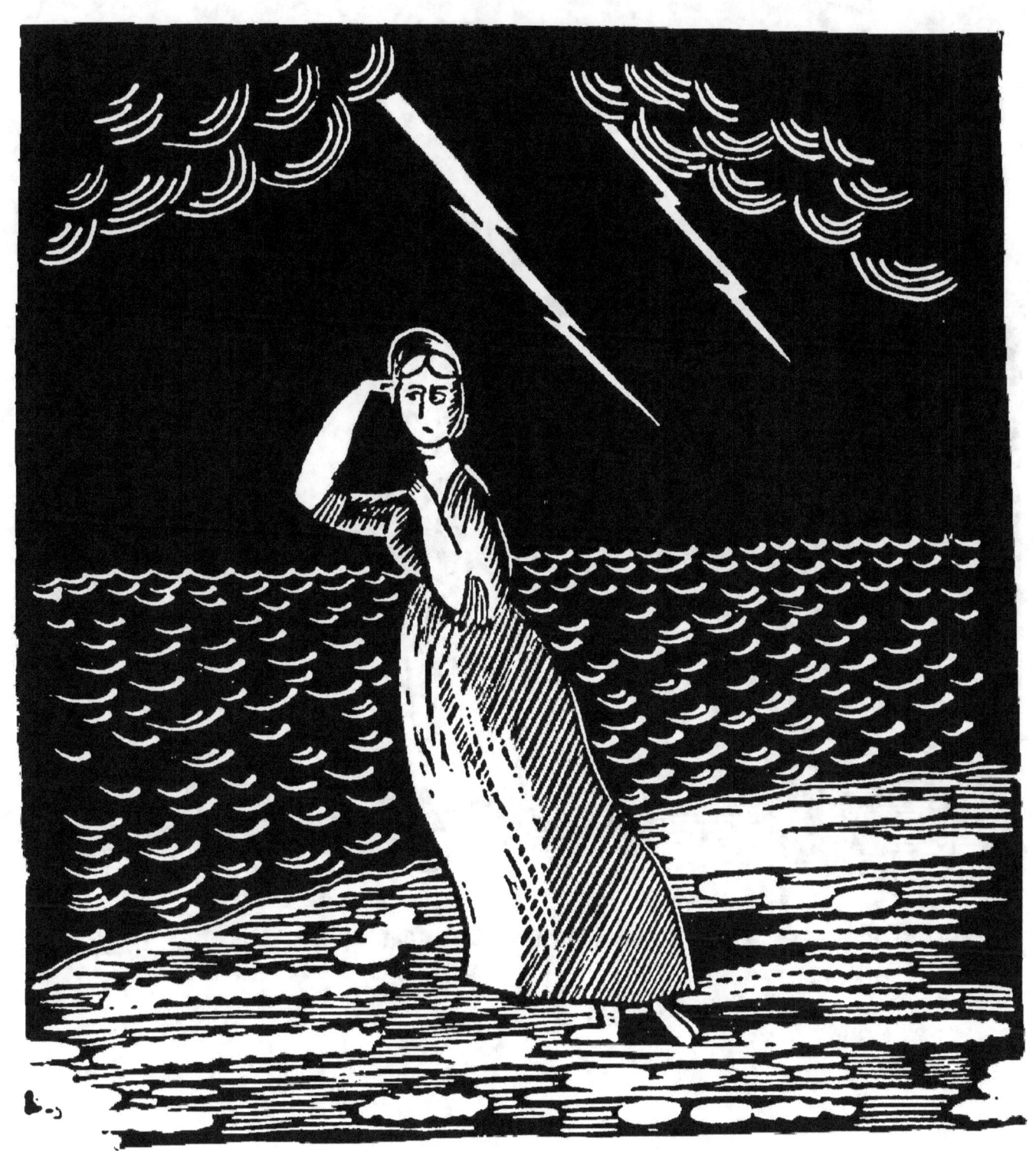

The RUMRUNNER'S
SISTER-IN-LAW

ENGRAVED BY JOHN HELD JR

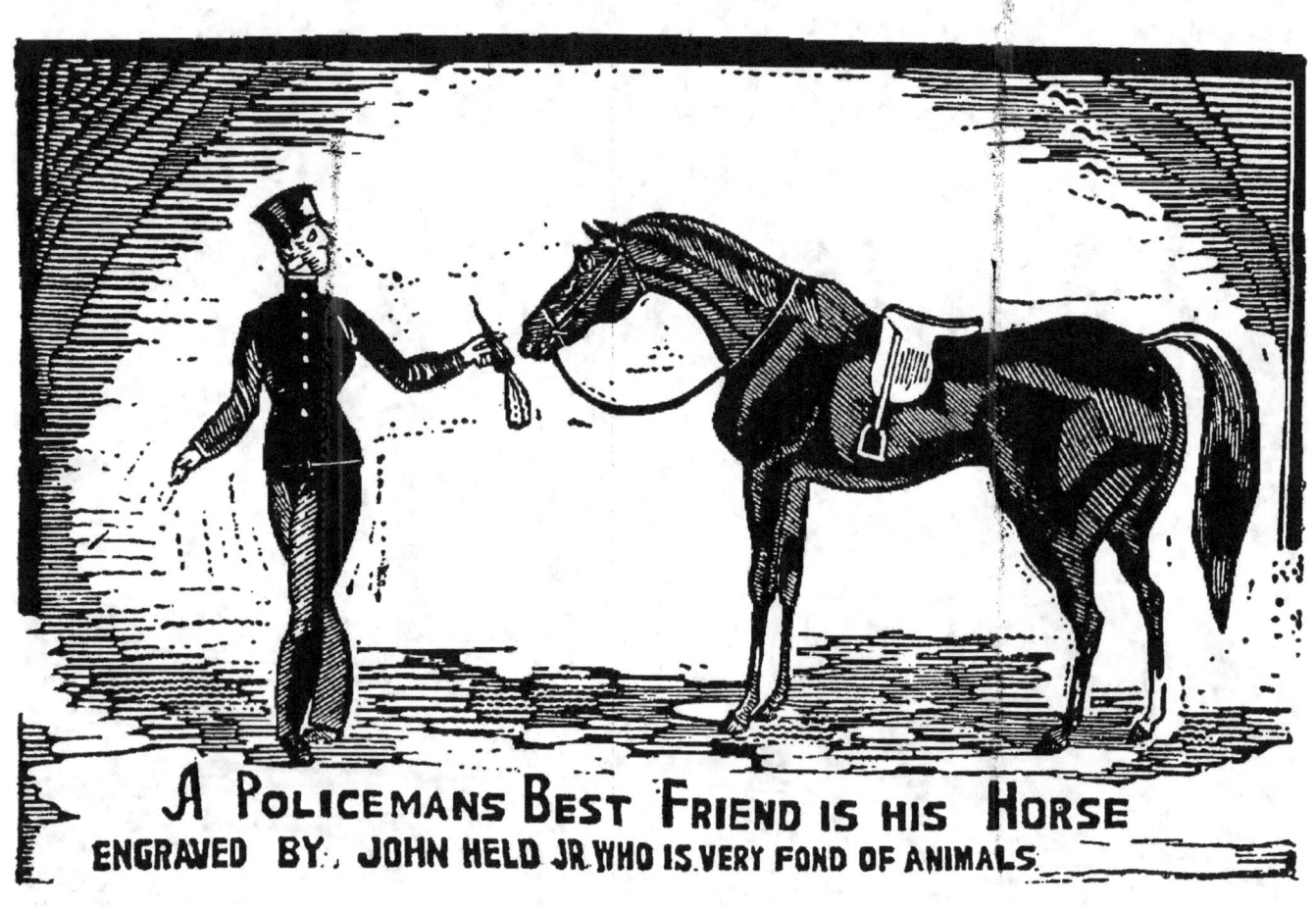

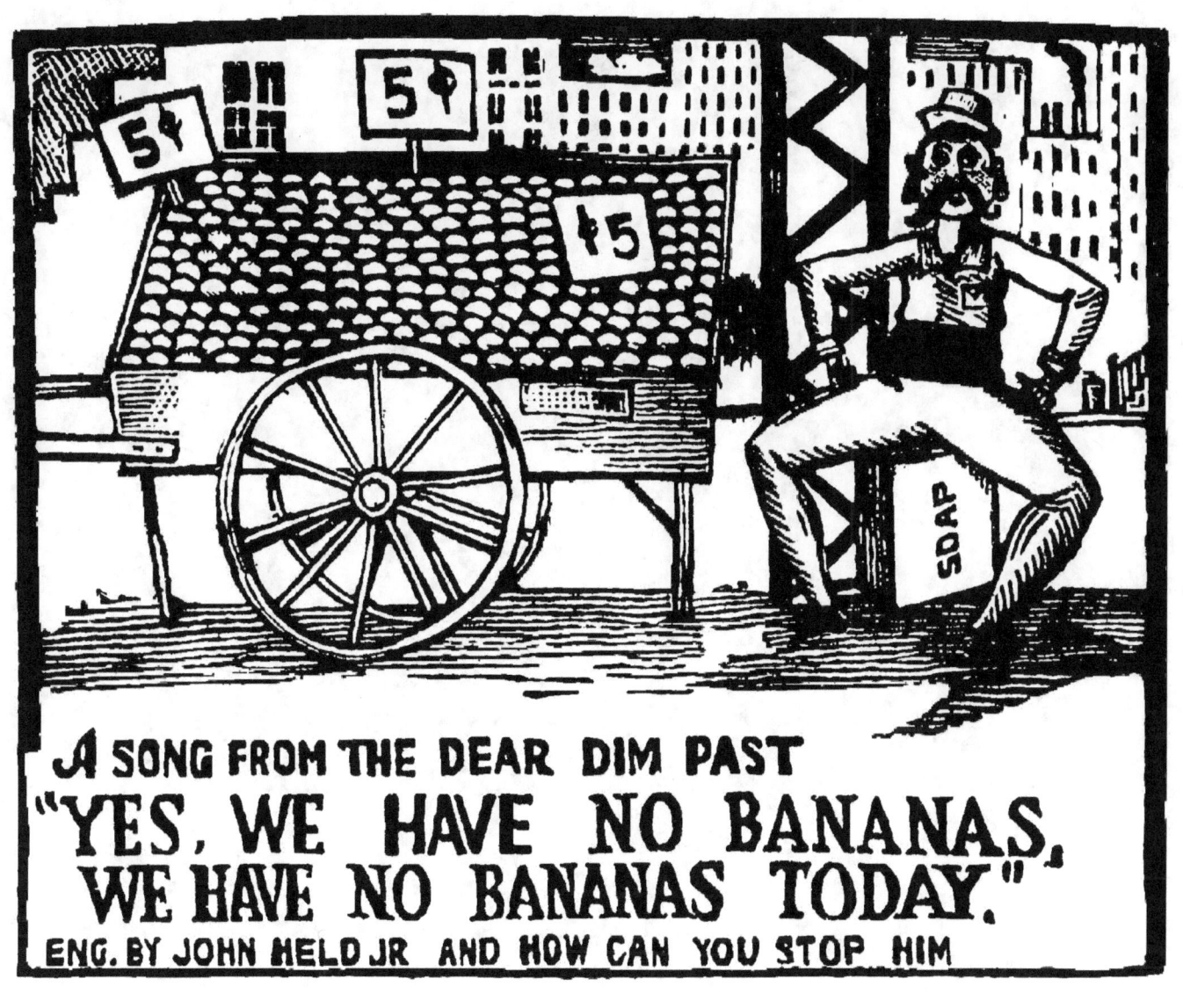

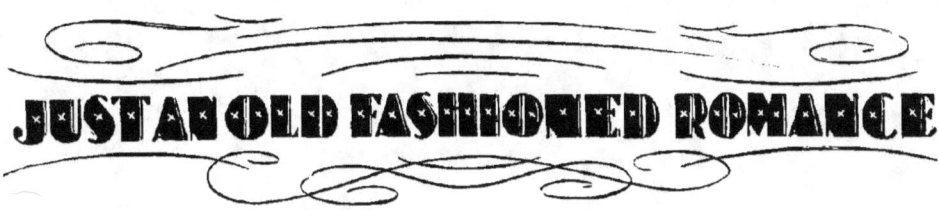

JUST AN OLD FASHIONED ROMANCE

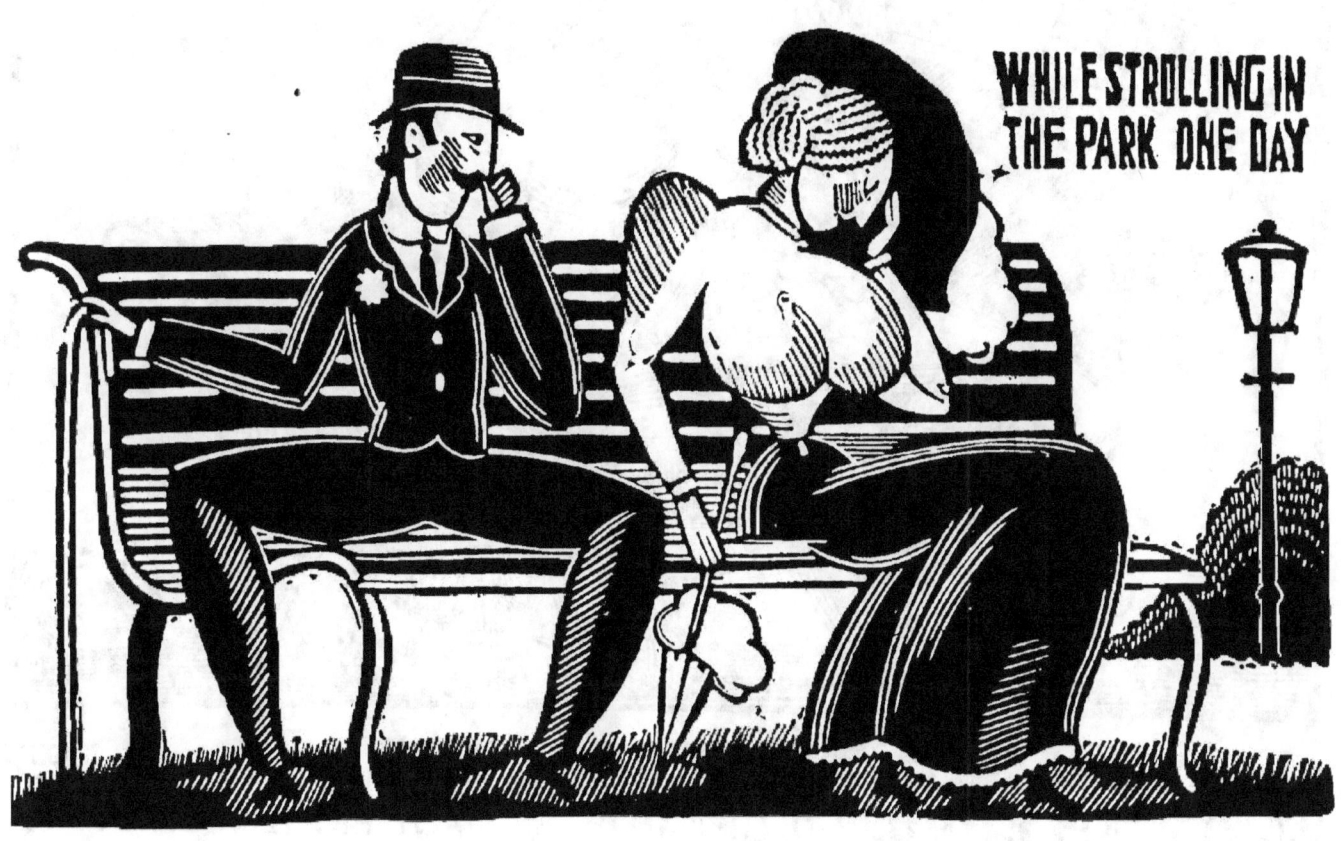

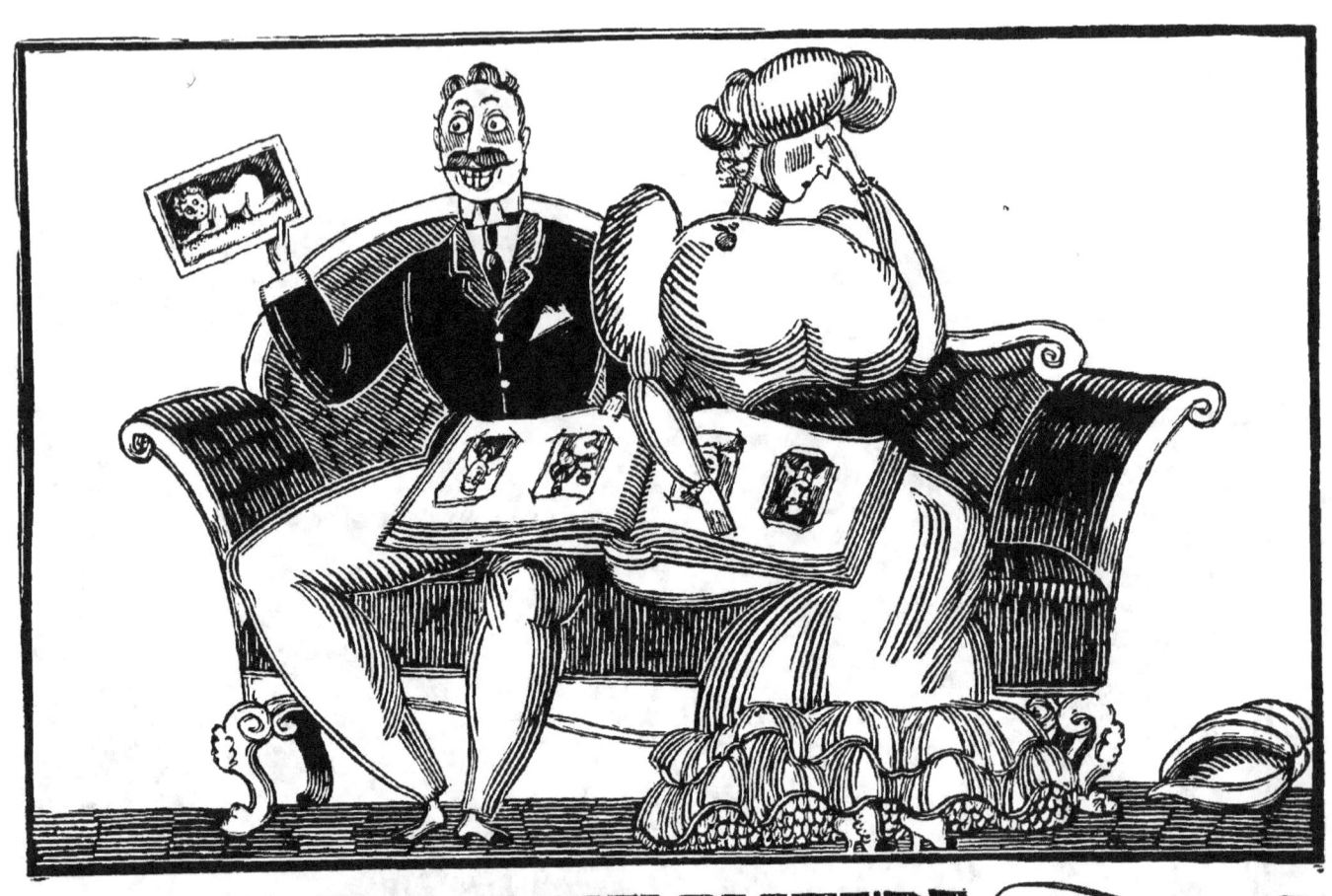

HER BABY PICTURE

ENG. BY **JOHN HELD JR** DELINEATOR of PAST-PRESENT & FUTURE

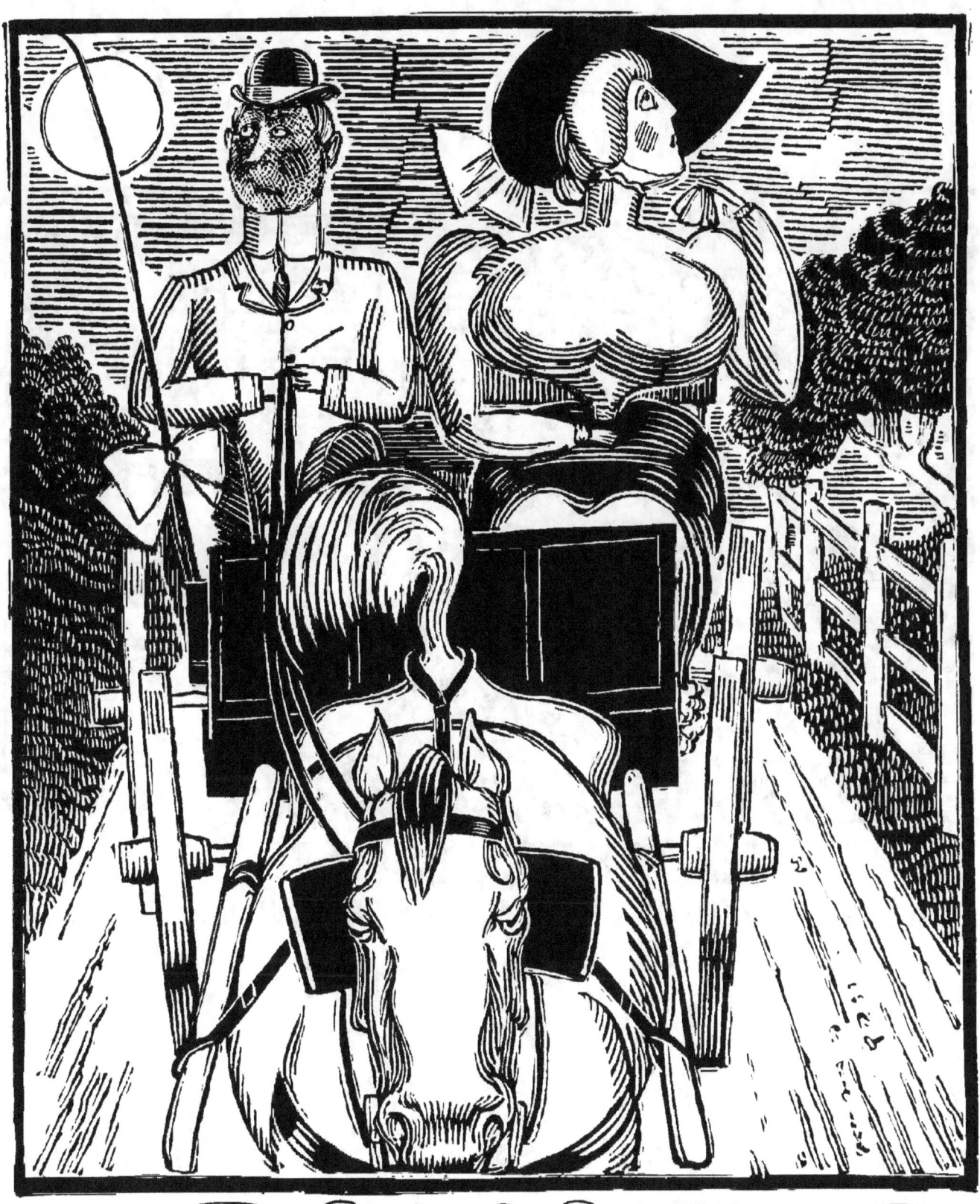

MOONLIGHT & ROSES

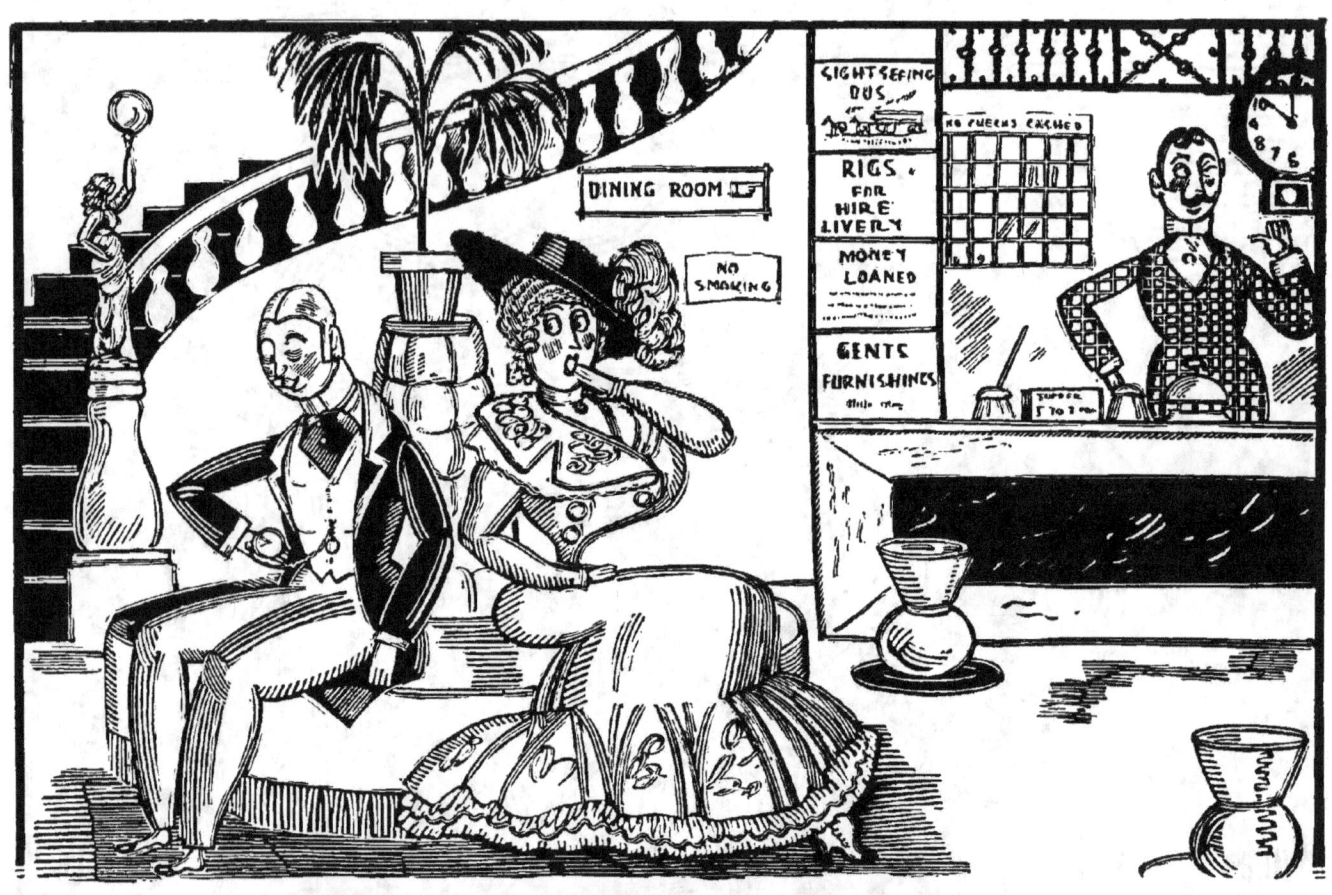

THE HONEYMOON

ENG. BY JOHN HELD JR WHO IS JUST AN OLD FASHIONED LAD

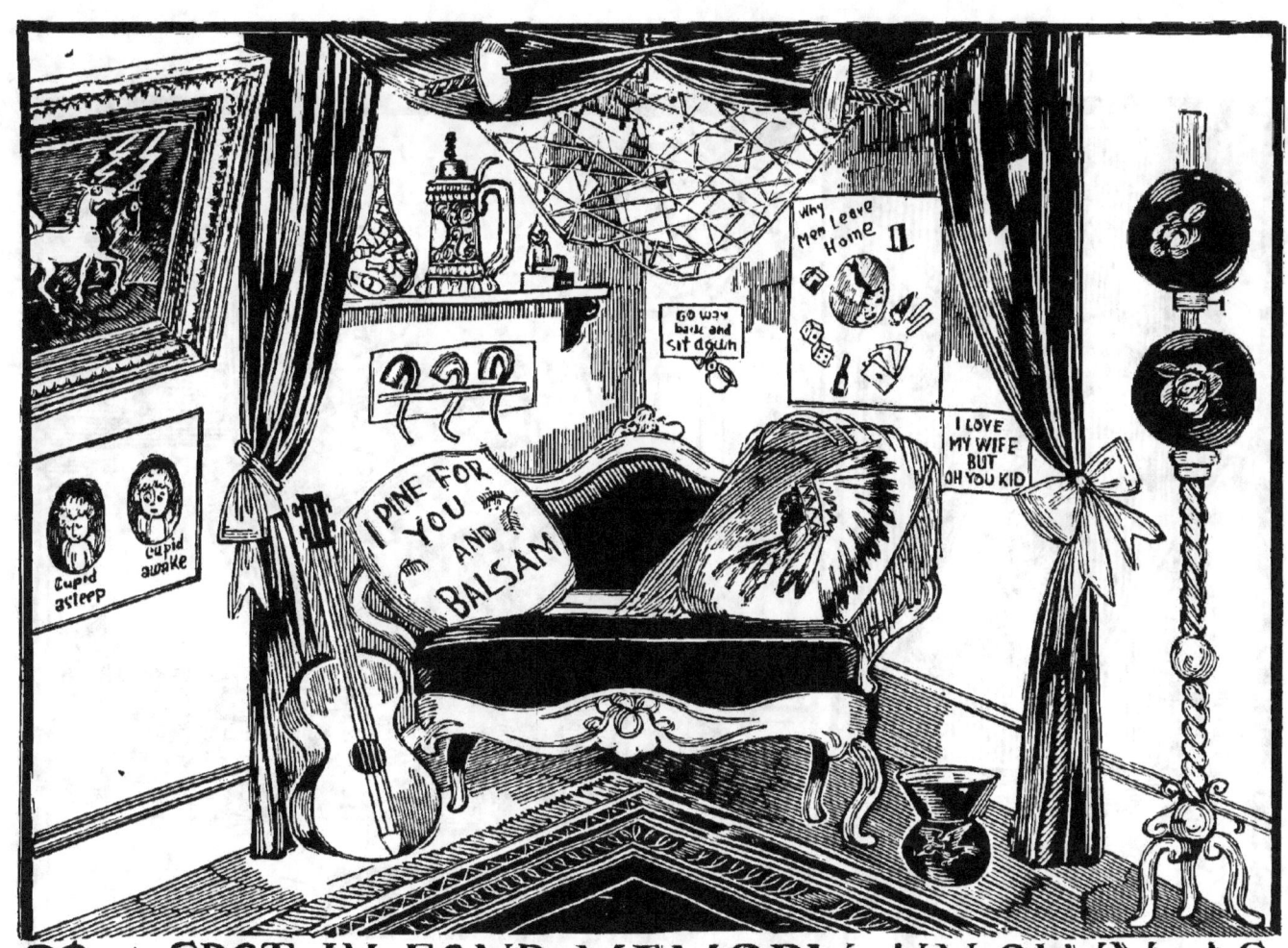

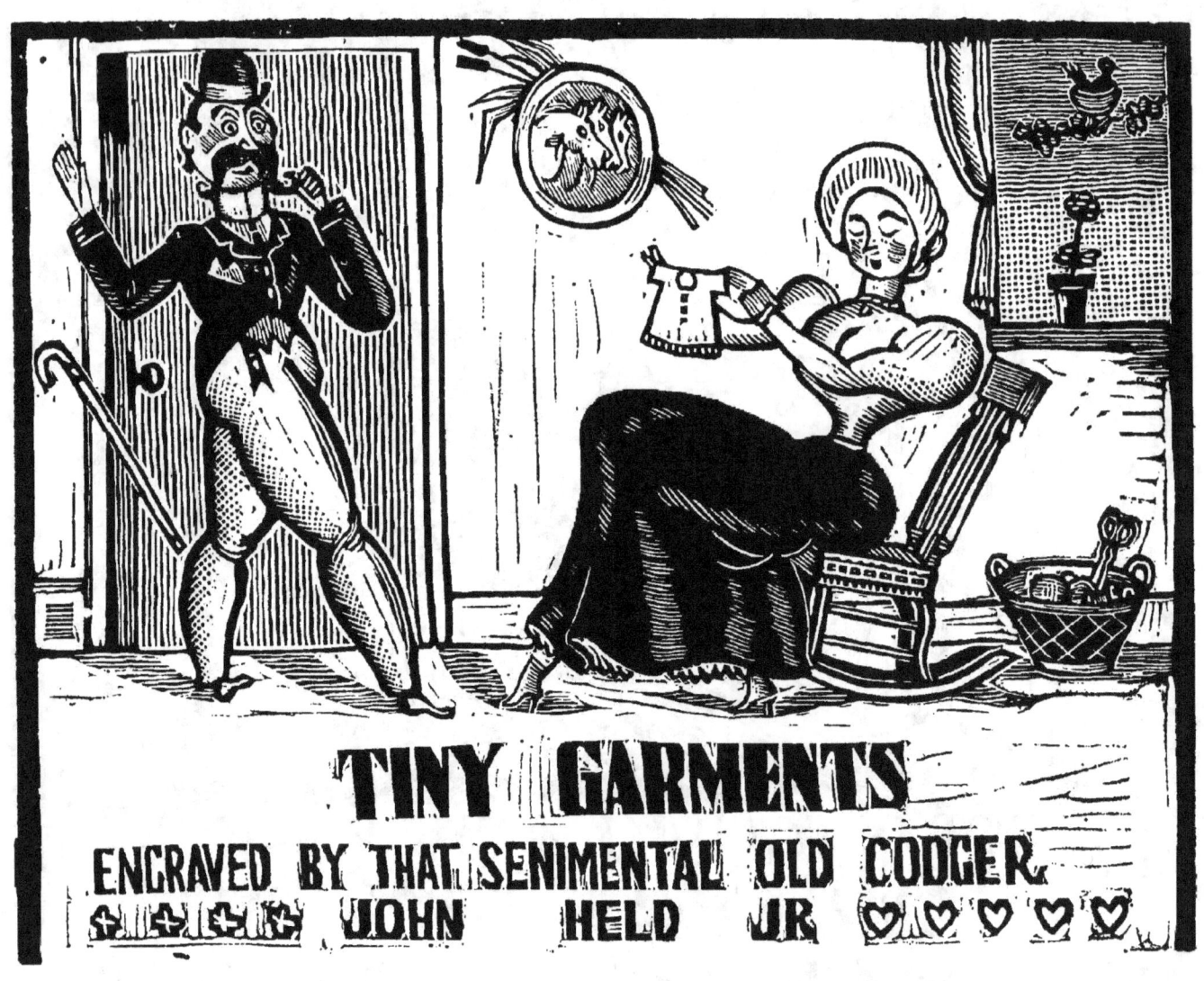

TINY GARMENTS

ENGRAVED BY THAT SENIMENTAL OLD CODGER JOHN HELD JR

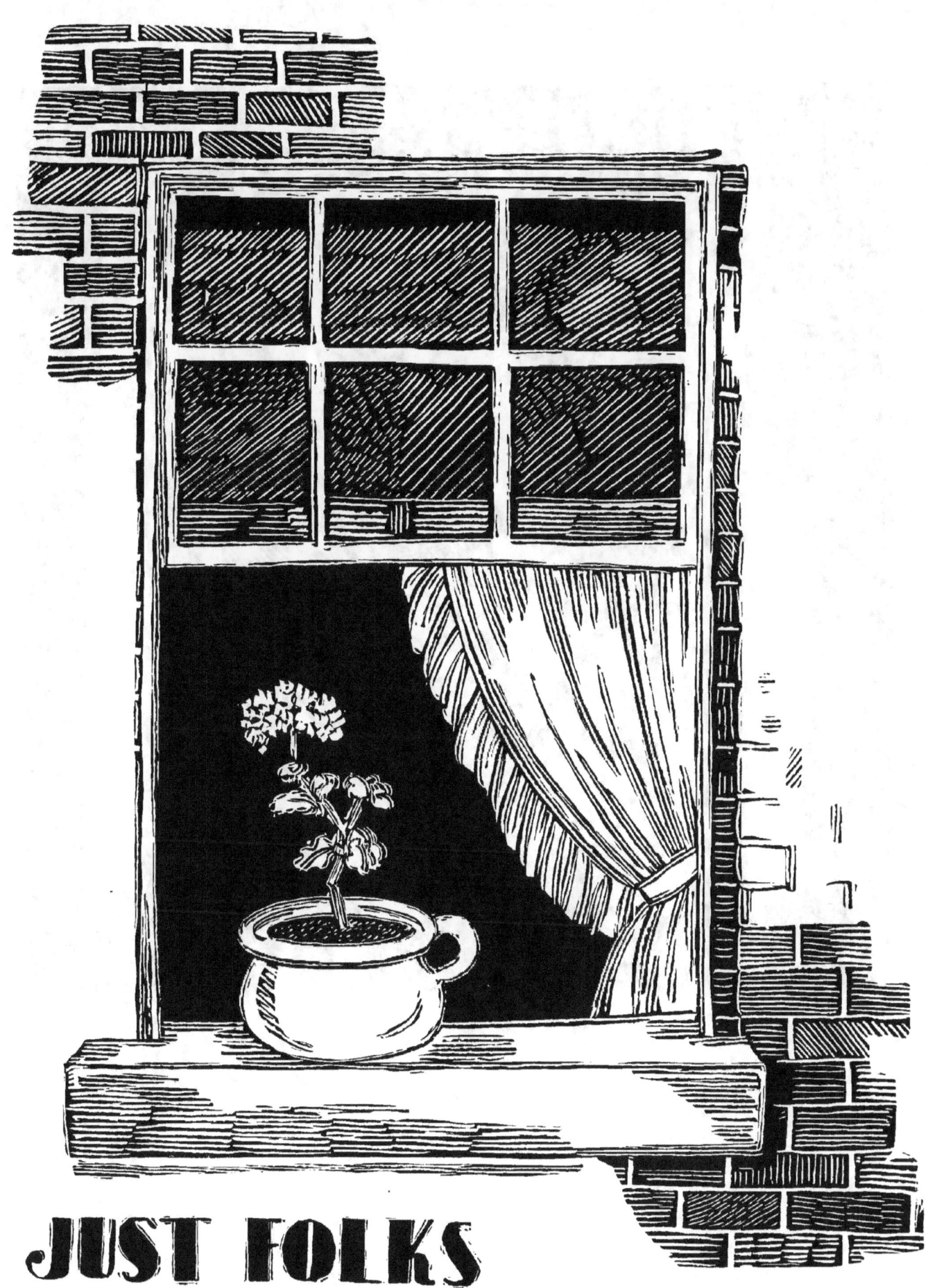

JUST FOLKS

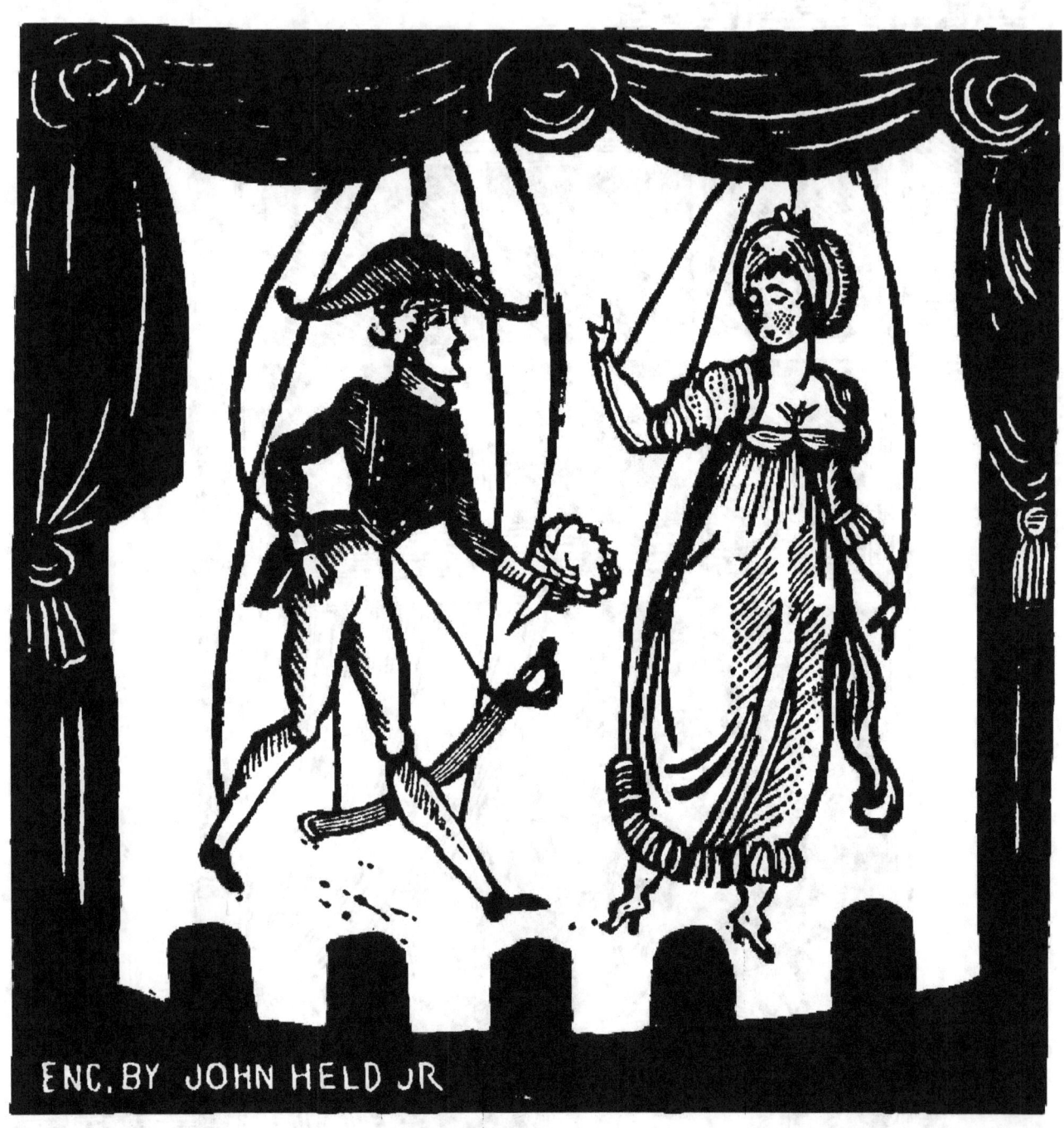

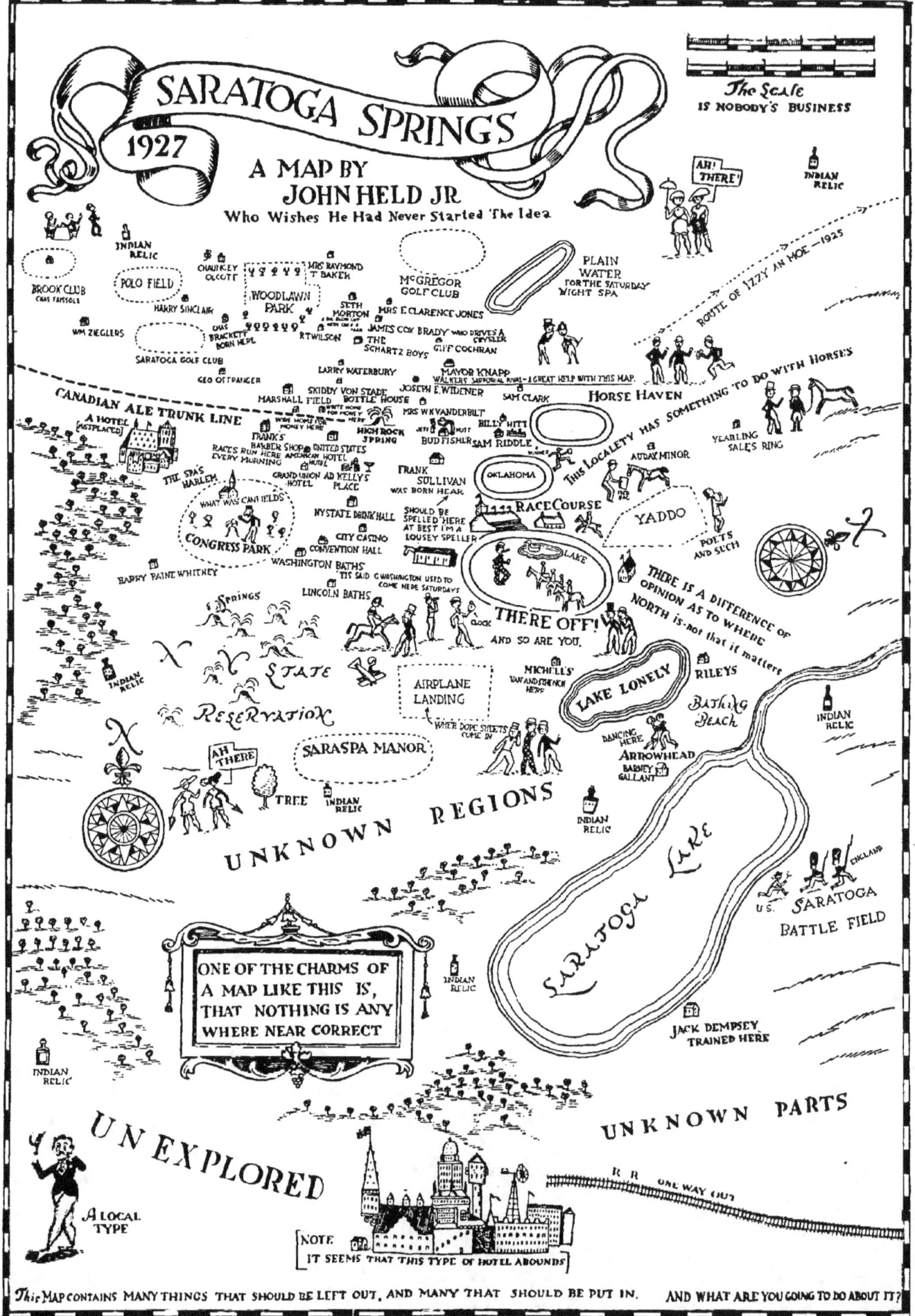

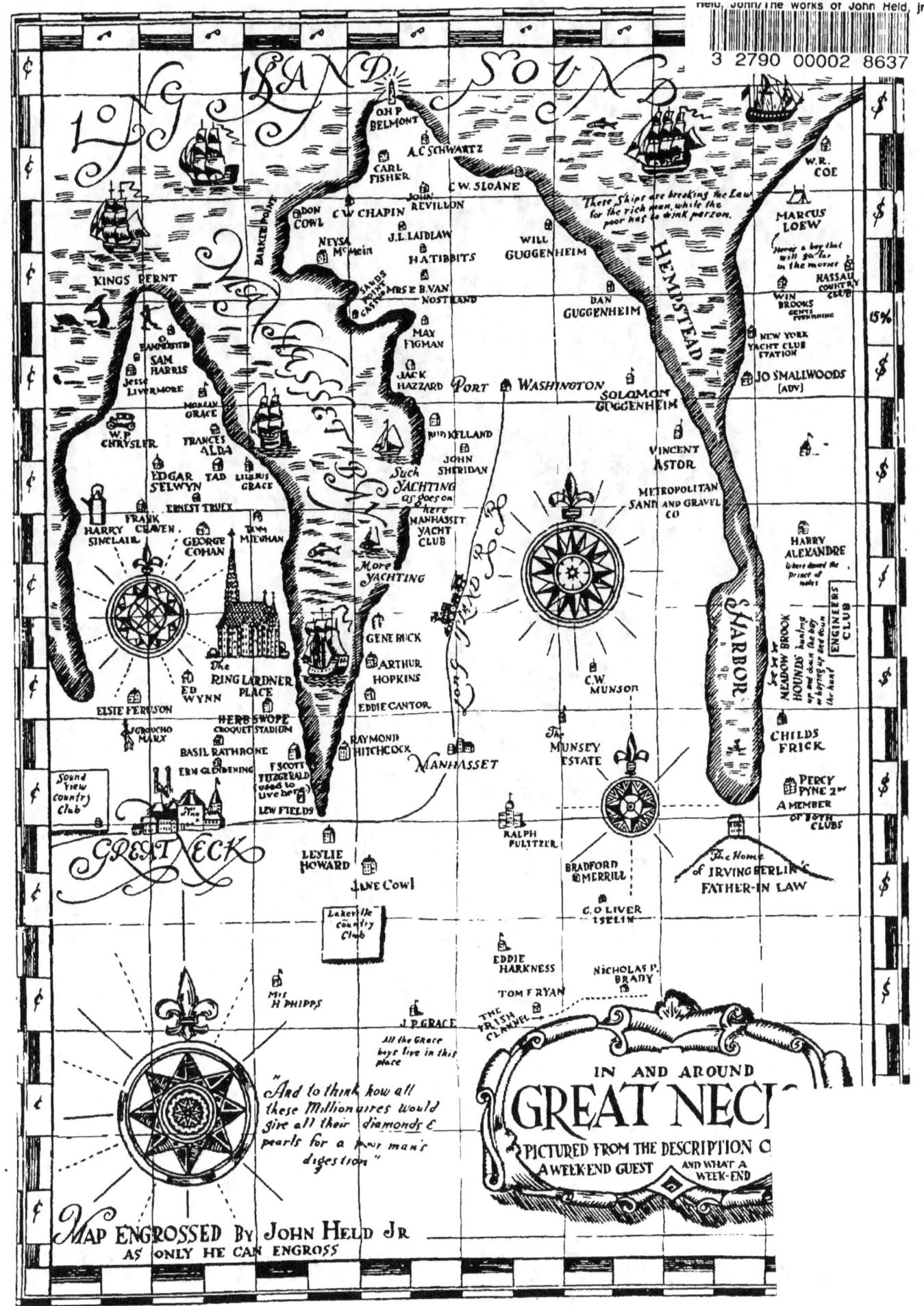

MAP ENGROSSED BY JOHN HELD JR
AS ONLY HE CAN ENGROSS

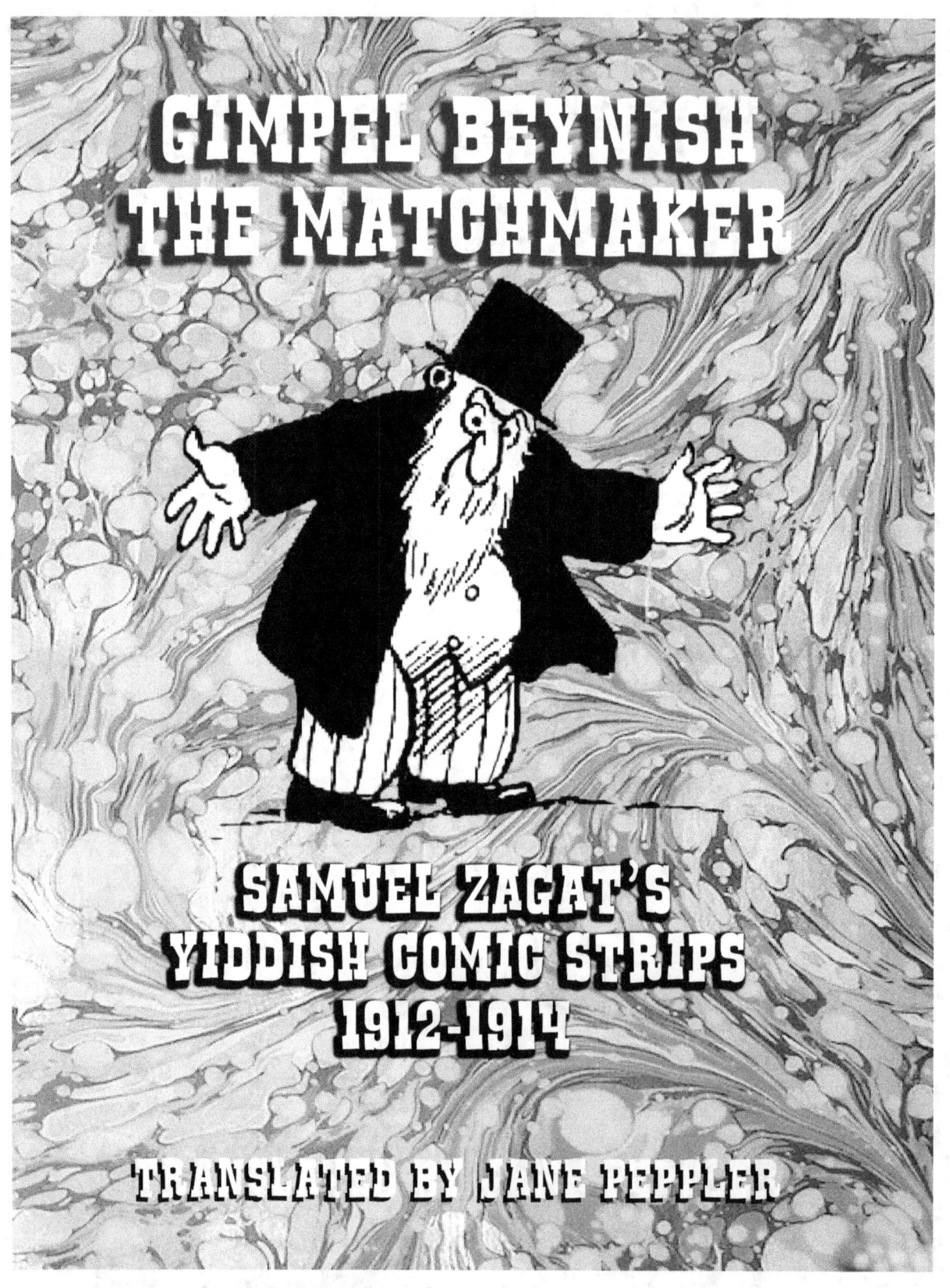